Hemingway:
The Homecoming

By Michael Reynolds

The Young Hemingway

Hemingway: The Paris Years

Hemingway: The Homecoming

Hemingway: The 1930s

Hemingway: The Final Years

HEMINGWAY: THE HOMECOMING

Michael Reynolds

W. W. NORTON & COMPANY

New York • London

Copyright © Michael Reynolds 1992
First published as a Norton paperback 1999

The text of this book is composed in Garamond

Library of Congress Cataloging-in-Publication Data

Reynolds, Michael S., 1937–
Hemingway: the American homecoming/Michael S. Reynolds.
p. cm.
Includes index.
ISBN 0–631–18481–3 (alk. paper)
1. Hemingway, Ernest, 1899-1961. 2. Novelists, American–20th
century–Biography. I. Title.
PS3515.E37Z75467 1992
813'.52–dc20
92–11662
CIP

ISBN 0-393-31981-4

W. W. Norton & Company, Inc.
500 Fifth Avenue, New York, N.Y. 10110
www.wwnorton.com

W. W. Norton & Company Ltd.
10 Coptic Street, London WC1A 1PU

1 2 3 4 5 6 7 8 9 0

This book is for my daughters,
Dierdre Alisoun and Shauna Iseult

"Remember to forget I told you
To remember all I told you."

CONTENTS

Acknowledgements   vii

Chronology   ix

Maps   xv

List of Illustrations   xxii

Now and Then   1

  1   Then   3

  2   Sun and Shadows   15

  3   Summer's Lease   26

  4   A Pursuit Race   37

  5   Room With No View   51

  6   The Hundred Days   64

  7   Fortune and Men's Eyes   87

  8   Ritual Acts   110

  9   Pilgrim's Progress   129

10   The New Life   142

CONTENTS

11   A Piece of the Continent   168

12   The Dead   192

Envoi   218

Notes   221

Index   259

ACKNOWLEDGEMENTS

Like October light on certain afternoons, there is a sadness that some-times pervades acknowledgements, for they come last saying that the book is done, another chance exhausted for well or worse. Then to remember supporting friends is to admit that you will not pass this way again, lending a funereal cast to the writer's eye. I, however, write this section with a smile, thinking of my favorite reviewer who never reads past my acknowledgements, which he finds vastly entertaining. To focus his amusement on the index or perhaps the text itself, I will stop think-ing my wife, who knows her contribution better than I. The support of others cannot be dismissed so lightly.

For kind permission to quote from unpublished Hemingway manu-scripts and letters, I am deeply indebted to the Hemingway Foundation. I am equally in the debt of the Hemingway Estate – John, Patrick, and Gregory Hemingway – for opening materials to scholars and in whose name copyright in all previously unpublished Hemingway material herein rests. I also thank Harcourt Brace Jovanovich, for permission to quote from Nicholas Gerogiannis's edition of *Ernest Hemingway: 88 Poems*, and Charles Scribner's Sons, an imprint of Macmillan Publishing Company, for permission to quote from *Ernest Hemingway: Selected Letters*, edited by Carlos Baker.

The National Endowment for the Humanities helped with a summer grant to finish my research. John Bassett and the English Department at North Carolina State University provided research assistance, encourage-ment, and sabbatical leave when it was most needed. Charlene Turner kept me humble when I was in residence and informed while I was away, and Stephan Chambers never lost faith in the project. For primary and secondary materials, obscure interlibrary loans, and equally obscure microfilms, I am indebted to the D. H. Hill Library at North Carolina State University. Without the Hemingway Collection at the John F. Kennedy Library and its archivists, Megan Desnoyers and Lisa Middents, who never failed me, this book could not have been written. To the public libraries of Oak Park, Monroe County (Florida) Library, Piggott, Arkansas, and Santa Fe, New Mexico, to the libraries of the University of New Mexico and Princeton University, and to the Library of Congress, I am also indebted. To the Reader's Corner I am grateful for keeping me in mind.

Without more than a little help from my friends, this book would be far less than it is. Paul Smith was boundless in his sharing, firm in his critique, and exemplary in his scholarship. Matt Bruccoli, Bernice Kert, Barbara Ballinger, Rose Marie Burwell, and Fern Kory provided vital information on short notice. John and Marcia Goin, Maury and Marcia Neville, all shared most generously. Jerry Kennedy kept Paris straight; Linda Miller confirmed my guesses and corrected errors; and Don Junkins forced me to write at the top of my bent. Patsy and Hal Hopfenberg, Jen and George Bireline – crucial companions in all kinds of weather – kept my excesses to a minimum.

In Santa Fe, where I spent the year writing this book, many contributed to my well-being. Bob and Esther Fleming at the University of New Mexico did favors without end. Lee Martinez gave me fair housing. B. Calico-Hickey kept all my parts in place, and Mariel Webb kept things from falling down. For special effects, I thank Ross LewAllen, David Rettig, Sandra Martinez, and Arleen LewAllen. Charlie Carrillo, with his attention to detail, gave me inspiration and took me to the morada. For extraordinary food at El Farol, Wednesday afternoons at the track, and friendship always, David Salazar was matchless. For conversation, caring, and Fundador, I have Richard and Helen to thank behind the bar, Tom and Sandy in front of it, good friends all. Tom Riker, who remembered when Annie was still a working girl, must be thanked for all his favors, including books most rare. Without these remarkable friends, my year would have been quite lonely.

It was also the year I buried my father, Raymond Douglas Reynolds, a geologist and historian who never stopped dreaming. It came with the territory.

M. R.
Santa Fe / Raleigh

CHRONOLOGY

1926

March
2–3 Ernest returns to Paris from his New York trip.
4   Ernest joins Hadley in Schruns, Austria.
8   John Dos Passos, Gerald and Sara Murphy arrive in Schruns.
12–17 All go to Gaschurn for better skiing.

April
1   Hemingways return to Paris.
6   Hemingways attend six-day bike races in Paris.
24   Ernest mails typescript for *The Sun Also Rises* to Scribner's.

May
13   Ernest leaves alone for Madrid, arrives next day.
16   Hadley takes sick son to Antibes and the Murphys.
26   Pauline arrives at Juan les Pins.
28   Ernest joins Hadley and Pauline at Juan les Pins.

June
5   After Fitzgerald's critique, Ernest cuts the opening section of *The Sun Also Rises*.

July
1   Hemingways, Pauline, and Murphys arrive in Pamplona.
6–12 *Feria* of San Fermin.

ix

20   Max Perkins mails galleys of *The Sun Also Rises*, asking for changes.
24   Hemingways are in Valencia.

August
2   Hemingways back in Antibes when galleys of *The Sun Also Rises* arrive.
12   Hemingways return to Paris to find separate residences.
27   Ernest returns corrected galleys of *The Sun Also Rises*, and "The Killers."

September
7   Ernest finishes "A Canary For One" and begins "In Another Country."
24   Pauline departs Paris as the Hundred Days separation begins. Ernest accompanies her to Boulogne.

October
7   Anson Hemingway dies in Oak Park.
11   Ernest and Archibald MacLeish leave for Zaragoza, Spain.
16   Ernest Walsh dies.
19   Ernest back in Paris.
22   *The Sun Also Rises* published in New York.

November
8   Hadley visits Chartres with Winifred Mowrer.
16   Hadley releases Ernest from Hundred Days agreement.
19   Ernest sends Perkins "How I Broke With John Wilkes Booth."
22   Ernest mails out "Neothomist Poem" and "In Another Country."
23–24   Ernest writing "Now I Lay Me."

December
4   *Scribner's Magazine* accepts "In Another Country."
8   Ernest files for divorce in Paris.
24   Ernest visits with Sherwood Anderson in Paris.
25   Ernest leaves Paris on night train to Gstaad, Switzerland.
26   Ernest, Virginia Pfeiffer, and the MacLeishes are in Gstaad.
30   Pauline sails from New York.

1927

January
8   Ernest meets Pauline at Cherbourg.
12   Ernest and Pauline arrive in Gstaad.
27   Hadley receives preliminary judgment of divorce.

February
18   Ernest returns to Paris to take his son back to Gstaad.

March
9   *Atlantic Monthly* accepts "Fifty Grand."
10   Ernest and Pauline return to Paris.
15   Ernest and Guy Hickok leave Paris on Italian trip.
26   Ernest returns to Paris.

April
14   Hadley's divorce decree is final.
16   Hadley and son sail for New York.

May
10   Ernest and Pauline are married in Paris.
11   Hemingways depart for honeymoon at Le Grau-du-Roi.
27   Ernest completes "Ten Indians" and "Hills Like White Elephants."

June
7   Hemingways return to Paris.

July
1   Hemingways enter Spain.
6–12   Hemingways in Pamplona for San Fermin.
22–31 Hemingways in Valencia.

August
2–5   Hemingways in Madrid.
15   Hemingways in La Coruña.

17–31   Hemingways in Santiago de Compostela. Ernest mails corrected galleys for *Men Without Women.*

September
1   Hemingways arrive Hendaye, remain two weeks or more.
19   Hemingways are back in Paris in new apartment. Revolutionist novel begun.

October
14   *Men Without Women* published in New York.
20   Ernest says 30,000 words done on new novel.

November
3–12   Hemingways are in Berlin for six-day bike races.

December
13   Hemingways, son, and Jinny Pfeiffer leave Paris for Gstaad. Bumby scratches Ernest's eye.

1928

January
    In Gstaad, Pauline realizes she is pregnant.

February
1   Pauline and Jinny return to Paris. Ernest stays to cross-country ski.
12   Ernest back in Paris.

March
6–7   Ernest pulls skylight down on his forehead. Within week abandons revolutionist novel to begin *A Farewell to Arms.*
17   Hemingways sail on the *Orita* for Havana and Key West.

April
    In Key West, Hemingways are visited by John Dos Passos, Waldo Peirce, and Bill Smith.

10   Ernest's parents appear unexpectedly in Key West.

21   10,000–15,000 thousand words written on *A Farewell to Arms*.

May

20   Pauline leaves for Piggott, Arkansas by train.

25   Ernest and Paul Pfeiffer follow to Piggott by car.

31   Ernest arrives in Piggott.

June

7   Ernest has 279 pages of *A Farewell to Arms* written.

13   Hemingways drive to Kansas City for baby's birth.

28   Patrick Hemingway delivered by caesarean section.

July

1–18   Hemingways remain in Kansas City.

20   Hemingways return to Piggott. Ernest has 477 pages of *A Farewell of Arms* written.

25   Ernest returns to Kansas City.

28   Ernest and Bill Horne depart Kansas City for Wyoming by car.

August

3   Ernest in Sheridan for four days.

8   Ernest at Donnelly's Lower Ranch.

18   Pauline arrives in Sheridan.

20–2   First draft of *A Farewell to Arms* is finished.

September

25   Hemingways return to Piggott. Ernest works on "Wine of Wyoming."

October

17   Ernest arrives in Oak Park to visit his family.

30   Pauline joins EH in Chicago.

November

1   Hemingways leave Chicago for New York and Conway, MA to visit MacLeish.

12–16   Hemingways are in New York City.

17   Hemingways meet Fitzgerald for Princeton-Yale football game. Spend the night at Fitzgerald's after game.

18	Leave for Piggott via Chicago.
20/21	Leave Piggott by car for Key West.
25	Arrive Key West.

December

3	Ernest leaves Key West for New York to meet Hadley and take Bumby back to Key West.
6	Ernest leaves New York with Bumby. Clarence Hemingway commits suicide in Oak Park.
7	Ernest arrives in Oak Park.
8	Clarence Hemingway's funeral.
16/17	Ernest returns to Key West.

1929

January

22	Typed draft of *A Farewell to Arms* is finished.

February

9	Perkins leaves Key West with *A Farewell to Arms*.
13	Perkins wires serial offer for *A Farewell to Arms*.
20–8	Dos Passos, Waldo Peirce, and Katy Smith visit Key West.

April

5	Ernest, Pauline, Patrick, and Bumby depart Havana for France.

MAPS

Map 1   France   xvi

Map 2   Italy   xvii

Map 3   The Camargue   xviii

Map 4   Europe   xix

Map 5   Spain   xx

Map 6   Switzerland   xxi

Map 1 France
(copyright © Adrienne Louise Brennan)

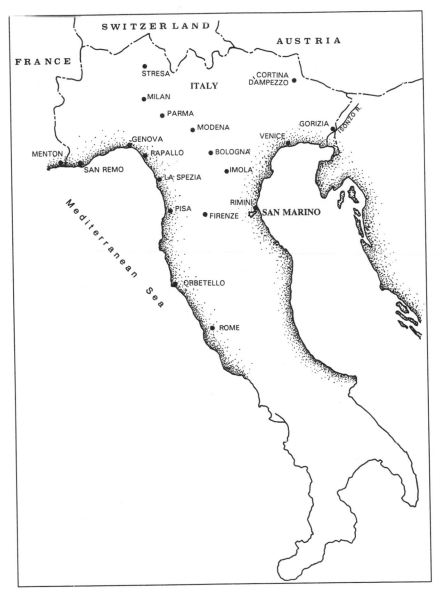

Map 2 Italy
(copyright © Adrienne Louise Brennan)

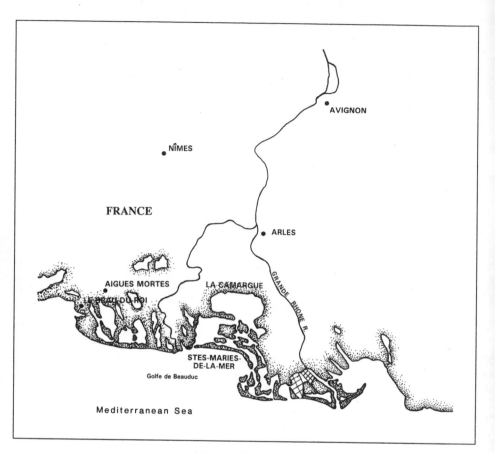

Map 3 The Camargue
(copyright © Adrienne Louise Brennan)

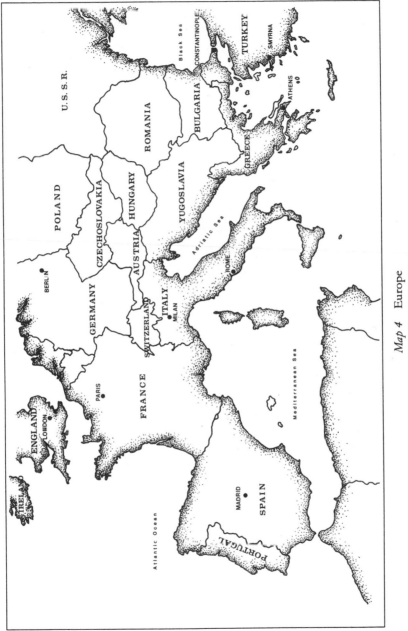

Map 4 Europe

(copyright © Adrienne Louise Brennan)

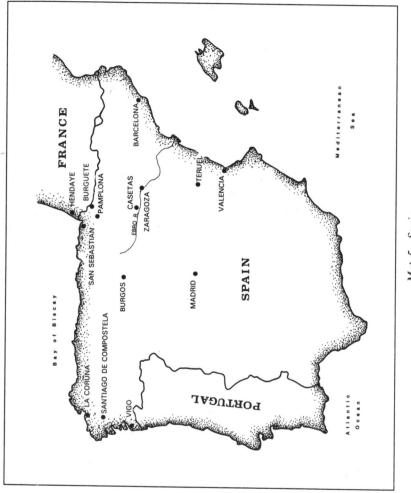

Map 5   Spain

(copyright © Adrienne Louise Brennan)

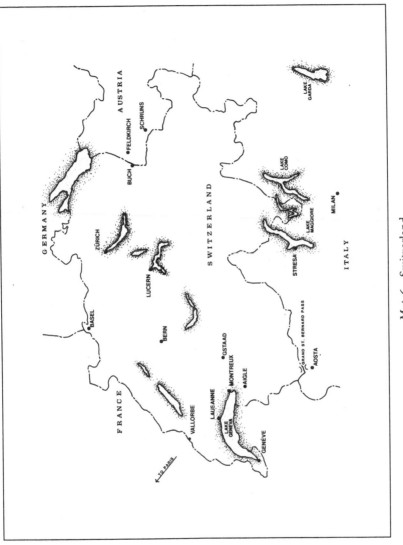

Map 6　Switzerland
(copyright © Adrienne Louise Brennan)

ILLUSTRATIONS

(plates between pages 104 and 105)

1 Ernest and Hadley with Bumby at Schruns the winter of 1925–6, just as their marriage was beginning to collapse.

2 Passport photo of Pauline Pfeiffer as she looked when Hemingway first met her.

3 Skiing up on the Silvretta, March 1926: left to right, ski instructor, Hemingway, John Dos Passos, Gerald Murphy.

4 Marie Rohrbach and her husband, Ton Ton, holding Bumby, whom they were keeping in Brittany during July 1926 while the Hemingway marriage was coming apart.

5 Gerald and Sara Murphy, Pauline Pfeiffer, Ernest and Hadley Hemingway in Pamplona during summer 1926. A month later Ernest and Hadley separated.

6 At the morning *amateurs* in the Pamplona bull ring, the men try their nerve against the padded horns of a cow.

7 Archibald MacLeish, poet and friend of Hemingway's, whose moral critical support helped him through his separation and divorce.

8 Ernest and Pauline in a photo taken either on their wedding day or shortly thereafter.

9 Ernest and Pauline on the beach at Hendaye in September 1927.

10 Virginia Pfeiffer at Gstaad during the winter of 1927–8.

11 Key West (ca. 1930). In the foreground are the ferry slips adjoining the rail lines to New York. The afternoon ferry from Havana has arrived next to the waiting train. In the upper right is the US Navy base with its submarine slips. The large building in the center of town is the La Concha Hotel.

12 John Dos Passos, the "old mutton fish" as Hemingway called him, displaying his tarpon catch in Key West, ca. 1928.

13 Uncle Willoughby Hemingway (far left), visiting from missionary work in China, with Ernest, his mother Grace, and Pauline standing against the Hemingways' new Model T Ford roadster. Pauline is seven months pregnant.

14 Father and son, Clarence and Ernest Hemingway, meeting for the first time in over five years. Place: Key West. Date: April 10, 1928. Eight months later Clarence committed suicide.

Now and Then

His friend once said that it was almost impossible to believe in the youth of one's parents; he could have said the same about Ernest Hemingway, who grew so tall on paper that it is hard to think of him as a young man in Paris, magnetic, brash, and bawdy, a writer on the edge of immortality. Later, speaking of himself, he would say it was always a mistake to know an author well. There were those who agreed, remembering him in all his flaws; others, no matter how badly he hurt them, never ceased to defend him. This literary pushing and shoving, which began early, did not thrive until he was dead and famous among his survivors. For some, he was the most important event in their lives. For others, he was only a summer storm crossing the bay. But no matter how he touched them, not the least of his commentators ever forgot the feel or look of him, ever forgot the way he could exhaust the oxygen by simply walking into the room.

Women, those who loved him and those who did not, remembered him in great detail. One woman said, "I wouldn't have been surprised at anything Ernest did. He was unexpected and temperamental, a lovable person who took a great deal of understanding. He was sensitive, although he didn't seem to be. If you didn't know him well, you'd think he was rather tough."[1] His first wife remembered him as "one of the most sensitive people I ever heard of, and easily hurt." She also said "he had the nerve of a brass monkey." He was "the kind of man to whom men, women and dogs were attracted. He was scornful of some people and would say outrageous things about them. He had a cruel streak. Yet his kindness went just about as far in the other direction."[2] Kitty Cannell

1

thought him phony, pretentious, and untrustworthy, but she could not forget his apple-cheeks, his infectious grin, or his boyish enthusiasms.[3]

The men drawn to him had difficulty performing at his level of intensity, for Hemingway did nothing halfheartedly. Many enjoyed the bullfights, but few followed them as he did all summer in Spain. Whether it was skiing, fishing, or drinking, he was competitive always. "He liked to win everything," Mike Strater complained long afterward, refusing to admit his own defeat.[4] For Gerald Murphy, who could not compete with the younger man so charming to his wife, the encounter with Hemingway changed him forever. He found the writer "huge and forceful, and he overstated everything and talked so rapidly and so graphically and so well that you found yourself agreeing with him."[5] Whether it was the bullfights at Pamplona, the ski slopes at Schruns, or an evening at a Paris dance hall, the Hemingway experience always demanded unexpected emotional resources. Few of his male friendships in those early days lasted longer than five years. Reading the letters, one can watch them burn up and out like incandescent lights. To whatever he touched in those days he added scale and a sense of importance. Murphy said, "The lives of some of us will seem, I suppose by comparison, piddling . . . For me, he has the violence and excess of genius."[6] It is not given to many men to imprint themselves so deeply upon their generation as did Ernest Hemingway in the first half of this century. Although he did not outlive either his friends or his enemies, who got in their last words, he burned so much more brightly than most that we still read their statements by his light.

We know so well the icon he became that it is difficult to imagine him unfledged, vibrant with energy, laughing and joking along the boulevards of Paris. Wearing sneakers, old trousers, and a patched jacket, his long hair sticking out from under his cap, he was six feet tall, broad-shouldered, mustached, and handsome, setting his own style. When the occasion demanded, he could put on his one tweed suit with its dark tie, but he never owned a summer straw hat in an age when only the poorest American was without one. For Nathan Asch, "It was an event when this towering figure passed the sidewalk tables at the Dôme. Arms waved in greeting and friends ran out to urge him to sit down with them . . . he wouldn't quite recognize whoever greeted him. Then suddenly his beautiful smile appeared that made those watching him also smile."[7] Continuously moving with his curious, slow-footed gait, he was a man on his way somewhere else, always.

Chapter One

THEN

He stands naked and dripping from the bath, a little too heavy from his recent trip to New York. Outside the warm room, where snow erases the Austrian landscape, a stream rushes through the village. As he dries his right foot, he fingers the welted scar tissue where they cut shrapnel out during the last war. He pulls the black rubber support band up over his knee, still weak from the mortar blast eight years earlier. In their bedroom down the hall his wife is reading one of the books he brought back from Paris. In the mirror he looks at his two-day growth of beard and his black mustache and then, without shaving, puts the straight razor back in its case. Downstairs a mountainous breakfast is waiting for him, and in the extra room across the hall, his typewriter is also waiting. Beside it are seven blue notebooks and a stack of typed pages. Today he will take up again the revisions he began before Christmas. Church bells begin to ring so close the window rattles.

SCHRUNS, AUSTRIA: MARCH 8–12, 1926

In his buckram notebook, he was listing various ways one might kill one self. The cleanest would be a night-time plunge from the stern of an ocean liner. "There would be only the one moment of taking the jump and it is very easy for me to take almost any sort of jump," he wrote. "Also it would never be definitely known what had happened and there would be no postmortems and no expenses left for any one to pay."[1] If ever a young man of twenty-five lacked apparent reason to think of suicide, it was Ernest Hemingway.

3

After seven lean years with no significant payments for his fiction, he had finally found the market he was aiming for all along. On the night stand beside the feather bed was a fresh copy of *In Our Time*, his collection of short stories which Boni & Liveright had published the previous October. Inside were clipped reviews, some of them so good that he could not believe them. The *New York Times* said that he packed "a whole character into a phrase, an entire situation into a sentence or two." He made "each word count three or four ways."[2] There were ambitious young men on the Left Bank who would kill for such a review. From his clipping service he read what Allen Tate said in *The Nation*: "The passionate accuracy of particular observation, the intense monosyllabic diction, the fidelity to the internal demands of the subject – these qualities fuse in the most completely realized naturalistic fiction of the age."[3]

He was glad to see the reviews, but they were old news. He and his publisher, Liveright, were through. Hemingway had seen to that with a satire on Sherwood Anderson that Horace Liveright could not accept, which Ernest knew when he wrote *Torrents of Spring*. In New York, he talked straight with Horace: You've got my next book that our contract called for. Publish it or give it back so I can take it somewhere else. And that was that. Now in the dresser drawer was his newly signed arrangement with Scott Fitzgerald's publisher, Charles Scribner's Sons. Max Perkins, his editor-to-be, gave him a wonderful deal, agreeing to publish *Torrents* and *The Sun Also Rises* without ever seeing the second novel. Hemingway would never break another contract.

Fitzgerald, who more than anyone else encouraged Hemingway to write *Torrents* and break his contract, was delighted when Liveright refused to publish the satire. Scott immediately wrote Max Perkins:

> Hemingway thinks . . . that their refusal sets him free from his three-book (letter) agreement with them. In that case I think he'll give you his novel (on condition you'll publish satire first – probable sale, 1,000 copies) . . . [Hemingway] and I are very thick and he's marking time until he finds out how much he's bound to Liveright. If he's free I'm almost sure I can get satire to you first and then if you see your way clear you can contract for the novel *tout ensemble*. He's anxious too to get a foot-hold in your magazine [*Scribner's Monthly*] – one story I've sent you ["Fifty Grand"], the other ["The Undefeated"], to my horror, he'd given over for about $40 to an "arty" publication called *This Quarter*, over here.[4]

So when Hemingway reached New York, everything went smoothly for him in the Scribner building: a $1,500 advance against both books to be published before the year was out and a 15 percent royalty rate. While waiting for the papers to be drawn up, Hemingway talked to Alfred Harcourt, for whom Louis Bromfield was scouting in Paris and who was most interested in signing Ernest, but it was only talk. As much as he liked Mr. Harcourt, he said he was bound to Scribner's by his promise of first refusal to Perkins. He told Bromfield that he "wouldn't have any fun writing the stuff if I did something that made me feel crooked inside."[5] Before Hemingway left New York, Perkins mocked up the cover for *Torrents* and the contract was signed.

Now, in his bare writing room at the Taube Inn, he stacked next to his typewriter the seven blue notebooks containing the novel written last summer; beside them was the typescript he was making himself, revising the text in process. The first page began

> This is a novel about a lady. Her name is Lady Ashley and when the story begins she is living in Paris and it is Spring. That should be a good setting for a romantic but highly moral story. As everyone knows, Paris is a very romantic place. Spring in Paris is a very happy and romantic time.[6]

Reading over the revisions made before going to New York in February, he worried about the self-conscious irony. Maybe he should try, once more, to put the novel into third person. He tried that in January, but gave it up. Maybe he should not start it in Paris, but at the bullfights in Pamplona where his first draft began. He tried it out to see what it looked like:

> I saw him for the first time in his room at the Hotel Montoya in Pamplona. Bill and I were going up to our room to get the wine skin to take to the bull fight and we met Montoya on the stairs. "Come on," said Montoya. "Would you like to meet Pedro Romero?"[7]

He typed on for two pages and stopped. Starting that way was asking a lot of the reader who didn't know Pamplona from Peking. The story had to start in Paris to catch the reader who knew all about Paris from the war vets, the magazines, and the movies.

But it was hard for Hemingway not to be satirical about Paris. His real story of the city was not about Lady Ashley, but about Pauline Pfeiffer, a story he could not tell anyone yet. It was not the trip to New York or his Scribner's contract that made him think about suicide; it was the firm, small body of Pauline Pfeiffer in her Paris bed that gave him dark thoughts. Ernest Hemingway was in love with his wife and her good friend, no uncommon thing that year in Paris. How he had gotten himself into this situation, he really did not understand, but he knew there was no good solution to it. He wasn't going to commit suicide; only think about it.

PARIS: MARCH 6, 1926

That evening after work, Pauline Pfeiffer crossed the river by taxi to rue de l'Odéon where Sylvia Beach ran her bookshop and lending library. She returned T. S. Eliot's *Sacred Wood*, which was on her bedside table when Hemingway came through Paris on his way to New York and was still on her table during the two days they had together on his return. "Major Elliot," Ernest called him. At Shakespeare and Co., she now checked out Virginia Woolf's newest novel, *Mrs. Dalloway*.[8] That night she started the story about Clarissa Dalloway's long day of party-planning with its attendant revelations of the human heart. By the second night's reading, she found Septimus Smith contemplating suicide: "and this killing oneself, how does one set about it, with a table knife, uglily, with floods of blood, – by sucking a gaspipe?"[9] Septimus had returned from the war a ruined man, having discovered that he did not care about anyone. Marriage had only made him bitter. In fact, none of Woolf's fictional marriages made Pauline feel the least bit good. "You'll get married, for you're pretty enough, thought Mrs. Dempster. Get married, she thought, and then you'll know . . . Every man has his ways."[10]

No one thought of Pauline Pfeiffer as gorgeous, but she was an attractive woman who looked younger than thirty in expensive, well-fitting clothes and fashion-model make-up. Small-breasted and slender, she was built for the jazz age. With her pixie face and her narrow hips, she had none of the matronly look of Hadley's generation. Behind her Twenties facade, she was smart and informed, well educated in a St. Louis girl's school and at the University of Missouri's school of journalism. After working newspaper jobs in Cleveland and New York, she was hired by *Vanity Fair* as a fashion reporter and publicist which she parlayed into a similar job as assistant to Main Bocher, the editor of Paris *Vogue*.[11] The new job required clothes and a certain flair. In her fashionable office on rue Édouard Sept, close to the Opéra, Pauline could not afford to appear dowdy or bohemian. Her Right Bank apartment on rue Picot edging the Bois de Boulogne was an appropriate address in a quiet, respectable arrondissement, unlike Hemingway's Left Bank flat on the rue Notre-Dame-des-Champs. When Hemingway went to the Dingo Bar, he was patronizing a neighborhood bar; when Pauline went there, she was slumming.

Later, some would say that Pauline's money took Ernest away from Hadley, as if he were up at auction to the highest bidder. Hadley remembered that she "was a poor young woman and Pauline was . . . from the Hudnut family, which means money. . . . I didn't have any money because Ernest hadn't clicked yet."[12] Hadley did not remember her own depleted trust funds, which still provided $2,000 a year. And as for Ernest not yet "clicking," he returned from New York with the $1,500 Scribner advance, enough for them to live another year in Paris with the franc at 29 to the dollar.[13] It was not for money that her husband lay down in Pauline's bed but for the excitement this new woman brought to his life. Hadley, tightly corseted now at thirty-four, seemed much older than Pauline at thirty. When the three of them were together, it was Hadley who looked out of place. Much as he loved his wife, Ernest was beginning to resent her dependence upon him, lose patience with her female friends, and wish for more intellectual support than she gave him. Where Hadley was passive, Pauline was active and athletic. Where Hadley was a nominal Protestant, Pauline was a devout Catholic, a mysterious religion with a strong attraction for Hemingway. That winter, the three of them were poised at a turning point. Hadley, a little weary of Ernest's emotional demands and his continual roving life, was ready for a more regular existence. Pauline, who not only loved Ernest but also recognized that his was an enormous talent which needed breathing room, was ready to give up her professional life and her soul, if need be, to marry this man and forward his career. And Hemingway, having exhausted the literary possibilities of Latin Quarter writing, was ready to move up to the next level of intensity. Of the two women, only Pauline was both suited and willing to take that step with him.

As he came back through Paris on his way to New York, Pauline was reading the documentation on her newly increased trust fund. Her uncle, Augustus G. Pfeiffer, who established the fund, explained to her that the total was now $60,000, so that her "income . . . should be approximately

$3,000 per year or $250 per month." It would be a year before the latest investments began to bear their full interest; by April of 1926, the fund would begin to pay about $150 a month. In the interim, Uncle Gus promised to send $100 a month "in order to make no lapse in your income." The gift from her childless uncle was given, as he explained to her, out of "love and affection" and a "desire to share the prosperity which has come to us." The most important motive, he told her, was to enable her "to better and more successfully evolve your personality and attain your hope and ideals. Our thought is that instead of losing your interest and endeavor in life's purposes, that it increase these and better enable you to work out your life's plans."[14] A married man was hardly what Uncle Gus imagined to be part of his niece's "hope and ideals," but, as time would show, he was a man liberal with his money and in his judgements.

Along with her money, Pauline carried a Catholic conscience that did not sleep. Some gossiped that she and her younger sister, Jinny, were in Paris looking for husbands, which was a joke to those who knew them well.[15] Virginia Pfeiffer, at twenty-four, preferred the company of women, and Pauline was in Paris to avoid an engagement with her cousin in New York.[16] Raised within the Catholic Church, these two sisters were not dizzy flappers out of Anita Loos's *Gentlemen Prefer Blondes*. In St. Louis, the Pfeiffer girls grew up fully indoctrinated by Catholic schools. In 1913, when their father, Paul, changed dramatically from a St. Louis businessman into a Piggott, Arkansas farmer (albeit on a large scale), Jinny moved with the family to the rural village while Pauline remained in St. Louis attending Catholic boarding school. Now, at thirty, Pauline may have been ready for a husband, but of all the men she met in Paris, Ernest Hemingway was the least likely prospect. If she were looking for a husband, a married non-Catholic with a two-and-a-half-year-old child and a doting wife was not the man. And yet she had taken him to her bed without remorse. Now, alone in bed, with only *Mrs. Dalloway* for comfort, she must have seen there was little prospect of a lasting relationship with Ernest. A mortal sin of sexual congress was at least forgivable in the Sunday confessional, but to destroy a marriage and then to live in sin with the husband was almost unforgivable. Not only would the priest insist that she give up the man before he would absolve her, but there was also the unimaginable confrontation with her mother, Mary Pfeiffer, who would be deeply hurt.

The more she thought about Ernest, the more impediments became clear. They lived on opposite banks of the Seine, hers rich, his poor.

Addresses, of course, were only symbolic, but she could not imagine Ernest ever living in some expensive flat like the Scott Fitzgeralds' on rue de Tilsitt, nor did she have any desire to live without hot water as Hadley did on Notre-Dame-des-Champs. By Right Bank standards, Ernest was frequently slovenly and poorly dressed. His four-year-old tweed suit was far too traveled to stand inspection. What possible excuse could she make for him to her parents? A married man with child, Left Bank bohemian, badly dressed and given to heavy drinking, a man with no means of support but his pen – this was hardly the man Pauline Pfeiffer should be choosing for a husband. And yet she could not forget the smile or touch of him any more than she could deny her heart which had its own reasons. For all his flaws and failings, she was deeply in love with Ernest Hemingway. If this were sin, then she would become a great sinner. "And if some one should see, what matter they?" the old crone in *Mrs. Dalloway* asks.

GASCHURN: MARCH 12–17, 1926

The first plan had been for everyone to meet in Munich where they would load up an airplane "with rich food, wine and condiments" and then fly into Madlener Haus, the skiers' hut on the Silvretta glacier high above Schruns.[17] It was a grand plan with their new friend, Gerald Murphy, paying for the trip, and their old friend, John Dos Passos, coming along for the food. Then Dos, who was the Murphy connection, wrote that he was cancelling out. He had to be in New York,

> where a play of mine is going on – abandoning Schruns . . . one hell of a note as I had my mouth all fixed for Voralberg schnitzels. Don't curse me out too much for going back on my plighted troth. . . . The Murphies allege that they can't go either. . . . I'm sore as a crab being made safe for democracy about not getting to the skiing to say nothing of the company and the Kirsch.[18]

That letter was waiting for Hemingway when he returned to Schruns, followed a few days later by Gerald Murphy's similar apology. Murphy said he and Sara felt "like skunks about Munich."[19]

Then, when the visit seemed definitely off, new word came from the south of France: the Murphys and Dos Passos were on their way to

Schruns. In his March 10 letter to Max Perkins, Hemingway said he expected the guests to arrive that day or the next. He still thought they were going "to Munich and fly from there to . . . the Silvretta." "Neither the Gerald Murphys nor Dos can ski," he said, "and that seems the simplest way of getting them up where the skiing is good now." Meanwhile, he was working hard on *The Sun Also Rises*, with only five chapters left to revise. At this rate, Max could expect the typescript some time in May. It did not surprise him, Hemingway wrote, that *Colliers* had rejected "Fifty Grand." Max was sending it on to *Saturday Evening Post* and *Liberty*, but Ernest, continually disappointed with American magazine editors, wasn't holding his breath on their acceptance.[20]

On March 11, the three visitors from Antibes arrived with fresh stories about Scott and Zelda but with little appetite for flying on to the Silvretta glacier. For Ernest, now an experienced skier from having spent the previous winter on the high slopes, it would be a great adventure; for Gerald and Dos Passos, it would be a survival situation. Not only were they innocent of all skiing skills, but they also arrived straight from sea level. On the 2,000-meter high Silvretta, such novices would be risking their lives. The next morning in Schruns, the Hemingways, the Murphys, and Dos Passos bundled on to the tiny electric train that ran up the Montafon valley to Gaschurn, where they were closer to better snow and serious slopes. Ernest and Hadley were welcomed as old friends by Arnold Kessler at his Hotel Zum Rössle-Post where Ernest, Hadley, and Pauline had stayed earlier in January.[21] Now at almost every corner of the small village and scattered commonly through its graveyard, Ernest encountered the local name of Pfeiffer. In his pocket he carried Pauline's note using the code word they agreed on: instead of Hemingway she would use Benchley's name. "This isn't a letter," she said, "but just written to tell you that I think your friend Robert C. Benchley is awfully swell. And I am very VERY fond of him."[22]

The snow at Gaschurn was not wonderful, but adequate for the beginners. In those days, there were no lifts or tow ropes. To ski, one put seal skins on the heavy, wooden skis and climbed the slope, earning every foot of the downhill run. After two days of skiing lessons, Ernest led Dos and Gerald up to Madlener Haus for a serious test, leaving Sara and Hadley to quiet days at the Rössle.[23] "Dos has always had hugely powerful legs and a tremendous restless energy," Gerald later wrote,

> and Ernest was an expert climber. I struggled along, trying to keep
> up with them, and felt terribly ashamed that I was holding them

up. . . . I was determined to learn how to ski in the two days we were up there. Ernest always gave you the sense of being put to the test, and he an absolutely superb skier. . . . I had spent two days doggedly practicing and falling down and learned the rudiments. . . . Dos didn't bother to learn, because his eyesight was so bad, he knew it was no use. When we started down, Dos just decided to go straight and sit down whenever he saw a tree. . . . I managed to get down the first part without falling. Then, in the second part, we had to go through a forest. I managed that pretty well too, falling only once or twice. Ernest would stop every twenty yards or so to make sure we were all right, and when we got to the bottom, about a half an hour later, he asked me if I had been scared. I said, yes, I guess I had. He said then he knew what courage was, it was grace under pressure. It was childish of me, but I felt absolutely elated.[24]

Murphy, older and ever attempting to be one of the boys, was determined to meet Hemingway on Ernest's terms, but always felt himself falling short of the younger man's expectations. Much as he admired the athletic Ernest, Gerald was never completely comfortable in his presence.

After two strenuous days at high altitude, the exhausted men were happy to warm themselves beside the green porcelain stove in the Rössle bar with a bottle of clear, smooth Kirschwasser for comfort. As they sat there drinking in Gaschurn, Dos Passos reminded them that he was supposed to be attending his new play, *The Moon is a Gong*, whose first performance was that very night in Greenwich Village. While they sat warm and well pleased, his vaudeville-like protest against the urban wasteland was awaiting an opening curtain. Dos was sure they would like old Death, the Garbage Man, who literally closed the show. They all drank to Death and *The Moon*.

Dos Passos, whom Ernest met briefly during the war in Italy and whose friendship was renewed in Paris, told fireside stories about his recent trip to Marrakesh, Magador, and Tangiers. In Fez, he said, there was some interesting if elderly local talent for sale, but he had led the life of a fifty-five-year-old virgin from Massachusetts. Algiers was interesting, gambling everywhere and no lights to speak of. Hoping to gather grist for his writing mill, he looked in on Abd el Krim's native revolt against colonial rule in the North African Riff. But not much was happening in the war because Primo de Rivera's Spanish troops had nailed down the lid on Krim's guerrilla operation.[25]

Amongst so much camaraderie and warmed with Kirsch, Hemingway, after some urging, got out his revised typescript to read aloud, something he had never done before. A lifetime later he would say that he had been "as trusting and as stupid as a bird dog who wants to go out with any man with a gun. . . . I even read aloud the part of the novel that I had rewritten, which is about as low as a writer can get."[26] At sixty he needed to explain behavior that had seemed perfectly reasonable at twenty-six. When he read the conversation between Bill and Jake, his friends got the joke about the Riff. Bill and Jake were eating breakfast in the village inn at Burguete:

> The coffee was good and we drank it out of big bowls. The girl brought in a glass dish of raspberry jam.
> "Thank you."
> "Hey! that's not the way," Bill said. "Say something ironical. Make some crack about Primo de Rivera."
> "I could ask her what kind of jam they think they've gotten into in the Riff."
> "Poor," said Bill. "Very poor. You can't do it. Thàt's all. You don't understand irony."[27]

More kirsch and more funny stories followed Hemingway's reading, stories about the Fitzgeralds and Antibes, stories about the festival of San Fermin at Pamplona. The Murphys wanted to join Ernest and Hadley there in July to see for themselves the wild bulls in the afternoon and the wilder nights that Hemingway described. Dos, who was never sure where his traveling itch might take him next, made no promises, but Gerald and Sara were eager for the experience. And with them was Pauline Pfeiffer, already committed to the adventure.

If Hadley had any second thoughts, she kept them to herself, but she could not forget the emotional disaster of the previous summer at Pamplona. Quite amazed, she had watched passively while Duff Twysden's sexual magnetism produced incredible and boorish behavior in the men. First the fights broke out after too much drinking, and then the hotel bill came with Duff unmoneyed and unworried. With all of the men, including Ernest, behaving like fools, Hadley pretended that it did not matter that her husband was so obviously taken with Lady Twysden, pretended that she did not worry about his fidelity. Her wounds were still raw from that experience. Now he was going to bring to Pamplona the petite Pauline who, unlike Duff, was neither engaged nor a drunk.

Afterwards Hadley watched the alchemy work as *The Sun* rose out of the ashes of those burnt-out relationships, but the emotional price was high. She could not imagine how much the summer of 1926 might cost.

PARIS: MARCH 16, 1926

That morning in the *Tribune* Pauline read the Latin Quarter Notes and laughed.

> Ernest Hemingway, one of the more promising Quarterites, is expected back from America where, it is reported, he has just concluded a most advantageous contract with Scribner's for the publishing of his books.

Usually the gossip column was right on top of things, but she and Ernest kept his return through Paris so quiet that no one on the Left Bank had noticed. Only the Fitzgeralds, before leaving for Nice, saw him, and they did not have time to spread the word. Pauline had not finished *Mrs. Dalloway*, but neither had she heard from Schruns since Ernest left Paris on March 4, so that morning she went by the bookshop Shakespeare and Co. looking for news. Sylvia Beach, den mother to the post-war literary generation that gathered in the City of Light, was usually the first to know of Hemingway happenings, for he used her shop as a mail-drop and base camp on his frequent European excursions.

It was threatening rain as Pauline walked up the rue de l'Odéon to the book-lined window where *In Our Time* was prominently placed among other recent fiction. Inside, Sylvia still had her stove burning against the lingering chill of the unfinished Paris winter. After checking out Virginia Woolf's *Common Reader*, Pauline casually asked about the Hemingways, but Sylvia had heard nothing. No, she wasn't sure how long they had sublet their flat. Pauline was only making conversation; she knew they were not due back until the first of April.[28]

That evening when she returned to her apartment, a Hemingway letter awaited her, telling about the Murphys and Dos Passos arriving and their planned Gaschurn excursion. Buried among the trivia were the code words she needed to hear. Pauline read the letter twice and then took out her pen. "Dearest Hadley and Ernest," she wrote.

13

So you turned out to be the Russians the Murphys went to see. Well, it's sometimes hard to tell who the Russians are. And Dos is back from Afrique. Hadley, this is of course private, but was there any where about him in addition to the regular luggage, anything resembling a jewel casket? Everything between me and the hot Spanish suitor has now been placed on the high love plane, and this I suppose must be maintained, but after all, enfin, au fond, and basically there IS the matter of trinkets. And remember you were to have – ARE to have half of these. . . . Hadley, sweet, I detect a falling off of the letters from your quarter. Isn't there something can be done about this? . . . Much love to you. Also, love to Dos.[29]

It was a charade about her being in love with Dos, a game she played to make herself less threatening to Hadley, who was, by all accounts, no fool.

When she finally snuggled down into her night covers, Pauline opened once more *Mrs. Dalloway* where Peter Walsh was musing on his various vulnerabilities. It was "quite ridiculous," he thought, "how some girl without a grain of sense could twist him round her finger. But at her own risk."[30] She closed the book and turned out the light. Outside a chilled rain was again falling. In the Bois de Boulogne, there would be no lovers on carriage rides tonight.

Chapter Two

SUN AND SHADOWS

He had been as surprised as anyone and terribly embarrassed when he opened This Quarter to find Ernest Walsh's poem.

ERNEST HEMINGWAY

Papa soldier pugilist bullfighter
Writer gourmet lionhead aesthete
He's a big guy from near Chicago
Where they make the shoes bigger and
It's a good thing that because he aint
Got french feet Napoleon and him
Wouldn't have said much together
He'd have pulled Buonaparte's [sic] *nose*
And absolutely ruined french history
In Solomon's winy days he'd abeen in court
A few times and the King of Israel would have
Said This kid knows a few things and given him
Two plump dancing jewesses to lean on
While he ordered up a fat roasted calf
For in those days Kings preferred art to business.

All he could do was joke with Walsh about the poem, saying Hadley wanted to know how the secret of the Jewish girls had slipped out of the family closet. How could he tell a man who was spitting his tubercular lungs out into linen handkerchiefs that he should keep his bloody mouth off of people he did not know well?

15

PARIS: EASTER WEEK, 1926

Ernest, Hadley, and their two-and-a-half-year-old son arrived back in Paris on the grey, rainy Tuesday of Easter week. Unable to move into their sublet flat until Good Friday, they took temporary rooms in the Hôtel Vénétia on Montparnasse. It would have been less expensive to have remained in Schruns, but with revisions done, Hemingway wanted to get back to Paris and to Pauline. That evening, to make their return official, Ernest and Hadley sat in their corner café, the Closerie des Lilas, and the next day "Latin Quarter Notes" announced that "Ernest Hemingway reported yesterday with an extra pound or two under his belt."[1]

On April 1, Holy Thursday, Hemingway answered Max Perkins's letter that was waiting for him in Paris. Max sent the galleys for *Torrents* with only a few suggested changes. With more tact than Hemingway was accustomed to, Max raised the point about Hemingway's use of Maud Adams's name in the text. Having once discussed with her the publication of her reminiscences, Max had been so impressed with her "extreme sensitiveness" that he now "was moved to suggest the removal of her name if you thought it did no harm. You must not remove it if it does, of course."[2] Hemingway may have smiled at Max's delicate diction. In the Scripps O'Neil and the Waitress passage in *Torrents*, he had been spoofing Sherwood Anderson's habit of having his characters think in silly and inaccurate ways, and at the same time he was mocking the literary crowd with their steady demand for gossip. In Brown's Beanery, Scripps looks at the waitress and thinks: "She looks a little like that actress that died in Pittsburgh. What was her name? Maud Adams? In *Peter Pan*. That was it. They say she always went about veiled. . . . There was an interesting woman. Was it Maud Adams? Perhaps not. No matter."[3] Hemingway told Perkins that Maud would be changed as soon as the galleys arrived; corrections would be done quickly. First, however, he had to find a typist for *The Sun*, which needed a professional to clean up his 330-page typescript. "Reading it over," he said, "it seems quite exciting."[4] It had taken him five years to learn how to write a short story; now he had this first novel written and revised in eight months from scratch (really in six months if distractions were eliminated). Start to finish, it was a learning experience, making mistakes and then turning them to profit as he could. Two months before starting to write *The Sun*, he had read Scott Fitzgerald's *The Great Gatsby*, from which he learned a good deal. In both books, despite their best efforts to tell the stories of

16

others, the narrators became the center of attention. Hemingway's sad story about the war generation and Fitzgerald's graveside eulogy for the Jazz Age, although played in different keys, were both working the same theme: the post-war world, at home and abroad, was sick at heart, its values defunct and its over-age children at a loss for purpose. Both men wrote better than they knew, creating the classics of their age.

But with rain steady in the Paris gutters and his typescript still awkward in its beginning, Ernest Hemingway was not thinking about classics or immortality. He was a young man among many, writing as best he could. Reading back over the story, making small changes for the typist, he saw he had been right in most of his revisions. Some of the awkwardness — scaffolding put up to support the structure — he took down in large chunks. What once had seemed good lines in colder light appeared self-indulgent, things he had to say to get the writing to flow. Sometimes he was merely talking to himself, as when he wrote

> Probably any amount of this does not seem to have anything to do with the story and perhaps it has not. I am sick of these ones with their clear restrained writing and I am going to try to get in the whole business and to do that there has to be things that seem as though they had nothing to do with it just as in life. In life people are not conscious of these special moments that novelists build their whole structures on. That is most people are not. That surely has nothing to do with the story but you can not tell until you finish it because none of the significant things are going to have any literary signs marking them. You have to figure them out by yourself.
>
> Now when my friends read this they will say it is awful. It is not what they had hoped or expected from me. Gertrude Stein once told me that remarks are not literature. All right, let it go at that. Only this time all the remarks are going in and if it is not literature who claimed it was anyway.[5]

He chopped the passage out, including the part about "special moments" which pointed directly at Henry James, who specialized in such exquisite moments. Gertrude, Ezra Pound, and Hadley kept after him about James, that grand master of the American novel. Although he tried, Ernest never was converted. James had a few good moments, but he was dead and so were his notions about writing. Who could sound like James after they'd been to the front lines of the war? So it was goodbye

Gertrude, goodbye Henry James. Now the only sign remaining from his literary feud with his past was in the Pyrenees section of *The Sun Also Rises* where Jake Barnes and Bill Gorton were joking over the breakfast table about American expatriates. Bill said:

"You don't work. One group claims women support you. Another group claims you're impotent."
"No," I said. "I just had an accident."
"Never mention that," Bill said. "That's the sort of thing that can't be spoken of. That's what you ought to work up into a mystery. Like Henry James' bicycle."[6]

Ford Madox Ford, who had known James, told Ernest that James had suffered some sexual wounding that left him unfit for the Civil War and unfit for marriage.

Other remarks he hacked completely out. Most of Jake's musing and most of Bill's funny lines about homosexuals were penciled out. At Burguete, Bill said, jokingly,

"Since Charley Gordon and I had an apartment together last winter I suppose I'm a fairy. That probably explains everything. . . . Sex explains everything. You may think you're having fun. You're not having any fun. Everybody's frustrated. Abraham Lincoln was a fairy. He was in love with General Grant. So was Jefferson Davis. That's what the civil war was about. Will Rodgers is unhappy. So is President Coolidge. So is the Prince of Wales. So is Jack Dempsey. Nobody has any fun. They only think so. Sex explains it all. The Colonel's Lady and Judy O'Grady are lesbians under their skin.
That's what's supposed to be the matter. My God it would make you sick. They don't talk about complexes anymore. It's bad form. But they all believe it. And every literary bastard in New York goes to bed at night not knowing but that he'll wake up in the morning and find himself a fairy. There are plenty of real ones too."[7]

It was ineffective slapstick that he wrote to get out of his system. He did not hate homosexuals individually, but in flagrant groups they still rubbed the vestiges of his Oak Park sensibilities raw. What remained, understated but perfect, was the scene where Brett arrived with Cedric Morris and Lett Haines.

Two taxis . . . stopped in front of the Bal. A crowd of young men, some in jerseys and some in their shirt sleeves, got out. I could see their hands and newly washed, wavy hair in the light from the door. The policeman standing by the door looked at me and smiled. They came in. As they went in, under the light I saw white hands, wavy hair, white faces, grimacing, gesturing, talking. With them was Brett. . . . I was very angry. Somehow they always made me angry. I know they are supposed to be amusing, and you should be tolerant, but I wanted to swing on one, any one, to shatter that superior, simpering composure.[8]

Jake, determined that his own grief not show in public, had reason to be offended at so much simpering. With his sexual wound leaving his desire for Brett forever unsatisfied, Jake was the right man to be standing at the door.

PARIS: APRIL 1926

When the six-day bike race began late Monday night, Ernest and Hadley, loaded down with blankets, a picnic hamper, and red wine, were seated in choice box seats at the Vélodrome d'Hiver. With them they had the galley proofs for *Torrents of Spring* which they read during the slow periods. For the next one hundred and forty-one hours, they dropped in and out of the dimly lit arena, five days out of six, as the teams of racers pushed toward the finish.[9]

Wednesday, sitting in the stands with the *Tribune*, Hemingway read that "Sliding Billy" Watson's wife had been shot to death out on Long Island in some road house she ran. He wondered what had happened to Billy, the old burlesque entrepreneur he met in Kansas City when he was working on the *Star*. There was also a story about H. L. Mencken being arrested on the Boston Common for selling his *American Mercury* which had been banned by the Watch and Ward Society. Mencken, Hemingway read, was "in the front rank of thinkers who oppose the growing wave of puritanism in America." Ernest had to grin. He had dedicated *Torrents* to "H. L. MENCKEN AND S. STANWOOD MENCKEN IN ADMIRATION." The first Mencken, peppery essayist and influential editor, Hemingway held personally responsible for the *Mercury*'s turning down his fiction. Stanwood Mencken was the president of the National

Security League, one of the numerous right-wing groups spreading fear of Bolsheviks in America's on-going Red scare. Stanwood was exactly the sort of man H. L. Mencken loved to attack. The next day Hemingway put his corrected galleys for *Torrents* into the transatlantic mail.[10]

When the French racing team took honors with a tremendous burst in the last few hours, Ernest was on his feet cheering with the other hard-core fans, cheering the winners on. Few of his American friends shared Hemingway's enthusiasm for the six-day events, which seemed to them boring and endless, but Ernest truly admired bikers of all sorts — pursuit racers, distance men, and grand prix riders. They were a small brotherhood living within a fixed code of ethics about which the average observer knew nothing. Bikers had their own rules, their own slang, and flashy jerseys. As with all of his enthusiasms, Ernest would have liked to have been a bike racer; he studied them with intensity and sometimes imitated their dress. At the end of *The Sun Also Rises*, when Jake was recuperating at San Sebastian, he crossed paths with roadracers eating and joking in the hotel dining room. "The bicycle riders," he said, "drank much wine, and were burned and browned by the sun. They did not take the race seriously except among themselves. They had raced among themselves so often that it did not make much difference who won. Especially in a foreign country. The money could be arranged."[11]

When the races ended, Hemingway carried the euphoric energy with him out into the Paris streets. Life was good: one book was finished, the second at the typist. Curtis Brown, who had responsibility for foreign rights on the Liveright line of books, had sold *In Our Time* to Jonathan Cape in London. On April 12, the day after the bike races, Hemingway accepted Cape's offer of a £25 ($125) advance against royalties on *In Our Time*, but wanted Cape to include in their contract a right of refusal on *Torrents* and *The Sun Also Rises*, about which the publisher knew nothing. Curtis Brown also told him the news that *In Our Time* was already translated into Russian and Italian. If he "had not yet received any payment from 'Il Convegno' for the part which they have published, perhaps" he would like them to "try to collect this amount" for him.[12] In Paris that spring, everything he had worked for was coming gradually true. The only dark part of his life was the guilt he felt when returning to Hadley after meeting with Pauline.

Then spring rains came to Paris, turning the days grey, chilly, and monotonous. In their damp and coal-smoked apartment, Hadley's sniffles, brought back from Schruns, turned into full-fledged grippe; Bumby started coughing and would not stop; and Pauline was planning a trip to

Italy. Meanwhile hundreds upon hundreds of American tourists poured into Paris, crowding the Right-Bank boulevards and gawking through Montparnasse, straining for a glimpse of a real bohemian. Every college sophomore felt he had to get drunk on the Left Bank. Armed with *The Paris That's Not in the Guide Books* and their pockets full of cheap francs ("How much does this cost in real money?"), the newest Americans in Paris were crowding all the old haunts. The Dôme and the Rotonde, they read, were no longer authentic but worth a visit. The "Closerie de Lilas, the oldest *brasserie* of the Montparno section" was no longer a literary café where one could see real writers. The Quarter was full of "stagy affairs, designed to invite and trap the credulous tourist – the kind of tourist that lives on atmosphere." There was plenty of such atmosphere, including fake artists, fake writers, and fake dope dealers, at places like "the Dingo, the Jockey, the Gypsy Bar . . . which are now the life and soul of the new Latin Quarter."[13] This Paris, with its Americanized Right Bank and its commercialized Latin Quarter and its phoney Montmartre, this Paris was not the town Hemingway had come to love in 1922. This was Paris of the dollar bill, Paris of the cheap trick. It was somebody else's town, not his anymore. He was already half planning to return to the States in September.[14]

Then "Chink" Dorman-Smith, his Irish war buddy from Italian days, came to town for a two-week visit, and they stayed up late drinking scotch like old times. The great Chink, hero of their trek across the St. Bernard Pass in the spring of 1922, did he remember how Hadley's oxfords had split at the seams, did he remember Hemingstein sick on altitude and Chink hauling everyone's pack? Did he remember? How could he forget? It seemed longer ago than four years, but they still could see the fields of narcissus above Montreux. Good old Chink, who had been with them at Pamplona for the bullfights in '24, was the right tonic for a rainy Paris spring. On April 19, Ernest went with Chink and his British Army friends out past Neuilly to the 1924 Olympic stadium at Colombes to watch the British Army rugby team defeat its French counterpart 19–13. The next evening he took Chink through the rain to the opening of the Walt Whitman exhibit at Shakespeare & Co. bookshop. Sylvia Beach made a fuss over him, asking him to sign the guest book on the first page which she had reserved for literary notables. There was his signature close to those of James Joyce, T. S. Eliot, Paul Valéry, and Jules Romain. Later that night Hadley, leaving Bumby at home with the two men, also got to the opening.[15]

For Chink to be in town as *The Sun Also Rises* was coming back from

21

the typist brought out Ernest's best comic spirit. When Scott Fitzgerald complained from Antibes about his money problems, claiming that the $15,000 movie rights to *Gatsby* would barely see his family through to Christmas, Ernest could not take the problem too seriously.[16] Hemingway said he would have Ernest Walsh give Scott the $2,000 *This Quarter* prize; Chink would leave him his Irish estate; Pauline would give him her job at *Vogue*; and Ernest would have Scribner's send Scott all the Hemingway royalty checks. *"So Don't Worry About Money,"* he told Scott. Ernest also told him that he was dedicating *The Sun Also Rises*

TO MY SON
John Hadley Nicanor
This Collection of Instructive Anecdotes

Which really was a joke, for he assured Scott it was not a collection of anecdotes, but Scott would have to wait until August, when the Hemingways arrived in Antibes, to read it. He said the book parodied Scott's novel in progress which had matricide as its central theme. "I've tried to follow the outline and spirit of the Great Gatsby," Ernest wrote,

but feel I have failed somewhat because of never having been on Long Island. The hero, like Gatsby, is a Lake Superior Salmon Fisherman. (There are no salmon in Lake Superior). The action all takes place in Newport, R.I. and the heroine is a girl named Sophie Irene Loeb who kills her mother. The scene in which Sophie gives birth to twins in the death house at Sing Sing where she is waiting to be electrocuted for the murder of the father and sister of her, as then, unborn children I got from Dreiser but practically everything else in the book is either my own or yours. I know you'll be glad to see it. The Sun Also Rises comes from Sophie's statement as she is strapped into the chair as the current mounts.[17]

On the following Saturday, Hemingway put the freshly typed manuscript of *The Sun Also Rises* into the mail, writing Max Perkins that someone needed to check its spelling and punctuation. Despite three weeks of steady rain, despite his and Hadley's colds and Bumby's ever-deepening cough, he was working on a short story and thinking about his next novel. It would not be a war novel, he told Max, because after reading *War and Peace*, he could see there was no need for another one.[18]

22

NEW YORK: EARLY MAY 1926

During the first week of May, Max Perkins opened the manila envelope containing the typescript for *The Sun Also Rises*, the pig he bought in a poke, as Hemingway called it.[19] With everyone in the Scribner's office eager to read Max's latest find, including Charles Scribner himself, Perkins must have been a little worried about the only novel he ever contracted completely unseen. About its content he had only the vaguest idea, based on his brief conversations with Hemingway in February. No one in the office had been terribly excited by *Torrents of Spring*, a slight book clever enough for the New York critics and insiders, but inaccessible to the general reader. Knowing that *Torrents* was a coterie book, Perkins hedged against Scribner's loss by printing only 1,250 copies.[20] Even if that first printing of *Torrents* sold out, it would bring Hemingway a scant $250 in royalties. To make back the $1,500 Scribner advance, *The Sun Also Rises*' first printing of 5,090 would also have to sell out.[21] In 1926, the chances of a new author attracting that kind of attention were slim; Perkins must have felt his stomach tighten just a touch as he extracted the typescript.

It opened with an entire page of epigraphs, one long one from Ecclesiastes and a short one from Gertrude Stein. Since T. S. Eliot's *Waste Land* had popularized the use of epigraphs, all the young literati were outdoing each other with pithy quotes, but by calling up religious authority and the matron saint of the avant garde in the same breath, Hemingway was asking for trouble. Max turned to the first chapter which still began, "This is a novel about a lady," explaining Lady Ashley's unfortunate marriages, her pitiful fiance, and her stunning lack of moral responsibility. Max read on. Quite suddenly Jake Barnes appeared to say that he was going to have to tell this story. "I wanted to stay well outside the story," Jake said, "so that I would not be touched by it in any way, and handle all the people in it with that irony and pity that are so essential to good writing." Max could see it coming now, another literary satire, this time on the New York crowd that had made "irony and pity" their catch phrase.

Jake Barnes was a newspaperman and a wounded war vet living in Paris. "Like all newspaper men," he confessed, "I have always wanted to write a novel, and I suppose, now that I am doing it, the novel will have that awful taking-the-pen-in-hand quality that afflicts newspaper men when they start to write their own book." In five pages nothing happened. Max read on. Jake started telling about the Latin Quarter where American tourists, who lived in expensive Right Bank hotels, went to slum but never saw from the inside. Jake described the contempt that the loafers felt for the working artists and that the young felt for the old. "Everybody seems to dislike everybody else. The only happy people are the drunks," Jake said, confirming much popular opinion about American expatriates in Paris.

Then, quite abruptly, there appeared a Jew with only two friends, Jake being one of them. For "two years Robert Cohn had lived with a lady who lived on gossip, and so he had lived in an atmosphere of abortions and rumors of abortions, doubts and speculations as to past and pro-spective infidelities of friends, dirty rumors, dirtier reports and dirtier suspicions." A long anecdote about a man named Braddocks led now-here except to Jake saying he would not have put Braddocks "into this story except that he was a great friend of Robert Cohn, and Cohn is the hero."[22] First the novel was about Lady Ashley; now it was about this New York Jew named Cohn. The story did not seem to be going anywhere. Then, quietly, it started to happen. Jake, less self-conscious, began to let the action flow, creating a series of quick studies that were tight and perfect: the streets of Paris, its sidewalk tables, its prostitutes and taxi cabs. It would take judicious editing to make the book work, but Perkins realized he could deal with the sticking points gradually.

First he had to face the editorial board meeting headed by Charles Scribner, who, at seventy-two, was not unmovable but was formidable on certain topics like obscenity. The old man was not about to publish anything he considered a "dirty book." As John Wheelock, Max's contemporary at Scribner's, remembered, "Charles Scribner would no sooner allow profanity in one of his books than he would invite friends to use his parlor as a toilet." And there was Lady Brett saying, "I'm not going to be one of these bitches that ruins children." And Mike Campbell yelling, "Tell him the bulls have no balls." Fortunately, Charles Scribner solicited an outside opinion from a friend and incom-parable judge of morals. Robert Grant told him, "You *must* publish the book, Charles, but I hope the young man will live to regret it." Max had to argue as strongly as he had for Fitzgerald seven years earlier when Mr. Scribner initially turned down *This Side of Paradise*. The old heads listened, dubious, to Perkins' account. They were debating, he told them, not merely one book, but the future of the publishing house. If they turned Hemingway down, young writers, who were the future of the firm, would avoid them for their conservative position, and Scribner's would suffer. When the meeting was over, the board accepted, with serious reservations, Perkins' recommendation. They would publish *The Sun Also Rises* in October.[23]

Not until May 18 was Max able to compose the letter to Hemingway, calling the book "a most extraordinary performance. No one could conceive of a book with more life in it. All the scenes, particularly those when they cross the Pyrenees and come into Spain, and when they fish in that cold river, and when the bulls are sent in with the steers, and when they are fought in the arena, are of such a quality as to be like actual experience." What he was saying, without saying it out loud, was that the opening Paris part of the novel was not as well written as the part set in Spain. All the mindless drinking, sexual permissiveness, and random profanity which so disturbed Mr. Scribner, Max for the moment did not mention. But he had agreed to take up with Hemingway the matter of Henry James and his bicycle.

Max said nothing about the abortion talk or about the habits of the Quarterites, but this slur on Henry James, the patriarch of American letters, was more than he could allow to pass. "There is one hard point," he wrote Hemingway,

a hard one to raise too, because the passage comes in so aptly and so rightly. I mean the speech about Henry James. I swear I do not see how that can be printed. It would not by any conception be printed while he was alive, if only for fear of a lawsuit; and in a way it seems almost worse to print it after he is dead. I am not raising this, you must believe, because we are his publishers. The matter referred to is a personal one. It is not like something that a man could be criticized for, – some part of his conduct in life and which might therefore be considered open for comment. I want to put this before you at the very beginning. There are also one or two other things that I shall bring up in connection with the proof, but there is no need to speak of them here.

Max ended the letter on his astonishment at the novel's "extraordinary range of experiences and emotions" for which he had the greatest admiration. Now he would hold his breath to see how young Hemingway responded. If Henry James was a negotiable item, then other points would follow easily enough.[24]

Chapter Three

SUMMER'S LEASE

Virginia Woolf, in her Common Reader, *told Pauline enough about Defoe and his heroine to prick her interest. The young woman, she read, has*

> *to depend entirely upon her own wits and judgement, and to deal with each emergency as it arises by a rule-of-thumb morality which she had forged in her own head. . . . she begins by falling passionately, if unfortunately, in love. . . . She has a spirit that loves to breast the storm. She delights in the exercise of her own powers. . . . Shrewd and practical of necessity, she is yet haunted by a desire for romance and for the quality which to her perception makes a man a gentleman.*

Six days after returning the collection of essays, Pauline reappeared at Sylvia's bookshop and lending library. Sylvia wrote down on Pauline's check-out card Moll Flanders, and the date, April 26. No, Sylvia did not think it was the proper book to take on a driving trip to Chartres, but then whom, besides Henry Adams, could one rightly take to that unprecedented cathedral?[1]

MADRID: MAY 1926

He had been alone now for almost two weeks, but it seemed longer, living in another country where conversation was impossible.[2] Never a man to suffer loneliness well, almost every day he wrote Hadley in Antibes and Pauline in Italy where she was visiting Italian relatives with

26

her rich uncle. Every day the mail brought letters and telegrams from both women, but they did not cheer him up. The more letters he wrote, the more impossible his situation became, for to each woman he had to lie a little even if it was only by omission. Hadley knew about Pauline's feeling for him, but he could not tell his wife how desperately in love he had become with "Fife," as they both called her. Pauline thought Ernest had told Hadley more than he actually had. Remorseful but unrepentant, Hemingway was engaged in a very old game to which there could be no pleasant conclusion.

He tried not to think about it during the day when there were bull fights to watch, a walk to the Prado to see the three new Goyas, a café on the sunny side with a brandy to sip. He had come to Spain for the San Ysidro bull fights, but the first afternoon he arrived too late, the second day was cancelled by bad weather, and on the third day Nino de la Palma, who had been spectacular at Pamplona the summer before, was only adequate.[3] Days were one thing, nights quite another, with heavy suppers not ending until midnight followed by an empty bed. Ever since being blown up in the Italian night, he was vulnerable to sweats and terrors when alone in the dark. So at night in Madrid, despite the pledge with Hadley that they would never drink alone, he drank too much, felt sorry for himself, and could not stop the dreams.

On good days and bad he wrote, starting a new story and reworking two begun earlier. On that first cold Sunday, so cold they cancelled the *corrida*, he typed all morning on "Today is Friday," a five-page treatment of the Crucifixion with Roman soldiers rehashing the day as if it were a sporting event.

1st Roman Soldier:	You see his girl?
2nd Soldier:	Wasn't I standing right by her?
1st Soldier:	She's a nice looker.
2nd Soldier:	I knew her before he did. [He winks at wine-seller.]
1st Soldier:	I used to see her around the town.
2nd Soldier:	She used to have a lot of stuff. He never brought her no good luck.
1st Soldier:	Oh, he ain't lucky. But he looked pretty good to me in there today.[4]

On good days, dialogue flowed so smoothly that it needed no revision. This was a good day, maybe not a great story, but a good day.

After lunch he reworked a story begun the previous fall about Nick Adams's encounter with mobsters in upper Michigan. Composing on his portable typewriter, Hemingway lopped off the first two pages of the old draft and picked up the story when "The door of Henry's lunch room opened and two men came in. They sat down at the counter."[5] He did that a lot, cutting the beginnings of stories to start at a dramatic moment. Max and Al, the two hired assassins, were in town to kill an Italian boxer, Dominick Nerone, who had double-crossed the mob. The two gangsters ate their sandwiches, talked tough, and waited for the "wop" who never appeared. Nick asks,

"What are you going to kill the wop for? What did he ever do to you?"

"He never had a chance to do anything to us. He never even seen us."

"What are you going to kill him for then?"

"We're killing him for a friend. Just to oblige a friend, bright boy."

As the wall clock passed through the dinner hour when Nerone is expected, customers are turned away, told the cook is sick. Finally the two gunmen give up. As Al comes out of the kitchen, "The cut off barrels of the shotgun made only a slight bulge under the waist of his too tight fitting overcoat. He straightened his coat with his gloved hands." The door closes leaving Nick, George the owner, and Sam the cook alone with their fear. Nothing happened in the story: Nerone did not come to supper, no one was shot. The story was all in the waiting. He stopped there on page ten of his typescript, thinking the story was finished. He called it "The Matadors."[6]

Full of juice, as he later described it, he "got dressed and walked to Fornos, the old bullfighters' cafe, and drank coffee, and then came back" to his hotel where he began revising a story written the previous September about Nick and Prudie Mitchell, a young Indian girl.[7] After spending the Fourth of July in the village, Nick returned to the family cottage on the lake where his father was waiting supper for him: cold chicken, milk, and huckleberry pie. During the night Prudie came scratching at Nick's window in tears. It ended with Nick and Prudie kissing in the rowboat, and Prudie saying, "I had to come. They all came back from town drunk."[8] That early draft now seemed sentimental and misfocused.

Retyping the story, he saw how smoothly the first part read and made few changes. Nick was riding back from town in the Garner family's wagon, and Joe Garner was hauling drunk Indians out of the road. "Them Indians," said Mrs. Garner, which led to Joe teasing Nickie about his Indian girl friend. Back at the Adams' cottage, the Doctor is alone, waiting for Nick, who asks his father what he did that day.

> "I went for a walk."
> "Where did you go?"
> "Up back of the Indian camp."
> "Did you see anything?"
> "I saw something I didn't like," his father said.
> Something in Nick stopped. He did not know why.
> "What was it?"
> "The young Mitchell girl was in the woods with Frank Murphy from Dugan's. I ran onto them."[9]

Then Nick began to cry and his father felt sorry for him, trying to assure his son that people weren't rotten, but it was too late. "You've got no business to open your mouth to a kid," Nick's father says to himself.

> His father blew out the lamp and went into his own room and undressed sitting on the bed. Then he got into bed. He slept crossways in the big double bed to take up as much room as possible. He was very much alone.

Hemingway ended it there, knowing it wasn't exactly right but very close. Father and son, both alone, without women, the father knowing that lesson for a long time, Nick getting his first dose. "Ten Indians," as he finally called it, was a story of loneliness and betrayal that he had not understood until that moment alone in his cold Madrid hotel bed.[10]

Everything he wrote in Madrid played on lonely or betrayed men, a theme much on his mind. Christ on His cross, the boxer alone in his rented room, Nick crying himself to sleep. He learned that lesson one way from Joyce, who wrote about betrayal so lovingly, and learned it another way in the mirror. He could see it each day in the letters he wrote, and it made him sick but he couldn't find a way to stop it. He didn't want to stop it. All of April in Paris, he had been able to keep his two lives as husband and lover equally viable. Pauline was in and out of the Notre-Dame-des-Champs apartment as their good friend, whom he would walk to the metro in the dark. If Ezra and Ford could have both wife and mistress, his relationship with Pauline seemed reasonable enough. But then Pauline became unreasonable.

During a brief break in the rainy weather, Hadley took an overnight drive with Pauline and Jinny down through the Loire valley, leaving Ernest to care for Bumby. Later Hadley remembered the trip quite clearly.

We had lots of fun together, stopped at good places and ate deliciously, and of course the old castles were a delight. Pauline would get very moody, and quite often, snap at me, and I felt most uncomfortable. Jinny noticed this, told me Pauline had always been subject to this kind of mood. I asked Jinny then if she thought Pauline was falling for Ernest. Her reply was, "I think they are very fond of each other."[11]

It was an old story that Hadley knew only too well. Women were continually falling in love with Ernest and he with them. Before they were married, it was Katy Smith and Irene Goldstein; in Paris he was a constant attractor of young women and old. Whatever the cause and no matter how innocent the guise, her husband needed women around him. She watched it happening with Pauline, even encouraged it. In Schruns they had been Doula and Double Doula to his Drum, nicknames and love games but not serious games. At least she had not thought so until the Loire.

Back in Paris she asked her husband straight out what it was between himself and Pauline. Then did anxiety and remorse begin, silly words and slammed doors. He could not help it, he claimed. It happened, it was happening, and there was nothing he could do about it. If Hadley had not brought it out in the open, it would not have become a problem. Somehow it was Hadley's fault. She recognized the ploy but did not forgive it. They were both hurt and uncertain, cold-ridden under grey skies, their child crouping in the next room. Where would they find a face to face the summer? Pauline was planning to join them at the Murphys' villa in Antibes before the five of them went to Pamplona for San Fermin.

At their lending library Hadley checked out Nietzsche's *Thus Spake Zarathustra* and another volume on philosophical problems.[12] When Paul Mowrer first met her that spring, she asked him what he was reading.

Philosophy, he told her. "That's just what I want to hear about," she said. Paul said to himself, "Here is a young woman in trouble."[13] The trouble was not completely of her making, but she was a party to it. In Schruns, when she first saw the pattern forming, she could have challenged her husband's fascination with Pauline, but that was not her style. She had let the games go on, and he knew it. When he came in from moonlight walks with Pauline, she had made light of it.

If Hadley had joined him in Madrid as planned, they might have worked the problem out in bed as they had previous problems, but Bumby's sickness and her misunderstood letters kept them separated. The original plan was to leave Bumby at Antibes with the Murphys, go to Madrid for the San Ysidro bull fights and then return to Antibes until it was time for Pamplona in July. With his son's hacking cough and erratic fever growing worse in the filthy Paris weather, Ernest was eager to be elsewhere. The slightest possibility of flu often sent him scurrying for healthier conditions, for he had a particular horror of drowning in his own fluids.[14] On May 13, Ernest departed for Madrid alone, leaving Hadley the chore of taking Bumby to Antibes. Had they not argued about Pauline, he might have gone with her, but they had and he didn't.[15] From Madrid he wrote Fitzgerald to complain about the cold weather, the lousy bull fights, and how much he missed his wife. He said he had changed the dedication of *The Sun Also Rises* as Scott had suggested. "It is so obviously *not* a collection of instructive anecdotes," he explained, "and is such a hell of a sad story – and not one at all for a child to read – and the only instruction is how people go to hell . . . that I thought it was rather pleasant to dedicate it to Bumby. If you're right I won't put in the anecdote part – but I'll dedicate it to him for reasons that will be obvious when you read the book and also for another reason."[16] He could not yet tell Scott about Pauline and what the two of them were doing to his marriage.

Now he was in his cold room at the Pension Aguilar, and Hadley was living in the vacated Fitzgerald villa which Scott insisted she use as soon as Bumby was diagnosed as having whooping cough. Sara Murphy, with her usual good sense, did not want to expose the Fitzgerald, MacLeish, and Murphy children to Bumby's infection. On May 22, Gerald wrote Ernest, telling him not to worry, Bumby was improving under the care of their British doctor and was much better off sick in Antibes than sick in Paris. "All this you know," he said, "but I somehow wanted to write you. At a distance, things look so funny. If H[adley] stays I'll send the bike with P. Pfeiffer."[17] In his gentle way, Gerald was telling

Hemingway not to be so hard on Hadley; they were all doing their best in an unplanned and unpleasant situation.

Things did not look funny to Ernest, only inconvenient. He wanted Hadley with him in Madrid, not spending their summer money in Antibes. Like his father, Hemingway worried a good deal about money, keeping account books and expense lists and expecting Hadley to do the same. The Murphys had asked them down with no expenses attached, but he could see it was not working out that way. Not only were there Hadley and Bumby's expenses, but she had to take Marie Rohrbach, their maid, cook, and nanny, with her. Hadley tried, in as good a humor as possible, to explain.

> It was good old Scott, our six-o'clock-in-the-morning-drunk, who tho't of giving us the use of this villa that they have just left but which is theirs until June 17th. . . . It's adorable here and there's room for Fife if she wants to stop . . . As to money – Gerald insisted on paying my hotel & the doctor won't let me pay him so I suppose Gerald did that also. I paid everything before I left – two months of bakery, milk bill, dressmaker, 400 to Marie . . . and a lot of small necessities, cleaning too, so now with tips and all I am down to 440 francs. I am charging at the grocery but later I will need more – leave it to you. I can borrow from Scott & Gerald of course. . . . there's a letter for me at Murphy's from Pauline – will write her tonight or tomorrow.[18]

In response, Ernest mailed Hadley their joint passport, insisting that after sending Bumby and Marie back to Paris, she come to Madrid where he was having no fun alone.

On May 21, Hadley's telegram arrived:

> Impossible to leave before fumigation. If not cured June tenth must find place until Bumby can go Murphywards. No cause worry. Passport letter received Thurs morning Antibes.

That afternoon, feeling misunderstood by her husband, Hadley tried to explain the situation in the same loving language they always used in their private letters:

> Dearest & well beloved Waxin,
> You are so small & and what hard luck has come your way – you poor impoverished kitten. Of course the thing I want to do

worst in the world is leave Schatz safe & sound in the hands of the
Murphs & and haste to Waxin – but I can't consider him safe &
sound at present, you see, and as all our friends here are open to the
disease & all have children who are open to it they cannot come
near Marie to help her . . . If Bumbie is not completely cured by
then [June 10] . . . I may have to find a small villa or apartment. . . .
Letter from Pauline this morning . . . I told her she could stop off
here if she wants – it would be a swell joke on tout le monde if you
& Fife & I spent the summer at Juan les Pins or hereabouts instead
of Spain – Mummy may have to – anyway you're all invited.[19]

That same day in Madrid, Ernest was trying, in a letter, to explain his
situation to Sherwood Anderson, his earliest literary benefactor and role
model, and the man Ernest relentlessly satirized in *Torrents of Spring*.
Hadley and Dos Passos both warned him that Sherwood would be
deeply hurt and that Ernest would appear churlish and ungrateful if the
book were published. He had not listened. Now, with the parody about
to appear in New York, Hemingway somewhat belatedly, admitted that
it probably would hurt Anderson's feelings. That wasn't what he was
trying to do, he insisted. The book was a sincere joke, not meant to be
mean. Among themselves, he said, authors didn't have to mince words.

If when a man like yourself who can write very great things writes
something that seems to me, (who have never written anything
great but am anyway a fellow craftsman) rotten, I ought to tell you
so. . . . It looks, of course, as though I were lining up on the side of
the smart jews like Ben Hecht and those other morning glories and
that because you had always been swell to me and helped like the
devil on the In Our Time I felt an irresistible need to push you in
the face with true writer's gratitude. But what I would like you to
know, of course that sounds like bragging, is – oh hell I can't say
that either.[20]

The more he explained, the worse the letter became with sentences
twisting themselves into knots and every remark needing qualification.
Breaking off abruptly, Ernest asked Sherwood to write whether or not
he was hurt by *Torrents*.

The next day Hadley wrote that Pauline, who had already suffered
through whooping cough, was arriving in Antibes on May 26.

33

If you feel you'd like to come your whatyoumacallit would be hailed by all and us four . . . would swim & drink our heads off in great comfort here and later in a Pension considering it all in light of Spanish summer expenses.

    OR

Pfeiffer & I can leave here as soon as health and comfort [of Bumby] is assured and join Waxins.

Whatever they did, Bumby could not be left with the Murphys; according to the doctor, the boy could be contagious for two more months. Hadley planned to stay in Antibes past June 10, making sure that Bumby was well enough to leave with Marie, and then she and Pauline would travel to Madrid.[21]

On May 23, Hemingway wrote his father, thanking him for the "many fine Sports magazines" and surprising him with the news that Ernest was bringing his family back to the states to winter in Piggott, Arkansas. First they would visit in Oak Park and St. Louis before moving to Piggott, where he could write undisturbed. Pauline Pfeiffer, he said quite casually, was getting them a house there. In the next breath and with no explanation, he said, "Having been to mass this morning I am now due at the bull fight this afternoon. Wish you were along."[22]

Their son's casual reference to attending the Catholic Church may have surprised his Oak Park Congregationalist family but would not have surprised Pauline Pfeiffer. The next day Hemingway received an answer from her to a question he had asked in an earlier letter.

And the Eucharists, my dear, tho I hadn't heard them called that, are evidently those going to the Eucharistic Council that, you are right, is going to be held in Chicago this year. It is the important Church Conference held every ten years (or some such period) in, I think, the interests of progress. It says "Whither are we drifting," and shifts the sail to the leeward. You will probably get to Chicago just in time for it, and won't that be fine.[23]

Hemingway was quietly engaged in a conversion to Catholicism, the religion of bull fighters, painters, and soldiers; the religion of Joyce, Fitzgerald, and Pauline Pfeiffer. His earliest Catholic experiences came during the war in Italy. The night he was blown up at Fossalta, an Italian priest anointed him at the field station as he lay on his stretcher, seriously wounded, in shock, and not certain he was going to live. He was now powerfully drawn to the Church's ritual as well as its power and dogma, to its humbling cathedrals as well as its insistence on mystery and faith. In Italy, France, and Spain after the war, he found there was no serious religion but Catholicism. No other faith had raised up the glory that was Cologne, Burgos, and Chartres.

But not even the benefits of the Church could mitigate his loneliness in Madrid. On May 22, he wrote Fitzgerald what a lousy time he was having in Madrid while Hadley was luxuriating in Antibes. He also wrote Hadley another letter, enclosing 1,200 francs for her expenses, once more telling her to come to Madrid. On May 24, when Hadley sat down to answer his letter, her feelings boiled over.

> Scott has just brought your disheartened letter full of how lonely you are and how I must be having such a good time and don't seem to mind being away from you and am not wrenched at the tho't of staying away so long from you and Spain! . . . I'm *not* having a good time, not seeing anybody and very, very lonesome and faced by a *bunch* of problems. I should have tried to force you to come as best for me only I didn't want to break up your Spanish plans even for so short a length of time. We are not in the hands of Scott & Zelda but I am using their villa at *no* cost (they are *giving* it) and being largely supplied with food even by Gerald & Sara . . . I don't even spend money on drink, however bad I feel – until yesterday when I had the curse and got so low I went downtown and spent 8 francs on whiskey & felt repentant. I don't talk to a soul except Marie all day. . . . I'm living here the cheapest possible and *not* being bad. I've got a headache & a heartache and I work for the common good and am sorrier than I can say I havn't been able to expend myself more on you and not so much on the Smaller Shad. I probably have just written Shit letters and that's the truth. My hand shakes writing most of them.

She also told her husband that Pauline would be glad to come to Madrid to comfort him. If he thought it "wisest" not to use the passport she mailed him, Pauline would "make Madrid a place of pleasure instead of the awful strain of a place it's been to you alone." Hadley's sarcasm gave Ernest some indication of how far he had pushed his wife in this game they were playing.[24]

When he received their joint passport and Hadley's letter on May 27, Hemingway immediately telegraphed his Paris bank to forward mail to the Villa Paquita at Juan les Pins and telegraphed Hadley that he was joining her as soon as possible. She wired back that she and Pauline were awaiting his arrival with joy, and signed it Kitten.[25]

Chapter Four

A Pursuit Race

Zelda Fitzgerald remembered that summer at Juan les Pins with its fog of parties filled with people now mostly forgotten. "At the Villa Paquita I was sick," she wrote Scott.

> Sara brought me things and we gave a lunch for Gerald's father. We went to Cannes and listened to Raquel Miller and dined under the rain of fire-works. You couldn't work because your room was damp and you quarrelled with the Murphys. We moved to a bigger villa and I went to Paris and had my appendix out. You drank all the time and some man called up the hospital about a row you had had. We went home, and I wanted you to swim with me at Juan les Pins but you liked it better where it was gayer at the Garoupe with Marice Hamilton and the Murphys and the MacLeishes. Then you found Grace Moore and Ruth and Charlie and the summer passed, one party after another. We quarrelled about Dwight Wiman and you left me lots alone. There were too many people and too many things to do: every-day there was something and our house was always full. There was Gerald and Ernest and you often did not come home. There were the English sleepers that I found downstairs one morning and Bob and Muriel and Walker and Anita Loos, always somebody – Alice Delamar and Ted Rousseau and our trips to St. Paul [de Vence] and the note from Isadora Duncan and the countryside slipping by through the haze of Chamberry-fraises and Graves – That was your summer. I swam with Scottie except when I followed you, mostly unwillingly.[1]

These were the new summer people, and this was the end of the line for Ernest and Hadley.

A Pursuit Race

South Coast of France: Summer 1926

Three changes of trains and a little patience brought Hemingway in the afternoon of May 28 to Juan les Pins where the Murphys, Pauline, and Hadley met him at the station. That evening, at a small night club, Sara and Gerald hosted a champagne and caviar party to welcome Ernest and to celebrate the publication that day in New York of *Torrents of Spring*. Ada and Archie MacLeish were there with Pauline, Hadley, and the Fitzgeralds for an evening that started well and ended badly. No gaiety, no rhetoric the Murphys devised could reduce the tension that no single participant fully understood.

Between Pauline and Hadley there was a forced, lip-tight levity; Ernest tried to offset their disturbing smiles with his own humor, but having had no time alone with either woman, he was at a disadvantage. The three of them were beginning to understand the stakes of the strange game they played. Even without Pauline's presence, there would have been between Ernest and Hadley a residual tension from their separation and the misunderstandings generated through the mail. Ernest sensed Hadley's hurt and anger, but he did not appreciate exactly how much burden had fallen on her with Bumby's illness, nor was he yet satisfied with their presence in Villa Paquita, which placed him in Fitzgerald's debt, a position he resented. Then there were the Murphys picking up the other expenses, and he had to smile and drink their champagne. Sitting among them but not with them was Zelda Fitzgerald, deadpan and intense, her dark eyes staring holes in Hemingway.

Dog-tired from his train trip and too tightly wound, Ernest was the center of attention. It was obvious to all, particularly Scott, that Sara and Gerald doted on the young writer who already had Pauline on one arm and Hadley on the other. It was more adulation than Fitzgerald was capable of watching without sharing. Never one to sit still gracefully and easily bored, Scott had developed an irritating repertoire of attention-getting tricks. That was the summer he began introducing himself, "I'm Scott Fitzgerald, and I'm an alcoholic." On a earlier evening in a similar club, he "followed two young French boys around the dance floor asking them if they were fairies." As Gerald Murphy said later, the Fitzgeralds "didn't want entertainment, or exotic food; they seemed to be looking forward to something fantastic . . . something had to happen, something extravagant."[2]

That night at Juan les Pins, much as he admired Hemingway, Scott managed, in his search for extravagance, to ruin the celebration. First he insulted Gerald, saying loudly that his champagne and caviar were an affectation terribly out of date, an opinion which did not slow Scott's consumption of the same. Then, when a particularly attractive young woman arrived in the club, Fitzgerald stared at her so long and so rudely that others finally asked him to stop. Zelda, with a fuchsia peony on top of her dark blond hair, said nothing, not even when her husband began throwing ashtrays at a nearby table of strangers. Finally, Gerald Murphy lost his temper and walked out of his own party. As he left, Scott told Sara that he had never seen Gerald act so silly and rude. The next day Sara wrote Fitzgerald,

And if Gerald was "rude" in getting up & leaving a party that had gotten *quite bad*, – then he was rude to the Hemingways & MacLeishes too. No, it is hardly likely that you would stick at a thing like *manners* – it is more probably some theory you have – (it *may* be something to do with the book) – But you ought to know *at your age* that you *Can't have Theories about friends* – If you Can't take friends largely, & without suspicion – then they are not friends at all. We *cannot* – Gerald & I at our age & stage in life – *be bothered* with Sophomoric situations – like last night.[3]

It was going to be the kind of summer where interludes, no matter how pleasant, were tarnished by remembered acrimony.

If Hemingway was disturbed by Scott's behavior, it did not prevent him from appearing next morning at Fitzgerald's nearby Villa St. Louis. After sharing with him Max Perkins' letter of praise for *The Sun Also Rises*, he gave Fitzgerald, for his comments, the carbon copy of the novel. Returning to Villa Paquita, Hemingway read through the rest of his mail. Vernon MacKenzie of the Hearst organization wanted a story for *Cosmopolitan*; *New Masses* wanted a story; the Paris landlord wanted his key.

Outside, the sun was shining on a curving, white beach that cupped the Golfe de Juan where sea-blown pine trees grew down almost to blue water. Up the coast on the headland jutting out into the Mediterranean, the town of Antibes glittered atop its white sea wall. In the markets there were fresh fish and vegetables, tart goat's cheese, dry white wines, good olive oil, and crusty bread. Across from the train station, the Book Lounge and Library carried almost current English papers, magazines, and books. Inside Villa Paquita, Hemingway was immersed in the sweet, medicinal smell of eucalyptus from his son's sickroom. Marie, who shared Bumby's room at night, cared for the boy by day when she wasn't cooking for Ernest, Hadley, and Pauline. When the lease came due, the Hemingway party moved into the conveniently close Hotel de la Pinèda. "Here it was," Hadley said later, "that the three breakfast trays, three wet bathing suits on the line, three bicycles were to be found. Pauline tried to teach me to dive, but I was not a success. Ernest wanted us to play bridge but I found it hard to concentrate. We spent all morning on the beach sunning or swimming, lunched in our little garden. After siesta time there were long bicycle rides along the Golfe de Juan." Cycling down the coast road, Ernest, as usual, forged out into the lead; Pauline tried gamely to catch up to him, and Hadley, falling further behind, kept her own, more leisurely pace. It was not a pursuit race, but it looked like one.[4]

VILLA ST. LOUIS: JUNE 2, 1926

It did not take Fitzgerald long to read the *The Sun Also Rises* typescript, for having made large promises about it to Max Perkins, he was worried that he might be wrong. When he finished the first ten pages, he was deeply worried. Nothing was happening except Latin Quarter gossip. He tried to talk to Hemingway about it that day, saying that he found in Ernest the "tendency to envelope or . . . to *embalm* in mere wordiness an anecdote or joke" the way he, Scott, tried to preserve a piece of "fine writing." Hemingway, a little hurt, wanted specific examples. Now Scott was writing it out in pencil, slashing, correcting, qualifying. It was not easy to find the right tone.

After an involved preamble, trying to soften the blow, Fitzgerald said it straight. "I think parts of Sun Also are sloppy, careless and ineffectual," he wrote. "Your first chapter . . . gives a feeling of condescending casualness." Then he began taking apart Hemingway's over-written introduction. When Jake wasted words, Scott said,

> That's what you'd kid in anyone else as mere "style" – mere horse-shit. . . . you've not only got to write well yourself but you've also got to ~~not do what cheap people~~ scorn to do what anyone can do and I think there are about 24 ~~cheap jokes~~ sneers, superiorities and nose-thumbings-at-nothing that mar the whole narrative up to

p. 29 where (after a false start on the introduction of Cohn) it really gets going. And to preserve these perverse and willful non-essentials you've done a lot writing that *honestly* reminded me of Michael Arlen.

[You know the very fact that people have committed themselves to you will make them watch you like a cat & if they don't like it creep away like one.]

For example.

Pages 1 & 2. Snobbish (not in itself but because the history of the English Aristocrats in the war, set down so verbosely, so uncritically, so exteriorly and yet so obviously inspired ~~by~~ from within is *shopworn*. . . . Either bring more thot to it with the realization that that ground has already raised its ~~crops~~ wheat and weeds or cut it down to seven sentences. It hasn't even your rhythm. ~~It's bad Arlen~~ and the fact that ~~it's true~~ it may be "true" is utterly immaterial. ~~I'm not talking about her but about your book.~~

~~My God!~~ That biography from you, who always ~~believed~~ in the superiority (the preferability) of the *imagined* to the *seen – not to say to the merely recounted*. . . . [About this time I can hear you say "Jesus this guy thinks I'm lousy & he can stick it up his ass for all I give a Gd Dm for his 'criticism." But remember this is a new departure for you and that XXXXXXXXXXXXXXXXXXXXXXXXXXXXX XXXXXXXXXXXXXXXXXXXXXXXXXXXXX ~~just remember~~ I think your stuff is great.

Then Scott told Ernest to kill his darlings, to take out real names like those of Aleister Crowley and Harold Stearns, and to cut a long literary anecdote centering on Ford Madox Ford, which Scott said was "flat as hell without naming Ford which would be cheap." He said,

When so many people can write well & the competition is so heavy I can't imagine how you could have done these first 20 pages so ~~carelessly~~ casually. You can't *play* with peoples attention . . . I can't tell you the sense of disappointment that beginning with its elephantine facetiousness XXXXXXXXXX gave me. Please do what you can about it in proof. Its 7,500 words – you could reduce it to 5,000. And ~~don't~~ my advice is not to do it by mere parring but to take out the worst of the scenes.

The rest of the book, Scott said, was "damn good. The central theme is marred somewhere but what the hell!" Jake was more like a man in a moral chastity belt than one left sexually maimed by a war wound, but there wasn't much Hemingway could do about that now.

He closed the letter, "Station Z.W.X. square says good night. Good Night all."[5] Ten pages it had taken him to write the kind of advice he gave himself every morning he managed to face his work in progress, which Zelda said, "goes so slow it ought to be serialized in the Encyclopedia Britannica."[6] Exhausted and a little worried, knowing how easily Ernest took offense, he folded the letter and put it into the envelope. It was the best thing he would write that summer.

Hemingway took the criticism much better than Fitzgerald had imagined. The next day they discussed the novel's marred beginning: Scott said, revise; Ernest said, radical surgery. Two days later, Hemingway wrote Max Perkins that when he got the galleys, he was excising the first sixteen pages of The Sun's typescript. Everything they contained was either restated elsewhere or was unnecessary to the book. "Scott agrees with me," he said. "He suggested various things in it to cut out – in those first chapters – which I have never liked – but I think it is better to just lop that off and he agrees."[7] As a result, Jake Barnes's attitude toward the Latin Quarter – *I could sort of take it or leave it alone* – was somewhat softened; Brett Ashley's foreground was made more vague; and Jake's Catholicism, carefully laid down in those opening pages, would now come as something of a surprise to the reader. This massive cutting was the easy way out of his problem, and Ernest needed an easy way, for he had no stomach just then for detailed revisions.[8] There were other changes to be made, but this, the most important one, had been midwived for Hemingway by the same man in whose villa he had lived rent free, the man who brought him first to Perkins' attention and who told him to cut the opening joke from "Fifty Grand." Ernest Hemingway was deeply in the debt of Scott Fitzgerald.

That same week, having received Hemingway's Madrid letter enclosed with a copy of *Torrents of Spring*, Sherwood Anderson sat down to answer the young man whom he had not seen for almost five years.

About the book – your letter – all your letters to me these last two or three years – it's like this. Damn it man you are so final – so patronizing. You always speak to me like a master to a pupil. It must be Paris – the literary life. You didn't sound like that when I knew you.

You speak so . . . tenderly of giving me a punch. You sound like Uncle Ezra [Pound]. Come out of it man. I pack a little wallop myself. I've been middle weight champion. You seem to forget that. . . . About the plug I put in for you with Liveright [re: *In Our Time*]. I'm sorry I ever mentioned it. I've done the same for men I hated and I like you. The only reason I ever spoke of it was to let you know I liked your work.

Tell the truth I think the Scribner's book will help me and hurt you. Spite of all you say it's got the smarty tinge.[9]

The letter ended with an invitation to the Hemingways to visit Anderson in Virginia that fall on their way to Arkansas.

Anderson's letter arrived about the same time as the first batch of reviews of *Torrents*, most of which included the Ford Madox Ford statement that Hemingway was "the most promising American author in Paris," and all of which saw Anderson as the point of his parody. The *New York Times* liked it well enough, but thought the book "a somewhat specialized satire . . . almost in the nature of a literary vaudeville, which will appeal mainly to Mr. Hemingway's fellow craftsmen." The *Evening Post* called it "delicious fun . . . and one of the best recent books we have found for reading aloud (always provided those present know Mr. Anderson's work)." Only the *New York World* mentioned the relationship between the book and Hemingway's broken Liveright contract, noting that "when Hemingway published 'In Our Time' it was Sherwood Anderson who turned handsprings and welcomed this newcomer to the ranks of America's great men . . . and now Hemingway pays him back."[10]

JUAN LES PINS AND ANTIBES: JUNE 1926

Summer days dissolved in sunlight and bright water, leaving a residue of old newspapers, orange seeds on a garden plate, and blurred memories. Was it the summer of '26 or '28 we swam at Eden Roc? The young girl, now grown old, can still see Archie MacLeish high diving, suspended in air, his arms spread gracefully against blue sky. And Gerald remembers the night that Zelda dared Scott to dive with her in the dark and Scott's face white and grim, following her up the rock. But was that the summer that Zelda danced on the casino table and the stragglers stopped to watch? Who can say? One summer in the Twenties at Antibes was much like another.

The Murphys' Villa America contained fourteen rooms, carefully renovated in 1925 and its flat roof made sturdy enough to support sunbathers. "The downstairs floor was waxed black tile, the interior walls were painted white, and the fireplace was framed with mirror glass. The furniture . . . was covered with black satin. Outside the house was beige with yellow shutters." The whole place, house and seven acres of gardens sloping down toward the sea, cost barely $15,000 start to finish. It was the Murphys' private kingdom, where Gerald was director of activities, sometime painter and master of the costume closet. Sara managed the household, arranged flowers, made lists, planned meals, and shopped, as her daughter remembered, "with rare imagination." She was assisted by Celestine, the cook; Clement the chauffeur; Mamzelle the nurse; and Ernestine, the maid.[11]

In the heart of the garden, their airy house opened on to Arabian maples, desert holly, persimmon, palms, and cedars of Lebanon, terraced and cared for by three gardeners. On the far side, adjoining the old French farmhouse turned guest cottage, were the vegetable garden, orange, lemon, tangerine, olive, and nut trees. At the bottom of the hill there was a renovated donkey stable, La Ferme des Orangers, where Gerald housed his overflow of summer guests. MacLeish remembered that the Murphys "knew how to live without throwing money around. For example, one of the best luncheons I ever ate in my life was eaten under a linden tree outside their little villa on d'Antibes. It was served on a blue china dish on which were some perfectly boiled new potatoes and some butter. There was a white wine, probably something like muscadet – at that time very cheap. And bread and butter."[12]

Life around the Murphys floated on an air of wonder and the possibility of the unexpected or the unlikely. Gerald, who would go to great lengths to astound his children and amuse his guests, delighted in games and costumes of all sorts. In the old photographs we see him equally poised in his French sailor suit, his Apache outfit, or his impeccable vested suit and banker's bowler hat. But try as he might with various disguises, he was never quite one of the boys, never quite certain of male acceptance. Besides his Mark Cross, Boston money, his many talents should have sustained him better than they did. Gerald Murphy was a first-rate painter who studied with Fernand Léger and exhibited in the Paris salons. In 1923, he collaborated with Cole Porter on a satirical ballet, *Within the Quota*, which they produced at the Théâtre des

Champs-Élysées in Paris. No mere dilettante despite his dandyish manners, Murphy tried too hard to meet what he thought were the expectations of others. This trait was particularly obvious in his relationship with Ernest Hemingway, whom he came close to worshipping.[13]

In those summers of the Twenties, while the Murphy children were growing up and the world was reeling blindly toward the Great Depression, Villa America was a way station for writers and artists whom Sara and Gerald attracted with their impeccable taste. They came for the company, the food, the beach, and the parties. They came to sail on the racing sloop, *Picaflor*. They came singly and in groups, and they all became famous in their time. Pablo Picasso and his wife Olga, a Diaghilev ballerina, came to the Villa. Philip Barry, the playwright, came and used the Villa as a setting for a new play. John Dos Passos, the MacLeishes, the Fitzgeralds, and the Hemingways all came to Antibes. Robert Benchley, Dorothy Parker, and Marc Connelly came. Fernand Léger came to look at the large canvases in Gerald's separate studio. Rudolph Valentino, the silent Sheik, came, as did Cole Porter, the songsmith of the era. These were the beautiful people, and as beautiful as any were Sara and Gerald, artists working in a most ephemeral form.

Dos Passos, remembering the guest house where he often stayed, said,

> It was marvelously quiet under a sky of burning blue. The air smelt of eucalyptus and tomatoes and heliotrope from the garden. I would get up early to work, and about noon walk out to the sand fringed cove . . . Gerald would be sweeping the seaweed off the sand . . . We would swim out through the calm crystal blue water, saltier than salt, to the mouth of the cove and back.[14]

In the summer photographs the beach is white with sunlight and Gerald, as poised as a dancer, holds his beach rake like an oar. Scott and his daughter sit hip-deep in the calm tidal pool; Zelda stands to their left, her finger tips almost touching the water. Slight distances separate all three. Arms cocked on his hips, right knee braced with a bandage, Ernest is thin and handsome in his striped swim shorts; Bumby perches on his father's shoulders; his fat legs hang down over Hemingway's chest.[15]

Laughter came easy and often that summer to everyone but Zelda Fitzgerald, who seemed to live within her own strange cloister. In the home movie she sits beneath the beach parasol, wearing "a bright striped French sailor's jersey, and her short hair is blowing back from her face and looks springy and dark. Nervously she plays with her hands on the table top." She "was aloof and remote," Ada MacLeish said. "It was not that she did not pay attention to what one was saying, but a strange little smile would suddenly, inexplicably cross her face. She answered questions if they were put to her, but otherwise she remained distant." What once had been her beauty was quickly hardening into something remote and even scary. "Gerald," she said without provocation, "don't you think Al Jolson is just like Christ?"[16]

That summer, before she went to Paris with troubled ovaries and lost her appendix in the operation, Zelda made it clear, once more, that she had little respect for Hemingway. Maybe she resented Scott's adulation of the younger writer; maybe she was too much like Ernest in her self-centered hardness. Whatever the reason, it made for unpleasant moments in all that sunlight. When Sara Mayfield asked her what Ernest's new novel was about, Zelda replied, "Bull fighting, bull slinging and bullshit." Scott stepped in to defend Hemingway, but never changed Zelda's mind. No one, she was certain, could be as masculine as Ernest projected himself to be. The man was a phoney. Frequently needling the Hemingways, she told Hadley one day, "I notice that in the Hemingway family you do what Ernest wants." Hemingway did not much care for the remark, but, as Hadley said later, it was perceptive of Zelda about Ernest wanting everything his way. What Hadley did not say was that her own apparent complacency had, that summer at Juan les Pins, reached its limits.

PAMPLONA: JULY 1926

While anarchists in Paris were trying to assassinate the King of Spain, the Hemingways, the Murphys, and Pauline Pfeiffer were sitting under the Café Iruna's arcade, sipping Fundador brandy with soda, eating grilled prawns, and observing the friendly bootblacks at their trade. "My God, you could not get in all the bootblacks," Hemingway said a few years later, "nor all the fine girls passing; nor the whores; nor all of ourselves as we were then."[17] Especially ourselves, he might have added. He brought the group into Pamplona a week early to acclimatize them, bringing them gradually up to drinking speed. They lived in rooms he booked at the Quintana, the bullfighters' hotel he knew so well from three previous *ferias* of San Fermin. Later in the week, Villalta and Niño de la Palma, two of the San Fermin matadors, moved in across the hall from the Hemingway party.[18]

In 1923, they had come alone to the bull fights and street madness, Hadley pregnant with Bumby, Ernest unknown and unpublished. In 1924, they had come with friends: Chink, Dos Passos, and Bill Bird. That next summer of 1925 was the disaster: too much drinking, too little sleep, too many angry words, too much Duff Twysden. But it had given Ernest *The Sun Also Rises* as an unexpected dividend.[19] It was strange. The good summers produced no stories; the rotten summer birthed a novel. At their sidewalk table, with the afternoon sun turning the plaza white and the dust rising in the still air, they smile at the camera as they are able. Gerald and Ernest in coats and ties; Ernest wearing his black *boina*, Gerald, a tweedy cap. Concerned with Hemingway's approval of his dress, Gerald had vetted his father's old golf cap with Ernest beforehand. "I was relieved," he said, "with Ernest being a figure there, when he said, 'That's just the right thing to wear.'"[20] Sara looks unhappy in her flower print dress, a cigarette at her finger tips; Ernest is seated as he was all summer between Pauline and Hadley; both women smiling bravely, squinting slightly in the bright sun. On the table before them are the siphon bottle and almost empty glasses. No one can tell from the picture to whom Ernest is married or that the marriage is failing.[21]

During the leisurely days preceding San Fermin there were walks along the river that sided the town below the old walls of the French star fort; village women still pounded their sheets clean in the water, and small boys skipped stones across it. Outside Pamplona, heaving in the slight breeze, wheat was yellow in the fields and on the hill sides. It was Navarra in July: "the smell of olive oil; the feel of leather; rope soled shoes; the loops of twisted garlics; earthen pots; saddle bags carried across the shoulder; wine skins ... the early morning smells; the cold mountain nights and long hot days of summer, with always trees and shade under the trees."[22]

Everything they saw, every odor and sound, brought back to Ernest and Hadley earlier summers in Pamplona. Here they bought their first *boinas*, long since lost. On this corner they first saw the *riau riau* dancers leaping. And at this wine shop they filled their goatskin *bota* before the picnic. Here they first came alone and later with friends, each summer's response a metaphor and calendar of their marriage. Now into all those shared and private places came Pauline, with a forced brilliance and a witty, wicked tongue, too witty for Hadley to keep up with. If Sara and Gerald noticed, and how could they not, they made little of it. In the midst of San Fermin, it was easy for them to ignore wordless conversations taking place beneath the facade of small talk and commonplaces.

Always there was something to drink, something new to see, something strange to buy. Gerald bought a guitar for his oldest son, Baoth, and Sara purchased a San Fermin drum for herself. Ernest delighted in being their guide, the only one among them with enough Spanish to navigate the week of the *feria* which began, as always, on July 6 with the cannon firing, the explosion of fife and drum corps, brass bands, Moorish giants of papier mâché parading in the streets, laughter and lurching and nights with little sleep.

Afterwards Gerald and Sara said that the two weeks in Pamplona had been the most intense moments of their lives, an experience they owed to the Hemingways. The bullfighters, Gerald said, lived "in a region all their own – and alone each, somewhere between art and life, – and eclipsing at times each of them – make you feel that you are as you find most other people – half-alive. They are a religion for which I could have been trained. This knocked at my heart all the time at Pamplona." The first time Sara saw blue intestines come leaking out of the picador's gored horse, she left the bull ring in disgust, but returned later to cheer as loudly as anyone. "I shall *never* forget it," she told Ernest, "and no one has anything on me about liking bullfights – even if I don't like seeing bowels. But *that* is just a woman's whimsey and does not count."[23]

During the *encierro*, when Villar, Romero, and Clairac bulls came clattering down the Pamplona streets with the young men racing before them, Gerald wanted to join the runners but his better judgement and fear of appearing a fool kept him from it. Afterwards Sara told him that she was sorry he had not run, for "it would have been a great feeling afterwards." "Next year," he promised, "I will, and I'll do it well."[24] He had done well enough during one of the morning amateurs, when armed with his raincoat and eager to prove himself to Hemingway, he had taken his place in the Pamplona ring among the hundreds of younger men. "Ernest was watching me out of the corner of his eye," he remembered later. "He didn't want me to get thrown, but he did want to see how I was going to take it. . . . Then I saw this bull coming straight at me, and I held up the raincoat, but unfortunately I held it in front of me. . . . Ernest yelled, 'Hold it to the side!' I moved it just in time, and the bull went right by me, and Ernest said something about a veronica." Then Ernest got into the ring, with nothing in his hands to mislead the bull. "Just as the bull reached him, he threw himself over the horns and landed on the animal's back and stayed there, facing the tail."[25]

By night, complicated fireworks lit up the plaza, dazzling the eye, and there was music playing, drums and fife, and everywhere drinking and laughter. Who could remember which day the Murphys danced the Charleston before a delighted crowd or who paid for the *barrera* seats that put them as close to the ring as possible? The first day Lalanda caught a horn and Zurito substituted for him the next, and almost every day there was Niño de la Palma who had been so brilliant only the summer before. On the tenth, Juan Belmonte appeared at great expense but at no great risk to himself, earned his pesetas and took them to the bank. On July 11, Lalanda came back for the last *corrida* with Niño, Zurito, and Villalta, each with his own style and mannerisms. The Murphys were impressed that Ernest knew these men well enough for introductions, and that Hadley once owned a bloody bull's ear, a gift from Niño de la Palma.[26] And afterwards Villalta said, "I won't try to thank you for the flowers."[27]

On the morning after San Fermin, Ernest and Hadley were relieved to catch the San Sebastian train. Under cover of station noise and baggage bustle, the party from Antibes was subdued in post-fiesta shock, the experience already becoming unbelievable. The Hemingways were glad to watch the countryside go by the window without comment. Their public masks were still in place, but neither knew if he or she could keep up the charade much longer. Both needed time to assess their situation. Six weeks of Pauline Pfeiffer's tiny waist, close-cropped hair and funny remarks had pushed Hadley to her limits of grace. She had been so sure that her husband's infatuation with Pauline would wear away as it had with Duff Twysden and other women. Now she saw that she had been wrong to ignore the affair, wrong not to have seen at Schruns where this game was leading, wrong to have let it quicken in Paris. Angry with herself and Ernest, hurt, and a little scared, it was all she could do to be light and polite at San Sebastian where they detrained and the other three continued on to Bayonne, where the Murphys would switch for Antibes and Pauline continue on to Paris.

At 1.30 that afternoon, Sara wrote them a card from the Bayonne station buffet: "Well well it's all over," she said. "Three depressed voyagers think of you kindly. A bientôt." It was signed: Sara, Pauline, Dow Dow (as friends called Gerald). Pauline's was the largest signature. On Bastille Day, Gerald wrote them at San Sebastian:

As for you two children: You grace the earth. You're so right: because you're close to what's elemental. Your values are hitched up to the universe. We're proud to know you. Yours are the things that count. They're a gift to those who see them too.[28]

Nothing could have been more ironic or further from the truth. Following the July bullfights as they had in previous summers, Ernest and Hadley went south to Madrid and then on to Valencia, but it was not the same. There were arguments and bitter words followed by long silences in which it became obvious to Hadley that Pauline had won the pursuit race.[29]

On July 15, Pauline wrote from Paris that "Pamplona seems very very far away and I am smoking a lot of cigarettes." Her Uncle Gus would be in and out of Paris before the Hemingways returned, she said, telling Ernest without saying it that her apartment would be open to his visits. If Hadley missed that message, she could not have misread the closing statement: "I'm going to get a bicycle and ride in the bois. I am going to get a saddle too. I am going to get everything I want. Please write to me. This means YOU Hadley."[30]

Hadley refused to write, saying sharp hurtful things to Ernest that she later regretted. "If I'd had any sense at all," she said later, "I'd have let him go with Pauline and burn himself out and then we could have begun again."[31] But there was not going to be any beginning again in this marriage. This marriage was finished. They celebrated Ernest's birthday in Madrid and then went on to the eight-day *feria* at the coastal port of Valencia. On July 24, two days after her birthday, Pauline received a telegram: TODAYS STILL PFEIFFER DAY IN VALENCIA. It was signed LOVE HADLEY AND ERNEST, but she knew whose love had signed the paper.

Chapter Five

ROOM WITH NO VIEW

August was no month to return to Paris: the boulevards were sweaty, waiters were surly, and the Closerie des Lilas was filled with corn merchants from Des Moines. Everyone, it seemed, came to Paris that summer; divorcees and debutantes, politicians and confidence men, song merchants and society sailors – they were all there. Frank Nelson Doubleday of the Literary Digest *came to Paris along with the president of Fisk Rubber and the Prince of Wales. Miss Yulande Eager arrived, as did Mrs. Isadore Sugar, Irving Berlin, Cole Porter, Colin Agnew the art collector, Lady Loughborough, and S. Jay Kaufman. Truxie Flagg and Jascha Heifetz were in town briefly, as were Drs. Charles Mayo and Sherlock Swann Jr., Ralph Pulitzer and Adolph Ochs, as well as Garrett Garrett, the author, looking for fresh material. Will Rogers came with his trick rope and jokes, and General Bramwell Booth of the Salvation Army arrived in uniform. Kiwanians and Legionnaires marched into town along with dentists and bankers, all leaving memorial wreaths in appropriate places. Others came to marry, several to divorce, but all came to play. The famous and would-be-famous, rich and not-so-rich were all registered bedfellows in Right Bank hotels, but not one of them knew the two Americans, who, in the August heat, went unnoticed among the throng arriving in Gare de Lyon. At the station exit, she went one way, he another.*

PARIS: AUGUST AND AFTER, 1926

Four days after they returned to Paris, Hemingway read in the *Tribune* about the train wreck outside of Gare de Lyon on the Pont de

51

Rambouillet. An early morning commuter smashed into the rear of a stalled freight, killing four and leaving two cars in shambles.[1] The image of splintered rail cars added to his storehouse of disasters just as he was beginning a new marriage story. Alone in the Paris heat that was driving record numbers to suicide, he was writing about a couple's return from Antibes. Twice before he had turned personal arguments into short fictions, but this time it was different. He tried not to think about how different it was, not to think about the emptiness he had created inside himself. The story was about that emptiness, only he did not show it directly. It was more like something small flitting past the periphery of one's vision. He knew how the story ended, if only he could get the reader there in proper shape to get the beauty of it fresh. "My wife and I are not characters in this story," he wrote in first draft. "It was just that the American lady was talking to my wife."[2] By the final draft, he did not need to say anything so obvious; the flat tone of his narrator and the irony of the wordy American lady missing the point were enough.

Nothing in the story was what it seemed to be. The train, a *rapide*, framed three characters in a story that did not move – the narrator stared blankly out the window while his wife listened with little comment to the older American woman, who talked endlessly. Beside her was her caged canary, a gift for her daughter whose love for a European man the woman has nipped in the bud. "American men make the best husbands," she said. "That was why we left the Continent you know. My daughter fell in love with a man at Vevey."[3] That was two years before at the Hotel Trois Couronnes where the narrator and his wife once spent their honeymoon. "Is your husband American too?" the woman asks, setting up tiny echoes from Henry James, who once began his unfortunate story of failed American liaisons at that same hotel. Daisy Miller's wart of a brother asked Winterbourne, "Are you an American man?" James was famous for stories in which the action was indirect; Ernest was doing him one better. Nothing happened in this story while the slightly deaf woman talked about her daughter's blighted love and the dull, flat country, like their flat, dull lives, moved quickly by the darkening window.

Outside of Marseille, they passed "a farm house burning in a field. Motor-cars were stopped along the road and bedding and things from inside the farmhouse were spread in the field. Many people were watching the house burn." He had been saving that image since his Chicago days when he and Bill Smith wrote some short sketches together.[4] Here it was exactly the image of domestic disaster he needed.

As his fictional train came into the Paris station, he used the real wreck from the *Tribune*: "We were passing three cars that had been in a wreck. They were splintered open and the roofs sagged in." A caged canary, love gone wrong, the deaf mother, a house fire, and a wrecked train: it all added up without him having to say anything until the end. There the story got really tough. He tried it five times before he got it right. Each time telling it but telling too much; each time he cropped until less said more.

They came into the dark of the station where the American lady "put herself in charge of one of the three men from Cook's" travel agency. The porter piled their bags on his cart. Then they said goodbye to the lady. No. "My wife said good-by and I said good-by to the American lady." That was it, not together but separate.

> We followed the porter with the truck down the long cement platform beside the train. At the end was a gate and a man took the tickets.
>
> We were returning to Paris to set up separate residences.

It took him two months to get the story right, and the revisions were good for him, using part of his grief. It was a piece of himself there on the page, a load of private ore he could refine only once. He left out the tears, the arguments, and the pain, transforming a piece of himself forever into his art.

PARIS: SEPTEMBER 1926

Ernest sat in the straight-back chair, staring at Gerald Murphy's thirty-foot-high studio wall where he had centered and hung Miró's *The Farm* to keep him cold company.[5] The huge painting needed such a wall to let it breathe, for hanging as it had above their bed, it was always cramped for space. He, on the other hand, was trapped by circumstances no longer within his control. Pauline was soon leaving for New York and Piggott, not to return until after Christmas. In Hadley's new apartment close to Gertrude Stein's place on rue de Fleurus, she and Bumby were living comfortably. "Nicely started here," she wrote him, "Will need pillow cases, towels, napkins." What didn't she need? She needed face towels and bath towels, the double boiler, the blue feather duster, and her razor. He couldn't find the razor. To hell with the razor.

Do *not need* kettle for a while nor coffee pot. . . . I want my beauty
Dresden teapot and about 8 Dresden cups & saucers & after dinner
coffee cups and all the old French blue plates and my ~~green tea tray~~.
For furniture – Chinese table, double decker mahogany bureau –
Breton folding table, Fauré picture, Mummy's baby portrait, little
teeny Hartman pictures.[6]

Every time he went back to their abandoned flat on Notre-Dame-des-
Champs, he felt absurd piling the residue of their lives into a cranky
wheelbarrow to push through the public streets like some junk man. He
was doing penance, sackcloth and ashes, announcing to the Quarterites
that he and his wife were separated.

They returned from Antibes on August 12 trying to be civil to each
other, but mostly being silent. Upon arriving in Paris, Hadley found
rooms for herself and Bumby in a nearby hotel, and Ernest moved into
the Murphy studio which he described later as being

at the end of a block of studios on a gravel courtyard. It was one
big room with a cement floor and a skylight. There was a gas stove
in one corner to cook on and in the other corner a stairway went
up to a little platform built across one end of the studio where his
bed and washstand were. There was a window and the washstand
on the other side. A curtain separated the platform from the rest of
the studio and made a room out of it. The walls were whitewashed.[7]

At first it was exciting, new, and romantic to live in monkish austerity by
day and to have Pauline in his hard, narrow bed sometimes at night. His
life was simplified, his possessions minimal, and his time his own –
exactly what he needed to correct the *The Sun Also Rises* galleys.

He knew there would be difficulties with the words that bothered
Perkins, but those were the easiest difficulties to face at the moment.
Words on paper he could control; it was the angry words in taxi cabs
that were complicating his life. Never take your separated wife out drinking was probably the answer, but what was the question? So she wrote
the next day, "My mind, as I recall things I said in that damn taxi, was
positively senile. I think however that I have forgotten most of what it
was that caused *our* bitterness and I hope that you can too darling. You
were really sweet and held yourself in *nobly*."[8] It was not going to be easy,
this divorce, particularly when his wife did not admit that divorce was
the point of their separation. She still believed that he would tire of
Pauline, and they would move back to rooms above the lumber yard. So

instead of one rent to pay, they now had two: Hadley's new apartment and their old flat.

With no near solution to his marital problems, Hemingway was glad for the escape offered by the galley proofs of *The Sun Also Rises*. With the light coming in through the French windows, he sat down to his task. In Valencia he had promised to eliminate as much potentially offensive material as possible, starting with the bulls' balls. Those could be changed, he told Perkins, to horns, "the bulls have no horns."

> But in the matter of the use of the word *Bitch* by Brett − I have never once used this word ornamentally nor except when it was absolutely necessary . . . one should never use words which shock altogether out of their own value or connotation − such a word as for instance *fart* would stand out on a page . . . Altho I can think of a case where it might be used, under sufficiently tragic circumstances, as to be entirely acceptable. In a certain incident in the war of conversation among marching troops under shell fire.

As for returning to the States, that did not seem possible for financial reasons, he said, not telling Max the whole story. "I can see no prospect of it," he said, "although I had hoped and counted on it tremendously. In several ways I have been long enough in Europe."[9]

On August 2, in Antibes, he had found the galleys waiting for him, along with Max's long letter of particulars which was both amusing and irritating. He had not understood how nervous New York publishers were in the face of conservative keepers of the public morals. Max warned him: "It would be a pretty thing if the very significance of so original a book should be disregarded because of the howls of a lot of cheap, prurient moronic yappers. You probably don't appreciate this disgusting possibility because you've been too long abroad, and out of that atmosphere. Those who breathe its stagnant vapors now attack a book, not only on grounds of eroticism which could not hold up here, but upon that of 'decency,' which means *words*."[10]

Ernest read quickly through the galleys on the train from Antibes and began working on them as soon as he settled into Gerald's studio. The work took his mind off the enormity of what he and Hadley were doing. On August 21, he wrote Perkins that he was almost finished with the corrections. The bulls were now "without appendages" as Max called them, too proper to write the word "balls". The Glenway Wescott character called Roger Prescott was now Roger Prentiss, and Henry

James was reduced to Henry. Hemingway affirmed that he was cutting the first fourteen pages to begin now with "Robert Cohn was once middleweight boxing champion of Princeton." He told Perkins, with a grin, that he had worked on the profanity "but I reduced so much profanity when writing the book that I'm afraid not much could come out. Perhaps we will have to consider it simply as a profane book and hope that the next book will be less profane or perhaps more sacred."[11] Working steadily, except for arguments with Hadley and meetings with Pauline, he finished his revisions on August 26, and mailed them to New York on the *Mauretania* the following day. The dedication now read:

THIS BOOK IS FOR HADLEY
AND FOR JOHN HADLEY NICANOR[12]

Along with the proofs, Hemingway enclosed the now completed version of "The Killers." To the ten-page typescript he thought finished in Madrid, he added in Paris another nine pages of holograph, turning the story away from the hired killers to their victim, whom he was now calling Ole Andreson. He sent Nick to warn Ole, but Ole didn't care. He lay in his rooming-house bed staring at the wall, knowing that his life was beyond his control. There was nothing he could do, no place to run, and no way to fix the situation. Ernest knew exactly how Ole felt; he could see him across the room on the bed, his feet touching the end and his back hunched a little. When Nick got back to the diner, he told George he was getting out of town.

"Yes," said George. "That's a good thing to do."
"I can't stand to think about Ole Andreson," Nick Said. "It's too damned awful."
"Well," said George, "you better not think about it."[13]

When he began typing the final draft, he made one small addition. As Nick was leaving Hirsch's rooming-house, he told the woman who let him in, "Good-night, Mrs. Hirsch."

"I'm not Mrs. Hirsch," the woman said. "She owns the place. I just look after it for her. I'm Mrs. Bell."
"Well, good-night, Mrs. Bell," Nick said.[14]

It was a nice touch and a subtle one. Henry's lunch-room was run by George; the clock was twenty minutes fast; the killers wanted supper but had to settle for breakfast, and when their orders came, they got them reversed. It made a good ending to have Mrs. Bell running Hirsch's rooming-house. Nothing was what it seemed to be in a world where all the signs were easily misread. Maybe the readers would get the point, maybe not.[15]

His bank account, however, was a sign he could not afford to misread. The summer in Spain had used up most of the $1,500 advance which he was drawing piecemeal from Scribner's. When he put the corrected page proofs into the mail, he asked "Mr. Perkins," as he still called Max, for another $200 of the advance.[16] For the first time in his married life, Ernest was almost broke with no immediate windfall in sight. Scribner's Magazine and several others had rejected "Fifty Grand" as too seamy a story for American homemakers, and no one wanted to buy "An Alpine Idyll," his tale of the Austrian peasant who kept his dead wife's frozen body in the woodshed all winter, using her open jaw as a hook to hang his lantern on. Even New Masses, after begging him for a story at paltry rates, rejected "Idyll" as an underwritten episode that "emerges as a stark shocker," and Jonathan Cape refused to publish Torrents of Spring because the objects of the satire were relatively unknown in the United Kingdom.[17] Perkins told him that he shouldn't be discouraged by these rejections, "except financially," which seemed to Hemingway as effective a way to be discouraged as any other. He wasn't giving up, he told Perkins, and if he could keep on writing, "we may eventually all make some money."[18] That was on a good day. On bad days he could feel discouraged as hell about it. In mid-August, Edith Finch sent him a copy of Gertrude Stein's Descriptions of Literature and asked him to be part of The As Stable Pamphlet series featuring unknown and "very well-known" authors, saying that Gertrude recommended him. Having no essays at hand, he sent instead "Today is Friday." The pay was only 400 francs, but he knew there was no American market for any story that took liberties with Christ's crucifixion.[19] Any day now he was going to write a story that Scribner's Magazine could buy. That was the idea that Scott had sold him on: go with a publisher that could buy the stories one at a time and then do the book of stories. But when he sent Perkins "The Killers," he had no great hopes for a quick sale. If "Fifty Grand," which was, after all, only about a fixed prizefight, was too tough for them, then hired killers and a fixed boxer were not going to be the answer. With the Dempsey–Tunney heavyweight fight making all the news, he thought the magazines would jump at a good fight story.

To Hemingway's amazement, Perkins wired immediately that Bridges accepted "The Killers" for *Scribner's Magazine*. As Hemingway wrote Fitzgerald, "Even cynical little boys like Ernest get pleasant surprises. Only I now wait to hear of the sudden death of Bridges, the losing of his job by Perkins and the suspension of Scribner's magazine. Otherwise may get published."[20] In what would become his first significant American payday, Hemingway eventually received $200 for "The Killers" in a year when Fitzgerald was paid $1,800 for a *Red Book* short story.[21]

With money borrowed from Scott and Pauline mostly spent, he was now living on $400 dollars that Gerald Murphy, without even asking, had deposited as a gift into Hemingway's Paris account. At the end of August, Sara and Gerald came up to Paris, concerned about how Ernest was weathering his separation. Whatever the Murphys saw that night at supper with Hadley and Ernest vindicated in their minds Ernest's complaints about Hadley. The same two people who, earlier in the summer, were so enamored of the Hemingway marriage, left Paris convinced that Hadley had never carried her share of the weight. Sara wrote Ernest, "In the end you will probably save us all by refusing (among other things) to accept any second-rate things, places, ideas or human natures. Bless you & don't ever budge."[22] Without mentioning Hadley's name, Sara clearly included her in the category of second-raters. Sara Murphy, the great mother and provider of Gerald's comfort, was tolerant of many but quietly judgemental of all who crossed her threshold. Ernest, who won her affection as he had won that of many another older woman, could do little wrong in those days. Pauline Pfeiffer, who was a friend of Sara's before Ernest appeared in the Murphy menagerie, was one of *them* – quick, witty, educated, and monied – a good match for Ernest in Sara's mind. Hadley, whom she barely knew, having seen her only in trying circumstances, was, Sara thought, responsible for the separation. Hadley should never have confronted Ernest with his affection for Pauline.[23] In this belief, Sara was taking her cue from Ernest's own version of his marriage. Gerald was less concerned with Ernest's wife, whoever she was, than with his art. Before leaving Paris, he told Ernest, "We believe in you in all your parts. We believe in what you're doing, in the way you're doing it. Anything we've got is yours: somehow we are your father and mother, by what we feel for you."[24]

From Antibes, Gerald wrote to explain the $400 deposit, saying that one got "through to the truth sooner" if not "hand-tied by the lack of a little money." The truth to which Murphy referred was neither particularly obscure nor difficult to derive. Hadley maintained that theirs was a trial separation, not a prelude to divorce. Ernest, she thought, needed this time to decide what mattered in his life: his legitimate family or Pauline. Knowing how lonely he became on his own, she felt certain he would realize how much he needed her support. That was Hadley's version of their situation, which, in public, Ernest supported.

Gerald told Ernest he was worried

> that you may temporize: first because Hadley's tempo is a slower and less initiative one than yours and that you may accept it out of deference to her, – secondly because of a difficulty in settling the practical phase of it all: Hadley's comfort, Bumby's. Should either of these things deter you from acting cleanly and sharply I would consider it a dangerous betrayal of your nature.

In Murphy's view, Hadley's neglect of her woman's work had forced Ernest to place himself "in the breach." To return to the marriage would simply be more of the same, with Ernest using his writing time to complete family chores. "For years," Murphy said, "conditions have allowed of Hadley's drawing upon your personal energy to face the efforts of the day. It's true that ¾ of the race lives upon the energy of the other ¼, – but when a man finds himself replacing woman in her own departments of life, – then it's a kind of death." Reviewing their lives and weighing options was well and good, but Murphy insisted that Hemingway's "remorse and self-reproach" were already blurring the facts. Gerald never used the word "divorce," but nothing less than that could define what he meant by "acting cleanly."[25]

Despite his complaints to the Murphys, Hemingway had not suffered greatly during the first month of his separation when he was alone only as much as he wanted to be. Hadley, who first moved into the Hôtel Beauvoir behind the Bal Bullier dance hall, was sometimes available for company when he needed her, and Pauline was there at night which was his worst time. He told Fitzgerald that since the previous Christmas he had been living in hell, with plenty of insomnia brought on by his failing marriage.[26] But he did not tell Fitzgerald that some evenings of insomnia were easier to bear in Pauline's rue Picot apartment, nor did he say that Hadley came back to the Murphy studio occasionally to do housekeeping.[27]

The awkward part was in the cafés where he could not avoid seeing Hadley and where their separation did not prevent him from feeling possessive toward her. To see her drinking in the Lilas with a table full of Quarterites was awkward and hard to bear. Afterwards they argued in private about many things, mostly about her money and his lack of it. She surprised him in the cafés, drinking more now and apparently enjoying herself. He saw her at parties with Don Stewart and his new wife, but did not see her in tears in the taxi afterwards.[28] He saw her frequently with Winifred Mowrer, now her closest confidant, and sometimes with Winifred's husband, Paul, who always treated him politely. On September 14, the four of them dined at the Lilas at Hadley's invitation and expense to complete negotiations on what she was calling "the hundred days."[29] If Ernest and Pauline would agree not to see each other for one hundred days, Hadley would agree to a divorce if Ernest still wanted one. It sounded like some chivalric test out of an old story book, but Hadley was deadly serious about it. It was, she felt, the only way to keep her husband. That night at the Lilas she added that she and Ernest should remain apart, seeing each other as little as possible. She was moving out of the hotel across the avenue and into an apartment on rue de Fleurus, not far from Gertrude Stein's.

The next day the *Herald* gossip column treated them as if their marriage were still intact:

> The poet, author, and composer, Ezra Pound, has become the proud father of a baby boy. Mrs. Dorothy Shakespeare Pound is at the American Hospital where she and the heir of her husband's glory have received many delighted friends. "He's just the finest baby," says Mrs. Ernest Hemingway – after which neither her husband nor Ezra himself need add a word.[30]

But less than a week later, the same columnist reported:

> One learns with regret that the old breakfast group which used to meet on the wide, shady terrace of the Closerie des Lilas has been broken up. The Lisle Bells, who formed so agreeable a part of the Quarter have returned indefinitely to New York, while Mrs. Hadley Hemingway whose name . . . reminds all youthful literati of her husband's distinguished books "In Our Time" and "The Torrents of Spring" has moved from the Boul'Mich end of Montparnasse down toward the Raspail section.[31]

Any Montparnasse insider could read between those lines: the Hemingway marriage was coming apart.

As unnecessary as their separation seemed, Ernest and Pauline agreed to Hadley's "one hundred days," for they would do anything to get the divorce. On September 16, following another of their arguments, Hadley wrote Ernest that it would be "the very best thing for you and me to keep apart ... When we are lonely we must take care of ourselves by seeing other people or something." When they argued, she usually said something to regret later. "I have had a terrible fear since I saw you last that you or Pauline would take very literally my having said that this affair of yours had almost killed my love for Umpster [Bumby]." She begged him not to tell Pauline, who was "so clever and quick" that she might use Hadley's admission in the divorce proceedings to take Bumby away from Hadley.[32] That night Ernest and Pauline went to the six-day bike races at the Velodrome where they could discuss their romance in public without fear of listeners.[33] What was one hundred days compared to the rest of their lives? The answer was simple: one hundred nights that they would not be together, but neither felt capable of keeping away from the other if both were in Paris, and Ernest could not leave until Hadley agreed to a divorce. Reluctantly, after alerting her parents in Arkansas and her Uncle Gus in New York, Pauline booked a passage on the Red Star line's *Pennland*, due to sail from Boulogne on September 24.

Three days after her Lilas supper with Ernest, Hadley sent her husband a letter filled with contradictory messages.

Dearest dear Palty,
    It's true we have to make a *very* clean break for us, don't know how long. You are just a Waxin that's all and all I want to know is will you be a seeker of this boy while Pauline is away so that Mummy can tear into this her Vita Nuova fresh and fine, sure that a hound is doing the same? You see at present I can't afford to think about you too much unless I'm to break down completely. Do you think you *need* Pauline to stay? I sort of hope not tho God knows what is best to do.
    Anyway here's my awfully tender, sorry love, dear Chickie and I don't think Pauline is a rotter and I'm sure some day – if let alone – my old ~~trusting love of~~ affection for her will come back in a measure. I promise to try for it. But to forget you both in the meanwhile.
    If you're afraid in the meanwhile, these coming three months – that you will come to see me too often – I think you had better keep her here. .... Mummy can't see you – definitely – for quite a long, long time.[34]

It was a tender and confusing letter, but Ernest had no trouble deciphering it. If he kept Pauline in Paris, the divorce agreement was off. If Pauline left, he would be absolutely alone, for there would be no more afternoons with Hadley. His most loving wife, in her newly decorated apartment, was eager for the "new life" as she called it. In his borrowed cold-water studio, Ernest was left staring at the Miró. At twenty-seven, he was long accustomed to being the focal point for attentive women. Now for over three months he would be a man without them, for he could not be untrue to Pauline, nor could he impose himself on Hadley, not after that letter.

When the Murphys returned to Paris to close up their apartment for their trip to New York, they found Ernest and Pauline happily morose as the beginning of their hundred-day separation approached. Sara and Gerald, who were sailing on September 22, tried to buck up the pair's sagging spirits and promised to visit with Pauline in New York. On September 23, the day before the *Pennland*'s departure, Ernest and Pauline made the four-hour train trip to Boulogne, the most British of French towns, where English was spoken in all the shops. The summer was over, tourists largely departed from the beaches, the casino running at half speed. In the warm dusk it was pleasant for the lovers to walk along the breakwater to the lighthouse where a slight breeze came off the calm Channel. That evening they dined on sole and partridge at the Hôtel Meurice, finished with a brandy, and climbed the stairs to their room.[35]

From Southampton, England, where the *Pennland* docked the next evening to take on more passengers, Pauline wired Ernest: AUVOIR ALL MY LOVE. She also mailed the euphoric, gloating, happy letter she had written while crossing the Channel. Beneath her pillow, she told her lover, she would place the expensive pen and cigarette holder which he had given her at the pier. "I love you more than ever," she said, "and I'm going thru these three months like mad. . . . I am a young matron who has left her husband in Paris while she goes on a visit to her parents in the mother country."[36]

After kissing Pauline goodbye in her cabin, Ernest caught the noon train back to Paris, arriving at Gare du Nord in time to make his way across the Seine to Shakespeare and Co. where he found, in the latest issue of *The New Republic*, a review of *Torrents* that made him feel better. The reviewer called it his "declaration of independence" from Anderson and Stein. "In writing Torrents of Spring he has weaned himself. That he had to do it so vigorously is the finest tribute Sherwood Anderson has received yet. That he chose to do it wittily is our good luck."[37] He checked out the magazine on his borrower's card. No, not *his* but *their* joint card, a piece of the marriage that remained intact. Taking the magazine with him, Hemingway cut through the graveled paths of the Luxembourg Gardens where old men were still playing boules in the evening air.

Chapter Six

THE HUNDRED DAYS

Turning right out the front studio gate into the street, he walked east along the cemetery wall until he came to the rue Richard cutting through to Raspail. With dew-wet headstones glistening in morning light and only the sounds of his own feet on gravel to distract him, it was pleasant to walk there between the graves, thinking on the dead and those yet to die. Passing the Jewish sector, he came to the graves of Guy de Maupassant and Charles Baudelaire, syphilitics both and both undone so early. They all had it, the old ones, writers and painters, burning out in night sweats, raving mad. Maupassant now lay beneath rail-enclosed shrubs above which an open bronze book told of two dates: 1850–1893. The writer of the beautiful stories had not lasted fifty years. On his left loomed the white Baudelaire cenotaph, from the top of which leaned out head and torso of the Genius of Evil, brooding above the poet's shrouded body carved atop the ground stone – 1821–1867. Nothing grew beside his grave, and nothing he wrote was inscribed upon it.

PARIS: OCTOBER 1926

Leaving Murphy's cold studio and trying to avoid his old haunts, some days he walked one way, some another. Turning west out the front gate took him to Avenue du Maine where there were one or two cheap cafés unfrequented by the Montparnasse crowd. From there it was a short walk to an excellent supper in Restaurant Lavenue close by the train station, but it was no good eating out alone, and eating his own make shift fare in the studio was worse. Where once in cafés he had sought

64

solitude in which to write, he now found solitude oppressive, and a loneliness set in, fed by his imagination, that was strangely exciting by day
and disturbing by night. At first he avoided most old friends, not wanting to explain what they already knew, and he was in no mood to make
new friends.

When Hadley met him in the street, he seemed as forlorn as she had
hoped him to be. "Your little face had a harrowed expression that I was
sorry to see," she wrote to him. "If it's loneliness and worriedness about
Pauline remember that it's only three months and that those three
months will make *her* happier ever after – she needs to establish her old
roots is it? I wish you could too. If I could help you now you *know* I
would. I long to and it's sad that we have found I can't make the grade."[1]
If he wanted her "help," all he had to do was give up Pauline. Hadley
made that obvious to one who remembered her "help" quite well. He
also remembered how Pauline looked at Boulogne, and he remembered
coming back from the six-day bike races on the bus where he was
"Paul"; she, "Ernest," and they, the same person, whole and together.[2]
He could not give up Pauline, no matter how lonely he felt; nor could he
forget Hadley, no matter how much he loved Pauline. To remember
either woman was to become morose.

Under those conditions he began his October poem about the Lord
being his shepherd:

> For thou art with me
> ~~You are not with me in the morning and in~~
> ~~the evening~~
> In the evening the wind blows and I do not
> hear it for you thou art with me
> ~~You have gone and it is all gone with you~~
> The wind blows in the fall
> and it is all over.
> ~~Surely goodness and mercy shall follow me~~
> ~~all the days of my life and I shall~~
> ~~never escape them. For thou art with me.~~
> ~~Though I walk through the valley of the~~
> ~~shadow of death~~
> ~~I shall return to do evil~~
> When I walk through the valley
> of the shadow of death
> I shall fear all evil

For thou art with me
In the evening
Especially in the evening.
The wind blows in the fall
And it is all over.
The wind blows the leaves
    from the trees
    and it is all over
They do not come back
And if they do
We are gone
You can start it any time
It will flush its self.
When it goes it takes
    everything with it.[3]

That was on a bad day. On a good day, warming up for his fiction, he could write quite jocularly about confessional authors, himself included:

And everything the author knows
He shows and shows and shows and shows
His underclothes
Are more important than the sun.
A work begun
Means many buttons more undone.
The author's wife or wives
Give me the hife or hives.[4]

For no matter how forlorn he appeared to Hadley in the streets, no matter how desperate he sounded to Pauline in his letters, he was not seriously depressed that autumn and early winter in Paris when chestnut leaves blew in the streets and the rains began to fall. Between the time he separated from Hadley and when Pauline returned, he revised the page proofs of *The Sun Also Rises* and completed five short stories, several poems, and one parodic essay.[5] Between times he attended boxing matches and six-day bike races, took dinners with old friends, and made a quick trip to Spain and bike trips to Meaux and Chartres. Lonely he was but not depressed, and he wore his loneliness like a Joseph coat in all kinds of weather.

Living behind the Montparnasse cemetery increased his sense of isolation, which he worried to good advantage. In his notebook he wrote

Now that I know that I am going to die none of it seems to make much difference there are a few things I would like to think about.

He crossed it out, unable to find words to catch the feeling he wanted, a feeling about the dead, about the rows of white crosses in the war cemeteries, that feeling. He tried again.

When you have them you can not keep them but maybe after you have gone away they are still there. You can not keep them but if you try but later when they have gone, they return, come again and sometimes they will stay.

It wasn't much better, but he saved the first line to try again.

You can not keep them but after you are gone they are still there. In the fall the leaves fell from the trees and we walked

He broke it off for the words were not working at all. No one would understand it. Say it straight without any preamble; get right to the place where the feeling was rooted. That was his talent, choosing the right places, the significant terrain. So let it start there where the feeling began and let the place become the feeling. He started over.

It was very dusty

No, not right. Again.

Toward evening it was not so hot but it was still dusty and the dust rose from the road

And again

When it was dark the dew came and settled the dust on the road that we marched on.

He started the sentence over one more time.

In Italy when it was dark the dew settled the dust on the road ~~and the men that the troops marched on in the dark and the~~ beside the road there were poplar trees in the dark[6]

He put the flawed fragments away for another day when he could write about the Italian war he knew.

He and Fitzgerald talked frequently about the war. Scott, who admired Hemingway's scars and damaged knee, felt he had missed the primal experience for his generation. Ernest tried to tell him that he could see more war than any front-line soldier by going to the cinema. As he explained earlier to Archie MacLeish, "There are a number of wonderful films that are always showing somewhere or other," including a three-part film on the Italian sector.[7] The previous winter he sent Scott two German war books, one of which dissected the Alpine fighting that took place before June, 1918 when Hemingway arrived in Italy.[8]

When Max Perkins sent him John Thomason's *Fix Bayonets*, Hemingway said the book disappointed him.

> There were too many bayonets in it somehow. . . . The bayonet is a fine and romantic thing but the very fact of its being attached to a rifle which is such a fine and practical thing automatically restricts its use in the hands of any practical man . . . to purely ornamental killing. . . . There was just that little journalistic something that was disappointing.[9]

With his ability to read terrain maps and absorb visual images, Hemingway was educating himself in military tactics far beyond his own experiences on the Piave river eight years earlier.

ZARAGOZA, SPAIN: OCTOBER 1926

On October 11, Hemingway dropped in at Shakespeare and Co. to check for mail, gossip with Sylvia, return a book, pay for a *Saturday Review* subscription, and check out *The Life, Work and Evil Fate of Guy de Maupassant*.[10] That evening he and Archibald MacLeish caught the night train for Spain, arriving late the next afternoon on the north bank of the Ebro where they joined the throng crossing the ancient stone bridge into the whitewashed town of Zaragoza.

Among the peasant women bearing market baskets, mules laden with firewood, children everywhere, Hemingway and MacLeish became part of Zaragoza's most important feast day, El Pilar, celebrating the appearance to St. James of the Virgin Mary atop a pillar of jasper. On their left, as they crossed the bridge, rose up the gloomy, gothic La Seu cathedral, that day almost deserted; on their right, the massive Nuestra Señora del Pilar, Our Lady of the Pillar, its domes brightly tiled in yellow and purple, white and green. Pushing their way forward into the plaza, they became one with the noisy crowd honoring the passing of the smoke-blackened statue of the Virgin bedecked in jewels, lace, and precious metal.[11] For MacLeish, recently returned from a League of Nations trip through remote regions of Persia, the confusion and religious ecstasy of Zaragoza was interesting but not extraordinary. For Hemingway this trip was a private pilgrimage with special meanings he could not explain to his friend. Pilar was the code name he devised for Pauline to use when the situation demanded secrecy.

In the afternoons, next to the military barracks at the edge of town, there were bullfights in the Plaza de Toros,[12] and at night, over late dinners at their hotel, Ernest and Archie talked about marriage and divorce, about the Persian opium trade, about bullfighting and other forms of artistry. Like most of Hemingway's Paris friends, MacLeish was older than Ernest and better educated. A Harvard graduate with a Yale law degree, MacLeish accepted the younger high-school graduate from Oak Park on equal terms. In 1923, after three years of Boston law practice and Harvard teaching, MacLeish had abandoned the law office to move his family to Paris for what he called his real education. On an allowance from his father, he lived frugally, read widely in Sylvia Beach's lending library, and kept much to himself those first two years, writing poetry and exploring the city. By the fall of 1926, MacLeish had four volumes of poetry and one verse play in print. Yet despite his seniority and his more numerous publications, MacLeish recognized in Hemingway's fiction and in his person something lacking in his own. Others were already calling it genius. By the time they went to Zaragoza, MacLeish, older and with two children to Hemingway's one, was calling Ernest "Pappy," a version of Hemingway's newest, self-selected nickname, "Papa." Archie thought it referred to Ernest's fatherhood, but he could not have been more wrong. To be "Papa" was to have authority over whatever the game happened to be.[13]

Coming so late in the year, the *feria* of El Pilar was devoid of summer tourists and European vacationers, leaving Archie and Ernest alone in the crowd. They talked about Hemingway's separation from Hadley and the war death of Archie's brother Kenneth. Hemingway felt guilty for destroying his marriage; MacLeish felt guilty that his admired older brother was dead while he survived. Eight years behind them, the Great

War remained an unhealed wound lightly scabbed over.[14] They also talked about religion, for Hemingway was convincing himself that he had been a Catholic ever since his 1918 night wounding at Fossalta. Having left young blood and part of his knee in Italian soil surely counted for something in these matters. MacLeish kidded Hemingway about the sexual lives of the more tawdry Catholic popes, some of whom, he said, were flaming homosexuals. That got them kidding back and forth about the homosexuals they knew and others they'd read about. MacLeish said that the Shakespeare of the sonnets was suspect, as was Julius Caesar. Hemingway complained that MacLeish had taken away several revered names, giving him in return only the "great" Yale football team.[15]

The night after they arrived, the two friends were among the 30,000 watching the *Rosario de Cristal* procession led by hundreds of carriage-borne lanterns. Like San Fermin, the *feria* of El Pilar was crowded and noisy with agricultural exhibits, mule judgings, public concerts, fireworks at night, awards for cattle and pigs in the afternoon, day and night street vendors, and numerous diversions: by night, a candle-lit procession; by day, giant papier-mâché kings and queens parading past, preceded by fantastic heads of dwarfs, all bobbing slowly down cobbled streets. Twice the statue of the holy Virgin, worker of miracles, was carried solemnly through the town, preceded by crosses and bathed with incense. By week's end, the *barrio* queens of the *feria* trailed dusty hems behind their long, white dresses.[16]

Somewhere between the bullfights and the church services, MacLeish managed one evening to expose Ernest's other self. Archie said that like Picasso, Joyce was changing the forms, making old ones obsolete in *Ulysses* and with his "Work in Progress." Hemingway, who actually admired Joyce a great deal and learned more than most realized from the Irishman's short stories, demurred that *Ulysses* was not as great as all the intellectual tourists were claiming. MacLeish said that Hemingway "should relax a little bit and give Joyce credit," for "there were some aspects of Joyce's work that Ernest ought to think about." Hemingway exploded with an anger more intense than the discussion warranted or MacLeish could understand, bringing the evening in their shared room to an awkward silence. Later MacLeish wrote:

He walks with Ernest in the streets in Saragossa
They are drunk their mouths are hard they say *qué cosa*
They say cruel words they hurt each other

70

Their elbows touch their shoulders touch their feet go on and on together.[17]

By the following evening, Hemingway's foul mood had disappeared, and he went on with their holiday as if nothing had happened.[18]

PARIS: OCTOBER 19, 1926

On his return to Paris, letters were waiting from Pauline, Dos Passos, Hadley, and his father. He liked the heft of the heavy ones, and he especially liked to get letters from Pauline, although they sometimes left him disappointed, for they were never as ardent as he anticipated.[19] He shouldn't worry about the divorce, she wrote him from the ship. Let Hadley take her own time on it. "We have everything," she said, "and we can wait." On the back of that first letter she said, "I don't care if you say to Hadley that we were living together in Paris. I don't care at all. I mean this. You tell anybody anything you want – Oh Precious!"[20] He read the letter several times.

In New York she stayed at the Waldorf Astoria, enjoying the largesse of her Uncle Gus while stepping out with Dos Passos and the Murphys. First they had Prohibition cocktails at Father Murphy's and then taxied down to Harlem where the jazz was hot and the blues low down. "*I'm a mighty tight woman*," said the big blues lady, tight like that. *What did she say?* In and out of "three nigger hives," Pauline found them all "swell." Sara and Gerald were "adorable" and "Dos was exactly like Dos." She was amused by the way he twitched over the news of Ernest's separation from Hadley. "*Make my bed, light the light, I'll be home late tonight, Blackbird, bye bye.*"[21]

Hadley's letter was newsy, friendly, and deceptive. He read it twice. She was "*so* happy" about his trip to Spain. With no indication that they were separated, without a word about a possible divorce, she bubbled on about her busy life filled with friends. Dossie Johnson was around; the Moores stopped by for coffee; Manuel Komroff, coming that night for supper, was leaving soon for Italy; she, Don Stewart, and his wife had been to the George Antheil concert. "Everything splendid except the Antheil – some of that quite good too." Hemingway's formerly dependent wife was leading a far more active life than she ever had before. If she missed him, it wasn't in the letter, not even between the lines. She was knitting him a sweater, she said, and playing the piano she had rented for two hundred francs a month.[22] For almost three years, unable to afford a piano in their Notre-Dame-des-Champs flat, Hadley had practiced in a dank basement on a cheap, badly tuned, and borrowed instrument. She could now afford a piano of her own. He got the message.

Neither letter cheered him up much, but the Dos Passos letter, including his review of *The Sun Also Rises* for *New Masses*, was really depressing. Dos, who never wanted to take sides, said Pauline was "an awfully nice girl. Why don't you get to be a Mormon?" Hemingway could not tell whether Dos was taking it out on him for leaving Hadley ("I'd like to knock yours and Hadley's heads together") or whether it was the weight of the world that embittered the letter. "I feel thoroughly sore about everything," Dos Passos wrote. "Everything I write seems to be crap and everything everybody I like writes seems to be crap. They're going to kill Sacco and Vanzetti . . . and everything is inexpressibly shitty." None of them – not Hemingway, himself, or Don Stewart – was writing worth a damn according to Dos, and his review enlarged upon this conviction.

The Sun Also Rises, according to the Dos Passos review, was a disappointing book that failed to meet expectations raised by Hemingway's short stories. It was "extraordinarily well written," and the characters were so vivid "you could recognize their faces on a passport photo." Yes, the style was wonderful, but a good novel needed more than style. After reading a page or two, he said, "the bottom begins to drop out." "Instead of being the epic of the sun also rising on a lost generation . . . this novel strikes you as a cock and bull story about a lot of summer tourists getting drunk and making fools of themselves in a picturesque Iberian folk-festival . . . It's heartbreaking. If the generation is going to lose itself, for God's sake let it show more fight. . . . When a superbly written description of the fiesta of San Fermin in Pamplona . . . reminds you of a travel book . . . it's time to hold an inquest."[23] That cheered Hemingway up no end. If a friend like Dos was going to say things like that, what could he expect from people who did not know him?

He folded the review back into its envelope and finally opened the letter from his father, expecting the usual pious rhetoric. Instead he read that his grandfather, Anson Hemingway, was dead in Oak Park. "He died," his father said, "with no suffering, slept away. The day before he had written several letters and paid up all his bills." Having said it without emotion, Clarence Hemingway hid his grief beneath the news from the home front. Their Oak Park home was not sold, but Clarence and

Grace were planning to move to Florida as soon as it was. Hemingway's father, who was already licensed to practice in Florida and had invested a good bit of money in the land boom, did not mention the September hurricane that wrecked Miami, knocking the bottom out of the land market.[24]

Three days later, when Ernest answered his father's letter, he could not bring himself to speak of his broken marriage or his separation from Hadley. He was "dreadfully sorry" not to have seen his grandfather again before he died, but "it is good he died as happily and peacefully." He apologized for not writing during the summer and fall, but the uncertainty of when he was returning to the States had held him up. Now it looked as if he would not be coming at all. "It was what I wanted to do more than anything else." Bumby and Hadley were both well, he said, and "we all send you and Mother our love and deepest sympathy on grandfather's death." For the return address on the envelope, he used Hadley's rue de Fleurus apartment.[25]

PARIS AND PIGGOTT: LATE FALL 1926

He lived that fall in continuous flux, for nothing in his life was ordinary, nothing average. On October 22, *The Sun Also Rises* was published in New York, and people he did not know in places he had never been began to talk about him. Some he once knew well began to resent his success; others he knew only in passing began to speak of him most familiarly.[26] The transition was gradual, that fall and winter of 1926, changing his public and private lives forever. On November 7, Edward Titus advertised that his Black Mannikin bookshop had copies of *The Sun Also Rises* for sale.[27]

On the Left Bank, inside gossip about the novel said that Hemingway had written a vicious satire and exposé about Montparnasse and its most treasured inhabitants. Finally the confirmation was at hand. The Paris *Herald* gossip column, reporting on recent books with Paris backgrounds,[28] said,

> The very latest is "The Sun Also Rises" by Ernest Hemingway. It contains a great deal of the Left Bank, a dash of the Grand Boulevards, and the great open spaces of the sanded arenas . . . One of the protagonists (and what a savage portrait!), is easily

recognized as one of Hemingway's literary pals. Several well-known habitués of the Carrefour Vavin are mercilessly dragged through the pages. Not very pretty reading, their recorded actions and reactions, but then Hemingway is noted for being an observant journalist and for not respecting the feelings of friends.[29]

No longer was Hemingway a name that needed Joyce or Pound beside to stand in print. Gossiping about Left Bank writers, the *Tribune* said,

> The person heard of as often as any one is young Mr. Hemingway, who apparently is arriving. It is now the right thing to mention his name casually, as if one had read his stories, and the cult is being founded. He is doing the really remarkable feat of making a reputation among his own countrymen out of his own country. The latest item we hear about him is that *La Nouvelle Revue Française* will publish a translation of a story to be called Cinquante Mille Dollars.[30]

Three weeks later the same columnist congratulated himself for his astute literary judgement:

> We said . . . that a Hemingway cult was in a fair way to being founded. Confirmation . . . appeared in one of the lofty New York periodicals. There Mr. Hemingway is called an inevitable best-seller. That seems now to be settled; a little more repetition and the state will be achieved. Incidentally, the review . . . puts Mr. Hemingway, or at least his latest novel, on the pan – even insinuates that he is writing facile caricatures of real people. Mr. H. should worry; the review takes him seriously and gives him plenty of publicity.[31]

The slightly acidic tone to the columnist's voice was another small signal that Hemingway's life had changed.

So long as he published with "little" and literary magazines like *This Quarter* and *transatlantic review*, or with Left Bank publishers of limited editions like Robert McAlmon, Hemingway was one of a crowd, a piece of the Montparnasse firmament, fitting comfortably into his niche. Of those Paris writers he knew, only Ford Madox Ford published books on a more than coterie basis. Ezra Pound, for all his stature, did not yet have a commercial publisher for his poetry. Gertrude Stein, the doyen and arbiter of rue de Fleurus, published with obscure presses at her own expense. James Joyce, modernist without peer, made more money from the charity of rich women than from Sylvia Beach's publication of *Ulysses*. Hemingway's move to Boni & Liveright with *In Our Time* raised him only slightly among his peers. However, when he signed the Charles Scribner's Sons contract, Hemingway moved into the major league. That this shift took place at the same time that he was ridding himself of Hadley and moving to a more sophisticated woman seems to have been coincidental, but it was all of a piece with his life.

Although a good many of his old friends were siding with Hadley during Hemingway's metamorphosis, he was not without support. Always there was Pauline's witty sister, Virginia, a friendly adviser and sound interpreter of Pauline's letters, who provided shrewd analysis of what Pauline was facing in Piggott. Another source of comfort was Archie MacLeish and his wife Ada, who were house-sitting a luxurious twelve-room apartment complete with a butler and maids. Many evenings Ernest biked across the river to the Avenue du Bois de Boulogne to have supper with the MacLeishes and to use their shower.[32] Archie's support never faltered during the hundred days, nor did that of Sylvia Beach or Louis and Mary Bromfield, to whose tables Hemingway accepted regular dinner invitations. Although his name did not appear on the party lists when Lewis Galantière left Paris permanently for a New York job, or when Ford Madox Ford gathered "fifty or sixty friends" to celebrate his departure for an American lecture tour, Hemingway was never without companionship when he wanted it.

But all his remaining Paris friends could not cheer him when Pauline's letters did not arrive. Like his father, who expected Grace Hemingway to write daily letters when they were separated, Hemingway became moody and dark when two days went by without a letter from Piggott. She did her best, writing often and making brave promises. On the train from New York to Arkansas, she ripped off a cheery note, reminding Ernest about "all the swell evenings" they had shared. Even though the hundred days were not up until after New Year's, she was going to be back in Paris before Christmas "without benefit of clergy or anyone else," bringing with her a new portable typewriter for Ernest.[33] In a moment of déjà vu, he must have remembered a similar letter from Hadley only six years earlier, and on the bare table before him sat the Corona she had given him as a wedding present. On it he had typed all of the *In Our Time* stories, *Torrents of Spring*, and *The Sun Also Rises*. First broken during their argument when he left to cover the Greco-Turkish war, it was now broken again, permanently.

By October 13, Pauline had arrived at her family home in Piggott, where she quickly ran out of new ways to say that she missed Ernest, and where the reality of what they were doing appeared more serious than it had in Paris. Immediately she confided in her mother, trying to explain how she and Ernest reached their dilemma. Mary Pfeiffer, an ardent Catholic, listened to her elder daughter, but could not approve of what she heard. Deeply hurt that her daughter was destroying another woman's marriage, she would neither discuss the matter, nor would she tell her husband, Paul. As far from Paris and Ernest's arms as she could be, Pauline Pfeiffer was alone in her family's house. To the east lay the rich Mississippi river-bottom land, thousands of acres of it owned by her father. To the west, the Ozark mountains and oblivion. With no one to confide in, she was deeply buried in the heart of despair. Every day she took strenuous bike rides to build up her stamina and to forget her pain. Every day she could read the moral weather report in her mother's face. In the afternoons she practiced her Spanish, determined to become Mrs. Hemingway.

"We must be very good to each other," she wrote Ernest, "because we have been very cruel to the people we love most. You got your most terrible hell being day after day with Hadley, and I think I'm getting mine with Mother. . . . I think I've probably broken her heart." Hadley herself, Pauline said, could not have made her mother more sympathetic to Hadley's position. That was fine. If Hadley hated her it didn't matter. "We'll always do and get whatever Hadley and Bumby want or need." The only thing she would not do was give Ernest up. Three days later she continued to repent of their treatment of Hadley, to whom they had not given a chance. "I think she was very wise," Pauline said, "to want to wait three months for all of us to think things over."[34] All the while her mother's silence worked on her, creating waves of black guilt.

Then, for several days, her letters stopped altogether, probably delayed in the mails, but Ernest reacted as if she had hung up on him in the middle of a phone conversation. In his dark imagination and on sleepless nights, he was certain he had lost her. "You have given yourself and your heart as a hostage to your mother," he complained. "The whole thing seems so absolutely hopeless." After her promise to write every day or to cable when she did not write, no letters came. One broken promise put all promises in danger. Maybe she was trying to give him up. They never should have agreed to the hundred-day separation, for it was killing their love for each other. "I know this is a lousy terribly cheap self pitying letter just wallowing in bathos," he admitted. "Oh

Christ I feel terribly. Just terribly Pfife." Then he said what he had not meant to say but it came out anyway. "Last fall I said calmly and not bluffingly and during one of the good times that if this wasn't cleared up by Christmas I would kill myself . . . to remove the sin out of your life and avoid Hadley the necessity of the divorce . . . then later I promised I wouldn't do it or think about it under any circumstances until you came back. But now it is getting all out of control again and you have broken your promises and I should think that would let me out. . . . But I won't and I won't think about it and maybe you'll come back and maybe there will be something left of you." Apologizing again for his "contemptible" letter, he signed off, calling himself, "your all shot to hell, Ernest."[35]

PARIS: LATE OCTOBER 1926

He felt terrible, but not too terrible to write. In the early morning he could usually escape into his fiction, living between and under the lines and knowing exactly how his characters felt to be there in the country he created. While the first loneliness of his separation was full upon him in September, he had written, "In the fall the war was always there but we did not go to it anymore." It was a story set in Milan during the war where recovered but not yet rehabilitated soldiers went each day to the hospital for physical therapy. "One of the boys wore a black silk bandage across his face because he had no nose and his face was to be rebuilt." Another was once a great fencer, whose war-ruined hand would never again hold a foil. The American narrator, with his wound-stiffened knee, walked with the war heroes but was not one of them.

> After I had had two or three aperitifs, I would imagine myself having done all the things they had done to get their medals, but walking home at night through the empty streets with the cold wind and all the shops closed and trying to keep near the street lights I knew that I would not have done such things and I was very much afraid to die and often lay in bed at night afraid to die and wondering how I would be when I went back to the front.[36]

In first draft the story used almost no dialogue and had little obvious direction; returning to it now in the full bloom of his own despondency, Hemingway drew on his own fears of losing Pauline to her mother and his real hurt at having destroyed his marriage, turning what looked to be a war story into one of his many marriage stories. With minor revisions to the opening section, he gave the story a dual focus. The young American, who at first appeared to be the central character, gave way to the Italian major with his withered hand. Now Hemingway was on familiar ground: the older man advising the younger, not, as one might expect, about war, but about marriage. "Are you married?" he asked the American.

"No, but I hope to be."
"The more of a fool you are," he said. "A man must not marry. . . .
He cannot marry. He cannot marry. If he is to lose everything he should not place himself in a position to lose that. He should find things he cannot lose."[37]

Finally the American and the reader are told that the major's wife, "whom he had not married until after he had been definitely invalided out of the war," has died from pneumonia. Hemingway left the reader there with the major sitting before the therapy machines that were curing no one. The major, like his creator, was "all shot to hell," but the story itself was perfect. Out of his hurt came Hemingway's art; out of his pain he was changing forever the American short story.

CHARTRES: NOVEMBER 8–17, 1926

Close to the train station and backed up against the old city walls of Chartres, the Grand Hôtel de France provided the "cosy, cheerful" shared room that Hadley and Winifred Mowrer needed. Close by at the city's center, the great cathedral of Notre Dame rose up above them, lovely and large in the clear, afternoon sky. After lunch the two women walked down the broad Boulevard Chasles and out into the open country along the rue St. Brice, which led them to the tiny Chapelle St.-Martin-au-Val, where Hadley and Ernest had prayed once before. Cathedral bells called them back into town for afternoon vespers where Hadley wrote Ernest a postcard, signing it "Catherine," their secret name for her. Back in Paris at her new apartment, he had moved in for nine days to care for Bumby, giving her the first quiet time in many months.[38]

The next day, November 9, Hadley received Ernest's birthday

78

telegram, and the day after arrived a new purse from her estranged but strangely affectionate husband who had not been this considerate for a long time.[39] Thirty-five years old and a long way from St. Louis, Hadley Richardson Hemingway was at another turning point in her life. During their shared days and nights, Winifred Mowrer made it clear to her that her marriage to Paul had become one of convenience. Both women knew that Paul Mowrer had been sending Hadley oblique signals of his interest in her. Winifred encouraged Hadley to become involved. It was all complicated, but not, as Hadley came to see, impossible. The five years of her marriage to Ernest had toughened her up more than she had realized. Now, for the first time in her life, she was free to live as she pleased and how she pleased, answering to no one. Her trust funds were depleted but they were still ample enough to support her comfortably in Paris. Despite the ache of loss, Hadley discovered a new wholeness to herself; she rather enjoyed the quiet days at Chartres, no longer tied to Ernest's emotional roller-coaster. Perhaps her highs would no longer reach the peaks they had with him, but then neither would she have to face his suicidal lows. Until they separated, she was determined to save her marriage; now, in that ancient pilgrimage site, she began to think of life without Ernest. During the Armistice Day Mass at the cathedral, she felt more peaceful than she could remember. Maybe it was time to declare their war at rest. On Sunday, as Winifred had arranged, Paul came to spend the day and to advise Hadley. That afternoon Hadley wrote Ernest two postcards, asking him to take some dresses to the cleaners and to send her a pair of pajamas, for she would probably stay until the end of the week.[40]

Following her Sunday in Chartres with Paul and Winifred, Hadley was no longer talking of saving her marriage; that was over. Her letter to Ernest was written in a detached voice he had not heard before. "My dear Ernest" it began; no "Dearest Chickie," no "Dearest Tatie," as on her earlier cards. This was business and she the aggrieved party. Ernest and Pauline had a problem, but she did not.

The entire problem belongs to you two. I am *not* responsible for your future welfare. It is in your hands and those of God (a pretty good scout and a *swell* friend). It is quite obvious about my not being further responsible from the length to which you have carried things in asking for a divorce. Because this is so, as near as I can see with my simple judgment, I am free to seek a divorce. I took you originally for better or worse (and meant it!) but in the case of your marrying someone else, I can stand by my vow only as an outside friend. That's quite all I want to say. Yes, but it's bound to be a peculiarly delicate outside friendship. It may never find a chance to express itself at all. You mustn't really mind or be hurt later if this is so.

Please, Ernest, get hold of some valid information about legalities. I want to find out several things from the States before I start on all this so things may go slowly for a while. However the three months separation is officially off.

Please for the sake of peace and on account of Bumbie put all discussion and arrangement of these matters into letters unless of course it is something that can be said in a few words and not involve a quarrel.[41]

She finally said the words that Ernest had been trying to force from her these last several months, and in doing so, let the responsibility slide from her shoulders. "Let's be impersonal!" she pleaded as she ended the letter, "Much Love, Hadley." She was not his "Cat," nor his "Kitten," nor his "Catherine." The Hundred Days War had ended early, but it was too soon to assess the damage.

PARIS: NOVEMBER AND DECEMBER 1926

The next day, he had Jinny Pfeiffer send the telegram to Pauline:

THREE MONTHS TERMINATED AT HADLEY'S REQUEST SHE STARTING IMMEDIATELY OWN REASONS STOP COMMUNICATION RESUMED STOP SUGGEST YOU SAIL AFTER CHRISTMAS WHAT ABOUT ME[42]

There were still misunderstandings to be cultivated and raw nerves to be irritated, but the first Hemingway marriage was over in all but the legal details. Ernest, still hoping that Hadley might file for the divorce, was on his best behavior, concerned and caring, anxious that nothing change Hadley's mind. He and Pauline were the cruel and selfish ones, he told her. If she wanted to hold them to the hundred-day agreement that was fine. If she wanted to start the divorce and visit the States while it was in process, she should do so, he would take care of Bumby. As for money, he had none, but he was giving her all the income derived from *The Sun Also Rises*, and he was making a will that left all income from past and future books to Bumby. "If you wish to divorce me," he wrote her, "I will start at once finding out the details and about lawyers."[43]

Hadley, still deeply wounded by Ernest's affair, was not going to make it that easy for him. Too well she understood his habit of forcing others to make his difficult decisions. He was divorcing her. "If you for any reasons that I don't know feel any hesitation I will start things myself," she told him, "tho I think you are much more likely to find a *good* lawyer quickly." She would accept the royalties and might go to the States for a visit, but she was not going to leave Bumby behind for Pauline to work on his affection. She wrote Ernest that his suitcases were piled in the dining room waiting to be picked up. "I'll send you a list soon of things (even furniture) that I want here before I make any trip."[44]

Outside the Murphy studio, all of Paris was drenched and shivering in its usual pre-winter weather, the weather Hemingway most disliked. The small stove barely heated the high-ceilinged room, and he was forced out to cafés and the hearths of friends. The day after Hadley's return from Chartres, he warmed himself beside Sylvia Beach's stove, browsing through her recent magazines and newspapers to read reviews of *The Sun Also Rises* that were now appearing. The *New York Times* appreciated his deft dialogue and his "lean, hard, athletic narrative prose," heading the review as "Marital Tragedy."[45] Conrad Aiken, in the *Herald Tribune*, saw the influence of Anderson, Stein, and Fitzgerald's *Gatsby*, but called Hemingway "the most exciting of contemporary American writers of fiction." The book's characters were unattractive, but "if their story is sordid, it is also, by virtue of the author's dignity and detachment in the telling, intensely tragic."[46]

No less sordid were his own night thoughts and occasional poems written that fall. Early in November, when Dorothy Parker passed through Paris on her way back to New York and her dying mother, Ernest was in attendance, sharing lunches and sending her off with some books from his personal library. She wrote him: "I was touched with your sweetness and sympathy – you know I appreciated it from the bottom of my heart and the books are going to help me thru the trip."[47] Because he was so nice to her with his public face, she had no idea how deeply she had offended Hemingway with her constant references to her half-Jewish background, her abortion, her suicide attempts, and her dislike for Spain. No sooner was she out of Paris than Ernest wrote a poem about a "Tragic Poetess," who waited "months too long" to abort her unwanted fetus: "you could see his little hands already formed." Her slit wrists and overdoses of veronal never produced the suicide she sought: "always vomited in time and bound your wrists up."

> you sneered your way around
> through Aragon, Castille and Andalucia.
> Spaniards pinched
> the Jewish cheeks of your plump ass
> in holy week in Seville
> forgetful of the Lord and of His Passion.
> Returned, your ass intact, to Paris
> to write more poems for the New Yorker.[48]

The poem went on to contrast the self-indulgent problems of Miss Parker with the gangrenous death of the bullfighter Litri, a true "desperado," and the eighty-year-old man in Valencia who smashed himself "completely on the pavement."

Had he kept the poem to himself, no harm would have been done, but one night at the MacLeishes' when Don Stewart was present he read the poem as a comic interlude. No one laughed. Don was appalled. Ada MacLeish could not believe her ears. Archie was offended. Unlike his satiric attacks on Sherwood Anderson, Ford Madox Ford, and T. S. Eliot, this poem was purely personal. Hurt by his friends' response, Ernest sent a copy of the poem to Pauline, asking for her judgement. "I didn't like the Dottie poem much," she wrote him. "About twelve tenths out of the water," she said, referring to his developing iceberg theory of writing in which the unseen part of the berg supports the exposed tip. A week later she called the poem, "shrill . . . clothes for an elephant on a mouse."[49]

On November 3, Ezra Pound confirmed that he was starting a new literary periodical and asked Hemingway for something he could not sell any place else. "If you feel like writing a life of Calidge Colvin or doing some other IMPRACTIcable or unpractical half sheet of verse, like the Peace Conference; don't sqush the impulse jess cause there aint no where to go." Pound said that the first issue would have no "lady writers." He admitted that it was "damn unjust to several of 'em and I don't mean seereeusly to make it a 'plank'; but it might be a tour de force to see how long one cd. silently run without 'em. . . . There are so few that one cd.

consider at all. Still, the ladies, gawdblessum." Remembering the irascible Ezra's penchant for George Antheil's music and T. S. Eliot's poetry, Hemingway asked if the periodical was going to be purely literary and what kind of literary. Pound said he could not promise an absolutely "non-musical review," but "I assure you, mon cher colleague, there shall be absolootly no neo-Thomism (will that content you?)."[50] Hemingway responded with the shortest poem he ever wrote, which, to underline Pound's promise, he called:

NEOTHOMIST POEM
The Lord is my shepherd, I shall not
want him for long.[51]

It was not the poem for a neophyte Catholic to be writing, particularly one who needed the Church's historic bosom upon which to rest his remarriage case, but he said it anyway. When he and Hadley were most happily married, he wrote stories of marriage gone wrong. His deep love for his father did not prevent him from using the Doctor in his fiction. Between life and writing there was no choice; his fiction came first so long as he called himself a writer. That winter in Murphy's cold studio, he wrote stories with the precise clarity of a master engraver.

While Hadley was in Chartres, Ernest was cutting another old relationship, this time with Gertrude Stein. From Sylvia Beach's, on November 3, he checked out Gertrude's *Composition as Explanation*, her latest attempt to justify her method and herself.[52] "Remarks are not literature," she had once told him, and now she gave the world her enigmatic remarks. The *Tribune* reviewer saw the difficulty as clearly as one saw a damp Cinzano sign on the sidewalk.

Those persons (and there are many) who have been confused, not to say appalled, by the writings of Gertrude Stein, will probably not be much wiser after they have read (or tried to read) this explanation of her theory of what composition is. As nearly as the present reviewer can grasp it (and he sets this down with extreme diffidence, quite ready to admit that he may be all wrong) her theory is that the difference between one generation and another is simply that each generation is looking at something different; that the difference consists in what is seen . . . Composition is the thing seen . . . and beginning again and again and again is a natural thing.[53]

Hemingway read the book as closely as he could, but Gertrude was no longer the writer he so admired on first coming to Paris. So he tried to write it out in a prose poem, parodying her style to explain what had happened.

It was happy and it was something and we all liked it. There were never any changes and as it came out was the way it was and people saw that it was a happy living and there was no explaining except simple explaining and the explaining was intelligent and it was something and we all liked it. It could be done anywhere where it was quiet and there was a pencil and a book to write in. It was done best where it was done and afterward it was copied on the typewriter and we all liked it. There were portraits and we were all in them.

At first it had been harder and for a long time it had been very hard and there was no reward and for lack of a reward it became easier and easier was a reward and it was a happy living with much writing. Now many who were there are gone and new ones have come in and they are applauding and many are giving explanations of just how it is done and it seems that is just how it is done and what it means.[54]

Having praised her in print and out, defended her in the cafés and to all his friends, it was not easy for him to call it quits with Gertrude. She, who was godmother to his son, was now taking the easy way to art after sending him down the rocky one. After eating her food, taking her advice, drinking her liqueurs, and learning her lessons, it finally came down to this.[55]

And now it is all over about a very great writer who had stopped writing because she was too lazy to write for other people because writing for other people is very hard because other people know when the things do not come out right and are failures, at least always some of them do, and that is unpleasant when you are a great writer and brings discomfort and one is not satisfied, but one can eliminate the need for it to mean anything and simply write and sometimes it will mean something and sometimes it will not.

Putting it on paper in Gertrude's way, he let the free association leap along, sometimes connecting with an idea, sometimes with a word. He tried to mitigate and explain, but there was no good explanation for what he was doing or what she had done. Finally, he wrote:

> Now we will say it with a small poem. A poem that will not be good. A poem that will be easy to laugh away and will not mean anything. A mean poem. A poem written by a man with a grudge. A poem written by a boy who is envious. A poem written by someone who used to come to dinner. Not a nice poem. . . . A small poem that does not say it about love. A poem written by someone who does not know better. A poem that is envious. A poem that is cheap. A poem that is not worth writing. A poem that why are such poems written. A poem that is it a poem. A poem that we had better write. A poem that could be better written. A poem. A poem that states something that everybody knows. A poem that states something that people have not thought of. An insignificant poem. A poem or not.
>
> Gertrude Stein was never crazy.
> Gertrude Stein was very lazy.
>
> Now that it is all over perhaps it made a great difference if it was something you cared about.[56]

He said it and put the paper away for the rest of his life.

In a less serious mood, he continued his literary house-cleaning with a satiric piece he called "How I Broke With John Wilkes Booth," subtitled "After reading the second volume of My Life by Frank Harris." He had browsed through the sexually explicit Harris autobiography in Sylvia's bookshop, where it sold quite well along with other erotica like Oscar Wilde's *Salome* and John Cleland's *Fanny Hill*.[57] When Harris was not seducing some teenage girl or a friend's wife, he was either explaining what a brilliant person he was or dropping names of famous people he knew. The satire was written in a voice similar to that of Hemingway's earliest published piece, "A Divine Gesture," but with the flavor of Scott Fitzgerald's letters making it funnier. Set in Lincoln, Nebraska, it opens with Hemingway questioning John Wilkes Booth.

> "Why did you kill him, Booth?" I asked bluntly. "He'd paid for his seat."
> "It was a matter of principle," Booth said. "It was a matter of principle and then suddenly everything seemed to go black. I had no time to think of the monetary angle."

When the tour de force finished in less than two pages, Hemingway continued with a new chapter headed: "The True Story Of My Break With Gertrude Stein."

Years afterwards he would write how once, while waiting for Gertrude to come downstairs, he overheard an argument between Stein and her lover, Alice Toklas, that so sickened him he could not return.[58] The early version he wrote in Murphy's studio was farcical, making fun of himself, of his knowledge of French, and a little of Stein. It began, he said, when he noticed he was no longer welcome at the Stein residence. No one would answer when he rang the bell, or the maid would tell him that Gertrude was not at home. Then he began dropping in unannounced when he saw others arriving for an at-home tea.

"Hemingway, why do you always come here drunk?" she asked me one afternoon.

"I don't know, Miss Stein," I answered. "Unless it is to see you."

Another time Miss Stein said, "Hemingway, why do you come here at all?" I was at a loss for an answer.

I tried to talk about literature to Miss Stein. "I am trying to form my style on yours, Miss Stein," I said one rainy afternoon. "I want to write like you, like Henry James, like the Old Testament and –" I added, "like that great Irishman, James Joyce."

"All you young men are alike," Miss Stein said. Frankly I was hurt.

On his next visit, the maid hit him with a bicycle pump; after that he found the door nailed shut and a bloodhound on guard to keep him out.

It was then that I broke with Miss Stein. I have never ceased to feel that I did her a great injustice and needless to say I have never ceased to regret it.[59]

It was all good fun, but barely beneath the smiles there was a sharpened knife, cutting the cord and putting the blame on Gertrude.

His many marriages, physical and literary, were done – Hadley, Gertrude, and Sherwood, the little magazines and the coterie writers. They were all behind him, and putting it on paper made it final.

Chapter Seven

FORTUNE AND MEN'S EYES

The pale American sat each afternoon with his back to the wall at Deux Magots, sipping a cassis and waiting for the burly author to appear. He revised and rehearsed his lines until he was reasonably certain that he would not forget or be unable to say them. Nothing would have been more embarrassing. When someone, no real friend to be sure, made him read the young author's story, he saw immediately how his dear and dead wife was maligned and he publicly humiliated. Spinoza, whom he read deeply, would have been more forgiving, and if this were a poem, the American could have been very mystical about the situation. But it was no poem, and Spinoza did not help. Contemptible worm was what he called the author in his letter, unable to find any worse epithet. After the first week, the waiters at Deux Magots paid little attention to the pale American. Had he asked them, they would have told him that Deux Magots was no longer the young author's café.

PARIS: ST. CATHERINE'S DAY, 1926

By noon the city descended into darkness, wrapped in a thick, muddy fog that stopped traffic and at Neuilly delayed the bankruptcy sale of Isadora Duncan's house. In the streets of Paris, however, lack of light did not prevent the St. Catherine's Day midinettes from kissing any passing stranger. On this day unmarried women over twenty-five, costumed and masked, snake-danced through their districts, announcing their spinsterhood and leaving kisses on any man they fancied. Beneath yellow and green caps, they came disguised as rabbits, dogs, vegetables, and

87

hat-boxes, pretending to seek a husband.[1] Ernest, who was not interested in discovering any new women, stayed in his studio to answer mail.

It was also Thanksgiving Day, and he had much to be thankful for: his divorce was in progress, Pauline would soon return from Piggott, and his name was in all the journals. On his makeshift writing desk, typed pages of new stories were piling up, and his humor was once more impulsive, a sure sign of his improved condition. He wrote Fitzgerald about reviews of *The Sun Also Rises*, "The boys seem divided as to who or whom I copied the most from, you or Michael Arlen, so I am very grateful to both of you – and especially you, Scott, because I like you and I don't know Arlen and have besides heard that he is an Armenian and it would seem a little premature to be grateful to any Armenian."

To Pauline he continued to complain about the nights when the horrors took him and he could not sleep. Despair, he told her, "comes up about five o'clock like a fog coming up from a river bottom."[2] A week earlier, he told Fitzgerald that he was working well: two stories sold to *Scribner's Magazine* and another in the mail to them.[3] His story of the Italian major and the young American reopened his war memories which he had closed off when his early, half-finished war novel was stolen in the Gare de Lyon. Out of memory's recess came once more the image of dust settling on troops marching down an Italian road and the sound of silkworms eating in the dark. No sooner was "In Another Country" finished than he was at work on an Italian front sequel about Nick, his fictional avatar whose mind he knew as well as his own, sometimes better. It was a strange story, doubly focused and drawing on his own night problems.

In the first pencil draft, Nick, unable to sleep, lay quietly retracing his earliest memories, which led him back to the attic in his grandfather's house where his father's pickled snakes were kept. When the family was moving to their new house, the jars were thrown into a backyard fire, popping in the heat and the snakes burning. At the new house, Nick remembered his mother, who was "always clearing things out and making a good clearance," once burned all of his father's Indian relics, "his stone axes and stone skinning knives and many arrowheads." He wrote

> When my father came back and got out of his buggy the fire was still burning in the road in front of the house. I ran out to meet him. He handed me his shotgun and looked at the fire.
> "What's this?"

"I've been cleaning out the basement, dear," my mother called from the porch, "and Ernie's helped me burn the things."[4]

Ernie? Not *Ernie.* Nick, it was Nick in the story, not himself, but Nick was a part of himself, living a separate and secret life that sometimes so overlapped with his other lives that it was difficult to remember what had happened to him and what had happened to Nick. He crossed out "Ernie" and put in "Nick."

In the second draft, typed on the borrowed typewriter, he started with the silkworms eating mulberry leaves, their droppings audible in the dark.

I myself did not want to sleep because I had been living for a long time with a feeling that if I ever shut my eyes in the dark and started to drop off to sleep my soul would sail out of my body. So while I am ~~quite~~ fairly sure that it would not have done so, yet then, that spring, I was unwilling to make the experiment.[5]

Holding on to his soul, Nick fished different streams that they both knew from up in Michigan, sometimes having to dig for fresh worms in difficult places. When that failed, Nick would pray for all the people he had ever known, which led him back to his grandfather's attic where his father's snakes lay coiled in their jars of alcohol. This time he did not tell about his mother burning anything.

The third draft was better, longer, and unhurried. He described the different baits Nick found along the river: worms, beetles in the swamp grass, grubs in rotten logs, wood ticks, "and once a salamander from under an old log. The salamander was small and agile and a lovely color and he had tiny feet that tried to hold on to the hook and after that one time I never used a salamander again. Nor did I use crickets because of the way they acted about the hook."[6] With the hook firmly set in both his bait and his reader, Ernest let the story develop unrushed. They were both fishing, he and Nick, for the fisherman was another metaphor for the writer, each working at his craft with reverence and a sense of ritual. "Some nights too," Nick said, "I made up streams and they were very ~~exciting~~ pleasant and it was like being awake and dreaming."[7] When he could no longer fish, Nick started remembering people and places and then back to the attic and the snakes and the burning artifacts with his father raking the blackened pieces out of his mother's fire. That was where the story began: mother on the porch, father in the road, Nick caught in between. Ernest was standing between Hadley and Pauline; Pauline was caught between her mother and himself. And, as Ernest saw all too clearly, his son was now standing as Nick stood, caught between himself and Hadley as their marriage went up in flames.[8] "The best arrow heads went all to pieces," Nick's father said.

Gradually the story shifted back to the night room in Italy with Nick and John, his orderly, talking to each other in the dark about home and cigarettes and silkworms and Nick not sleeping. "I got in pretty bad shape last Spring," Nick said, "and at night it bothers me." John's cure for Nick's problem is marriage. "A man ought to be married," he tells him. "You'll never regret it."

I had a new thing to think about and I lay awake in the dark with my eyes open and thought of all the girls I had ever known and what kind of wives they would make. ~~I had never been married~~ It was a very ~~exciting~~ interesting thing to think about and killed off trout fishing and interfered with my prayers for a while.[9]

Finally, when the women begin to blur, losing their appeal, Nick returned in the night to fishing the rivers of his mind, where "there was always something new." It was a marriage story, but not one particularly suited to St. Catherine's Day.

PARIS: CHRISTMAS NIGHT, 1926

Standing once again in the cold Gare de Lyon, waiting for his train to depart, he was following their old ritual. Around Christmas he and Hadley always escaped from the Paris rains into the mountains for skiing, but this time there was no wife, no son. He was going to Switzerland to join Jinny Pfeiffer and the MacLeishes while Hadley went to the snows of Savoie with the Mowrers and their children. It was so civilized, so surgically neat he almost did not feel the pain. In the large, half-empty station where the night train was making up, he stood apart among strangers and for bad company he counted the memories of his many arrivals and departures in this same station: Chamby, Genoa, Constantinople, Lausanne, Schruns, and their last return from Antibes. It was here that he returned repentant and sick from the Greek war. It was here that his manuscripts were stolen, and from here that he and Hadley had finally gone to their separate residences. The joint passport in his coat pocket bore stamped evidence of their joint lives. Burkhardt, the lawyer he hired for Hadley, handed him the papers to sign away his son and his wife. She got custody and the income from *The Sun Also Rises*; he got to pay the lawyer.[10] Now that the divorce papers were filed, setting the process in motion, he would have to do something about the passport.

He would have to do something about a lot of things – telling his parents, for example. Early in the month he wrote them that Bumby was living in "a comfortable, light, well heated apartment on the sixth floor with a lovely view and all modern comforts. . . . It is me that works in the studio where nobody has the address and can't bother me." Unable to tell them about the pending divorce, he pretended that he too lived in the apartment. "I have a fine new picture of Bumby to send you for Christmas," he promised.[11]

But his charade was too obvious for his mother's sharp eye:

> Dear Boy, we have heard rumors of the cooling off of affections between you and Hadley. I trust they are not true – but you have not mentioned her in any recent letter and I can't help but worry a little concerning your happiness. Perhaps there is nothing to it, and you will write me and tell me so.[12]

That was followed by his father's letter, arriving the day before Christmas:

> The gossip is about a serious domestic trouble, please write me the truth so I can deny the awful rumors that you and Hadley have had a break. I cannot believe a word of such gossip until I hear from you direct.[13]

It was like them, writing separate letters without telling each other. In Oak Park, where nice people did not divorce, his parents had been living separated lives for many years without admitting it. He could remember more than one Christmas when his mother was in California while the children and his father gathered at the Oak Park tree.

On Christmas Eve he had gone to Hadley's place to watch his son open presents, both he and Hadley knowing that this was the last Christmas they would share. It was too sad to think about and he tried not to; thinking about things that could not be changed never did any good. So he did not think about his marriage and tried not to think about Sherwood Anderson, who was vacationing in Paris, and whom people were asking, with a grin, if Ernest had seen him yet.[14] For eight days Hemingway avoided the meeting but could not avoid Anderson's presence announced broadly in the papers. The *Tribune* could not say enough about the author of *Winesburg*, featuring him in its "Who's Who Abroad" series and running a lengthy interview in which he said that the new Book-of-the-Month Club would "not make a dent on the spongy mass of general unintelligence" in America, and that the sexual permissiveness of flappers was misunderstood. "The only way in which our girls could be corrupted into general immorality," he said, "is to be convinced that it was their duty. Maybe immorality will become a new form of Puritanism."[15] Ernest had to admit that Sherwood still knew how to get a reporter's attention.

Nor did he miss the perverse irony when the *Tribune* ran the Fanny Butcher review of *The Sun Also Rises* on the same day it featured Anderson. (It was the only review his mother clipped and sent to him.) Butcher recognized his skills and his "remarkably restrained style," but could find no redeeming features in the fiction. "The book," she said, "is concerned with such utter trivialities that your sensitiveness objects violently to it." He thought the story tragic, she thought it trivial. It was exactly what she expected "a mediocre young man from Oak Park" to write, but not one with his talent.[16]

His mother loved the review, lecturing him at length on the talent he was wasting. "It is a doubtful honor," she said, "to produce one of the filthiest books of the year. . . . surely you have other words in your vocabulary besides 'damn' and 'bitch' – Every page fills me with a sick loathing." He, who had been dedicated to God before his conception, needed to find God again and find his "real work." He kept the letter close to the one she wrote him six years earlier when she evicted him from the summer cottage, telling him he was overdrawn on his emotional bank account with her. His father, far more religious and unbending than his mother, at least sent him a decent review from the *Kansas City Star*, hoping that his son's future books would "have a different sort of subject matter."[17] It was with his parents' letters and the *Tribune*'s review ringing in his ears that he went to see Sherwood. They shared a beer over small talk, neither wanting to drag up *Torrents* and neither having anything of substance to say. Neither their sad beer nor their remembered afternoons in Chicago could repair the damage done by Hemingway's satire. There, in the Paris café, Ernest's first literary father reached the end of the line.

Behind the young author stretched a string of broken friendships and burned bridges: Marge Bump, Sherwood, Gertrude, Lewis Galantière, Harold Loeb, Hadley – people who once helped and loved him. Afterwards, he regretted the breaks but something in him kept creating them, something he could no more control than he could master the cycles of depression to which he was prone. At twenty-seven he was writing bleak stories of failed marriages, lonely men, and washed-up professionals, a literature of loss from one who needed most to win. Three nights earlier at the Salle Wagram, Hemingway watched Bart Molina, the French middleweight champ, methodically, over ten rounds, take apart a Panamanian named Jimmy Brown. It was not a pretty affair according to the *Herald*'s reporter, who said, "At the conclusion of the rounds Brown received a volley of cat calls from all parts of the arena."[18] When Georges Carpentier, the not-so-old but nevertheless finished French heavyweight champ, got into the ring to referee, the crowd cheered, but it was still a sad thing to see.

Leaning his wooden skis against the station wall, Ernest jammed his hands against the cold deeper into his old overcoat, the same one he had worn at Schruns the two winters before. Maybe it would be different at Gstaad with Jinny and the MacLeishes. Archie knew a lot of interesting things, went along with Hemingway's enthusiasms, and usually liked his fiction. But in his suitcase, Hemingway carried the beginning of a war story he could never show MacLeish.

The idea for the story grew out of Archie talking about the war and his brother Kenneth MacLeish, a Navy pilot killed in combat. Archie talked about him in the Closerie des Lilas where the table was sticky with syrup and again in Zaragoza. *Never tell personal secrets to a writer, never be married to one, and never do one any great favors.* He should have that caveat printed up on a business card to hand out on first meetings. Archie shared everything about Kenneth with Ernest, including his guilt that his brother was rotting in a Belgian grave while he was still alive. In the MacLeish apartment, Ernest read the section in *The First Yale Unit* called "Kenneth MacLeish's Path to Glory," where Archie's poems and Kenny's letters were made embarrassingly public. On October 14, less than a month before the war's end, Lieutenant Kenneth MacLeish and his wing man, after downing two low-flying German aircraft, were jumped by eight German fighters. No one saw the end of it or could say how Kenny died. Three months later a Belgian farmer found the plane and the body in his flood-drenched field. They sent Archie a photograph of the body before they buried it. He wrote,

This other's afterward –
after the Armistice, I mean, the floods,
the weeks without a word. That foundered
farmyard is in Belgium somewhere.
The faceless figure on its back, the helmet
  buckled,
wears what look like Navy wings. A lengthened
  shadow
falls across the muck about its feet.[19]

Afterwards the Navy named a destroyer for Kenneth and gave him a posthumous Navy Cross.[20]

Hemingway now knew more about Kenny than he did about his own younger brother, and the details began to eat at his mind in November when the Armistice was celebrated and his own Italian war began to reopen like an old wound. Having once written such letters himself, Hemingway now distrusted war heroes who could write home with all sincerity, "If I must make the supreme sacrifice I will do it gladly, and I will do it honorably and bravely as your son should." The story, barely begun, he called "After the War."

Archie's brother Kenny was a pole vaulter at Yale and was found some distance from his plane after the armistice without a wound but having been dead a long time in the rain. He was very handsome and young, he loved his country and had flown with the British . . . He hated the Germans and believed in the war. He was very frightened before he died and the man who killed him looked nothing like my cousin Leonard. The man who killed him looked a little like Archie. He had a high forehead and a doctoral degree in Philosophy. He was not considered a good pilot and he killed Kenny MacLeish by accident. Kenny MacLeish was a good boy. He did not drink nor go with women and there was no way to relieve the tightening of his nerves so that they kept getting tauter so that he could not sleep.[21]

The story was in his suitcase with recent and unanswered letters, including Pauline's most recent one saying, "I read over 'In Another Country' last night and it re-reads swell." "What about the other story?" she wanted to know. "I'm sure it's swell, because you wrote the two in the same spirit."[22] Had he finished it, she would not have found the Kenny MacLeish story "swell," and had he read it, Archie would have been deeply hurt.[23]

What Ezra told Ernest about "An Alpine Idyll" was more specific. When he accepted Hemingway's "Neothomist" poem for the magazine he was now calling *Exile*, Pound requested a story as well, something that could not be marketed in an American journal. Hemingway sent his old friend the somewhat grotesque story of the Alpine peasant. With rejections from *Scribner's Magazine* and *New Masses*, the story could not be sold on the American market, but not because Ernest had not tried. "This is a good story," Pound told him, "but a leetle litterary and Tennysonian. I wish you wd. keep your eye on the objek MORE, and be less licherary. . . . the reader has to work to keep his eye on the page during the introductory pages. . . . Don't be so damn scared your 'effect' won't come off. ANYTHING put on top of the subject is BAD. Licherchure is mostly blanketing up a subject." Ezra's wife Dorothy was even more pointed: "She sez: It is an amazing story to have picked up, but it isn't right, it is all out of proportion."[24]

It was his own fault, using such a bizarre incident, for doing so covered up the subtle point of the story, which was its effect on the narrator who had been too much in the sun. "We oughtn't ever do anything too long," he tells his American friend John. They first see the peasant assisting with his wife's burial on a day too sunlit to be sad and later hear the story within the story. The narrator found it "pleasant to be burned black" by the sun, but there was nothing pleasant about the wife's face blackened by the lantern's lamp. When the peasant was asked how many times he had hung the lantern from her frozen jaw, he said, "Every time I went to work in the shed at night." The narrator does not know whether to believe the sexton storyteller or not; John, unable to understand German and bored with listening, wants to be fed. Hemingway meant there to be a trade-off, a balancing point between anecdote and listeners. For the four fictional crows walking in his green field, one crow watched from the tree: metaphorically much depended upon the crow in the tree. His narrator in the story and his reader off the page listened to the Gothic incident, as twisted a marriage tale as he knew, a woman used up in marriage, a spring burial too close to the sun. Did the peasant love his wife, the priest demanded? "*Ja*, I loved her," Olz said. "I loved her fine."

On first opening Pound's letter, he felt his anger rise up, but Ezra, knowing him well, anticipated and defused his wrath.

An he sez: vot, you tinkin?
"aidnt tinking nodink"
"I know vot you tinkin: tdamn your vater, dats vot you tinkin."

Ezra said he would print the story even though he knew Ernest could improve it. "Art is long," Ezra reminded him. Maybe Ernest could improve "An Alpine Idyll," but he would not.[25] Ezra was only right half the time. The trick was knowing when. At twenty-seven Hemingway had written and published in New York three commercial books of fiction, all showing a profit. He no longer needed anyone's advice, not even Ezra's, on how to write his stories; "Alpine Idyll" would stand as it was.

For a few dollars more Hemingway could have left an hour earlier on the Orient Express, but he was traveling second-class coach on the late train, as he and Hadley always did, carrying a blanket for his feet and legs. Cold, he sometimes thought, would not be a bad way to die. *Lonely author freezes to death in station Christmas night.* It sounded no more improbable than the three Left Bank suicides that month, one dead for lack of money, others for lack of love. In early despair over the hundred days, he remembered his own threat of suicide if it were not all settled by Christmas. Well, it was Christmas with the divorce begun if not settled, and he was alive except for his feet which were growing numb in the cold. At Thanksgiving he wrote Fitzgerald that he was "all through with the general bumping off phase and will only bump off now under special circumstances which I don't think will arise."[26] Then Pauline was offered a New York job with *Vogue* which she honestly wanted to take, and that had sent him into a pre-Christmas funk. He could not leave Paris until the divorce was final, nor could he wait any longer for Pauline's return. He sent the wire:

IF PROMISED VOGUE OR WANT TO WORK NEW YORK STAY OTHERWISE WELCOME BOULOGNE AFTER JANUARY FIRST VIRGINIA WORKING SORBONNE STOP AM GRAVE CONDITION STOP HURRY STOP DOUBTLESS PASSING LIKE ART CUBISTS[27]

It was the only time he had used their code word – "Hurry" – which meant that he could stand the separation no longer and that she should take the first ship back to France no matter where they were in the hundred days. Pauline, who said she'd had "enough suffering," needed no further urging. Having booked a passage on the *Cleveland* to arrive January 8, she said nothing more about the *Vogue* job.[28]

Finally the boarding call echoed through the station, and he badgered his skis, battered suitcase, and knapsack into the six-person compartment and his reserved window seat. In his knapsack he carried the latest issue of the *Saturday Review* where the Rapid Reader found his characters in *The Sun Also Rises* to be "wraiths blowing down the wind." The Reader said: "When he comes home (he is expatriate, too) it will be interesting to see what he does with the more solid, less subtle, American scene. He is gifted."[29] *When he comes home.* When indeed and where was home? Wind up the carved wooden drunk leaning against the tiny lamp post and he would whistle: *Show me the way to go home. I'm tired and I wanna go to bed.* On that cold Christmas night, there were few travelers, and with a little luck he would have room to stretch out on the seats. With even more luck the heat would be turned on. *And any place I hang my hat is home.*

GSTAAD: LATE JANUARY 1927

It was the year of the avalanches in the Arlberg and Vorarlberg, but not at Gstaad where the slopes were more gentle and the clientele more genteel. At Gstaad, Count Rupert and Princess Estelle could enjoy the curling matches or cheer the slalom racers. At Schruns there were no Counts or Princesses that year or before, no tea dances, no horse shows on ice. In previous winters Schruns was never news in the Paris papers. Now the reports were about nameless Englishmen, dying under tons of loose snow. "The features of the victims are not distorted and therefore it is supposed that they were soon suffocated without pain."[30] No one was suffocating at Gstaad except from being overly polite to strangers.

First at the Alpine with Archie and Ada, now at the Hotel Rossli with Pauline and Jinny, he was trying to make it work as it did before. In winter they always went to the mountains, skiing by day and reading books at night under goose-down comforters. In the mountains of 1922, '25, and '26 he did not need to shave, and his hair was long, almost down to his unstarched collar. This year his hair was trimmed; his winter beard reduced to a stylish mustache. In newly tailored trousers with a white sweater that matched Pauline's, he looked lean and handsome among the winter trade. The hundred days of erratic meals and insomniac nights had trimmed his weight and deepened his eye sockets. No longer did he have that "fat, married look" he once wrote about. In all the pictures he is smiling broadly, sometimes with Pauline, sometimes with Jinny. They are all smiling.

During the separation, he was frequently with Jinny at her Paris apartment or in a night café where no one knew them or dining with close friends who did. It was Jinny who sent Pauline his telegrams in French, and Jinny who interpreted Pauline's replies. Younger than Pauline, Jinny was attractive without being beautiful, quick-witted, sensitive in her observations, and drawn by preference to women. Ernest, for whom lesbians were a dark attraction, felt comfortable with Jinny's presence and appreciated her wry humor. Living with two women and sleeping with one was like old times in the mountains.[31] At the same time, less than 300 kilometers away in the snows of Savoie, Hadley was sharing Paul Mowrer with his wife, Winifred. Her New Year's greetings enclosed an ancient, uncashed five-dollar check sent by Ernest's parents at Bumby's birth, which Hadley discovered in the back of her trust account book. Now that the divorce mill was grinding out their severance, Hadley in her letters was once again his Cat, his Catherine, who did not let him forget their once shared life.[32]

But Gstaad was not Schruns, and the old life was disappearing quickly. Ernest and Pauline were no longer conspirators hiding their passion. Now they were merely two lovers with a sister on their way to a marriage as soon as his divorce was final. It was also clear that Pauline was a good deal more organized and less dependent than Hadley on Ernest's lead. Whereas Ernest tended toward tactics, Pauline relied on strategy. He was at his best in an emergency, quick to read the situation and respond; she was better at anticipating the crisis and at long-range planning. With no way to know it in advance, Ernest Hemingway had found, among all the available women in Paris, not the prettiest nor the richest, but the one best suited to his situation. With his career about to burgeon, he no longer needed a devoted Hadley leaning heavily upon his lead. What he needed now was a wife to help manage his career, a woman who could make decisions and take care of herself; a woman like Pauline Pfeiffer, who was already thinking about where they would live in Paris and how they would get married. At twenty-seven, Hemingway was about to wed a woman with an adequate trust fund and access to more money when needed, an independent, older woman who, after living eleven years on her own, was willing to quit her career to be his wife.

Pauline, better schooled than Hadley and a more critical reader, was to become a silent partner in Hemingway's literary career, the possibilities for which were multiplying daily. He had three stories soon to appear in *Scribner's Magazine* and what was quickly becoming a best-selling novel in the bookstores. The publicity generated by *The Sun Also Rises* was bringing him new offers with almost every mail delivery. There were foreign rights to be negotiated and translators to be selected. James Joyce recommended Hemingway to his German publishers and two French firms were also interested. Eugéne Jolas wanted him to do an essay on Gertrude Stein for the first issue of *Transition*, and Ezra was still harassing him to revise "An Alpine Idyll" for *Exile*.[33] The *New Yorker* accepted his humorous "How I Broke With John Wilkes Booth," and wanted more material.[34] Even *Vanity Fair*, after turning down one of his early stories, was now asking for his work. Sure that Hemingway would "get so rich in a year or two that you will look like Henry Mencken," the magazine wanted to help him reach that pinnacle if he would only send them two or three stories about anything "except abortion and allied subjects." Hemingway wrote his next three stories about alcoholism, homosexuality, and abortion.[35]

In New York, sales of *The Sun Also Rises* were exceeding Scribner's expectations for a first novel and making Max Perkins look very good around the office. Already he was asking Hemingway about his next book of stories, a book that Pound strongly advised against. "You will do no such GOD DAMND thing. You will publish ANOTHER NOVEL next, and *after*, and NOT UNTIL THAT you will make them pub. sht. stories. Wotter yer think yer are, a bloomink DILLYtanty?"[36] Whatever currency Ezra's advice once held for Hemingway it had lost through distance and lack of perspective. Having marked and remarked on almost every writer in Hemingway's generation, Ezra was growing gradually out of touch in fascist Italy. Hemingway, who grew up respecting middle-American hard-earned money and who never in his life intended to be poor, was trying to perfect a style that satisfied both his artistry and the general public.

He still enjoyed Ezra's strange letters filled with curious diction, but he no longer took his literary advice seriously or made any concessions to Pound's new magazine. The more Ezra advised him on the revision of "An Alpine Idyll," the more Hemingway tried to sell it unrevised to another American magazine. In late January, he instructed Max Perkins to send the much-traveled story to Alfred Kreymbourg for his *American Caravan*.[37] When Ezra asked for a story that would not sell in

America, Hemingway, who could have given him the much-rejected "Fifty Grand," put him off, for Ezra was his past, not his future. Pound thought that "Alpine Idyll" was wasted on *Caravan*, "but yr manipulation of the external woild is so much superior to mine, that I hezzytate to comment," he added. "I trust yr contract dont include turning over proceeds of ALL best sellers to your late consort."[38]

Hadley, who was back in Paris tending to their divorce, was about to become a modestly affluent woman from *The Sun Also Rises*, which by the end of January was in its fourth printing, having sold almost eleven thousand copies.[39] "It's perfectly great . . . how that book of yours is going," Hadley told him, "and yours truly is prostrate with joy at the prospect of such grand riches. Paul says he will let me know at what moment to invest, which will *not* be the present sez he."[40] In Hadley's world, Ernest had clearly been replaced by Paul Mowrer, which relieved some of Pauline's guilt while secretly galling him. He was now dependent upon Pauline's money, while his own earned royalties would be invested by the man who was apparently in love with his not yet ex-wife.

But, as Hadley made clear to Ernest, future royalties were not going to pay for their present divorce. Upon her return from Savoie with the Mowrers, she wrote Ernest that her lawyer, Burkhardt, wanted the rest of his fee up front before the first stage of the divorce was reached. Because the wife's lawyer should not receive money directly from her husband, Hadley asked Ernest to send the check to her to make the payment. She enclosed triplicate copies of official papers for Hemingway to sign and return, which he promptly did, enclosing a draft on his Paris account for 5,100 francs. On 27 January, Hadley received her official judgment for divorce giving her custody of Bumby. The final decree, having still several final steps to go through in the French court system, would not come until sometime in March.[41]

Hadley enclosed several Christmas cards that had arrived for them as a couple, and plenty of mail was being forwarded by Hemingway's Paris bank. Some came from almost forgotten friends like Frances Coates in Oak Park, who found the novel heart-breaking.[42] Lincoln Steffen's wife, Ella Winter, wrote that after reading *The Sun Also Rises* she now understood what Gertrude Stein was trying to say in *Composition as Explanation*. "You must have worked like hell at it, and when one reads it, one feels you just stuck it down between putting on your pants and your coat."[43] Even John Dos Passos was having second thoughts about his negative review of the novel. "I've sworn off book reviewing," he joked. "It's a dirty habit. . . . the funny thing about The Sun Also is that in sections it isn't shitty. It's only in conjuncto that it begins to smell. Of course it's perfectly conceivable that it's really a swell book and that we're all of us balmy." The part that galled Dos most was Hemingway's "rotten" tendency to use his friends full-face in his fiction. "Writers," he said, "are per se damn lousy bourgeois parasitic upperclass shits and not to be written about unless they are your enemies."[44] And out of the blue came a letter from Sinclair Lewis, then the hottest literary property in America. *The Sun Also Rises*, Lewis wrote, "was one of the best books I have ever read, and I want to have the privilege of sending my great congratulations about it. I know of no other youngster . . . who has a more superb chance to dominate Anglo-American letters. Jesus you done a good book!" In February, Lewis hoped to meet Ernest in Paris.[45]

Guy Hickok, his old drinking and journalist buddy, wrote from Paris that *The Sun Also Rises* was "a swell book. . . . Quite a feat to make drunks' talk sound as good to undrunk readers as this does." "I hear," he said in his next letter, "there are one or two guys looking for you with gats [guns]." Hickok and two men Hemingway did not know had been out to dinner with Hadley, whose "maternal duties" began to prey upon her late in the evening. "I got all four of us into my two place Henriette and we trembled off down the rue de Fleurus while Hadley, perched away up near the roof on a couple of laps, sang little French songs which she said the 'boys' brought back, but which I know were nicer than anybody in the A.E.F. ever learned." Hemingway read it slowly, and knew exactly which songs they were and when she had sung them to him. He did not blame Guy for feeling upset about their divorce. "Somebody looking for a degree," Guy said, "ought to trace the influence of whooping cough in history."[46]

Not all the incoming mail was quite so friendly. In Paris, Chard Powers Smith, a sometime acquaintance of Hemingway's during his 1923 Café du Dôme period, had finally read *In Our Time*, in which parts of "Mr. and Mrs. Elliot" bore an uncanny resemblance to parts of his own marriage to Olive MacDonald.[47] In the story, Hubert Elliot and his much older wife, after trying "very hard to have a baby," are sleeping in separate rooms of a rented chateau. Hubert stays up late, alone, writing long poems while his wife sleeps with her dearest girl friend in the big medieval bed. "They were all quite happy." Somewhat like Hubert Elliot, Chard Smith, after remaining a virgin during his Yale years, married an older, southern woman. Later Smith said that he was "ashamed" of his "premarital inexperience," about which he unfortunately told Hemingway and which Ernest used in his story. Like Mrs. Elliot, Smith's wife had a close and dependent female friend, whom Smith invited to Europe during his wife's pregnancy. Hemingway learned of her visit from Krebs Friend, who met her at the boat dock. She, too, appeared in the story. On top of all this, Smith was a heterosexual friend of Glenway Wescott's, whose affected homosexual mannerisms irritated Hemingway enough to satirize them in *The Sun Also Rises*.[48]

Still grieved by the death (in 1924) of his wife, Smith wrote Hemingway an angry letter, which said, in part,

> It is always difficult for me to admit that men can be false in their relationships, no matter how transitory. You and Krebs have done what you could to convince me of this. . . . he was able to hurt me. You, on the other hand, must remain a contemptible shadow to me . . . Nothing would please me more than an intimation of whatever reality may be yours, in order that I might understand and forgive this silly fiasco you attempted to perpetrate.[49]

Smith's letter could have been written by any of Hemingway's recent and involuntary models – Harold Loeb, say, or Kitty Cannell. Smith was not the only one taking him to task for his fictional use of real people. In a recent *Herald*, he read that

> Ernest Hemingway will never hear the last of his "The Sun Also Rises." As Christopher Morley makes some of his characters in "The Saturday Review of Literature" remark:
> "Boy, that bird can write; if he'll just learn not to shove in little topical jokes about individuals that have nothing to do with the story. Of course the material's pretty thin, but his technical dexterity –. I admit I don't get the Latin Quarter stuff. It seems too terribly like Greenwich Village to me, and . . . none of the characters is entirely imaginary.[50]

Hemingway could have left the Smith letter unanswered, for the rebuke was, in some measure, deserved. He could have, but he did not.

Two weeks later Hemingway typed his answer, finding it interesting that Smith identified with the characters, and hoping it would induce Smith "to purchase several copies" of *In Our Time*, which, on his next visit to Paris, Hemingway would be glad to inscribe. He also found Smith's letter "an interesting example of a letter written to some one you were sure was out of town." Warming to his task, Hemingway continued:

102

I remember the feeling of contempt I had for you on meeting you and regretted it intensely as a very cheap emotion and one very bad for literary production. . . . this feeling, contempt, has persisted, greatly to my regret, and has, in fact, increased the more I have heard of you . . . It will be a great pleasure to see you again in Paris and somewhat of a pleasure to knock you down a few times, or perhaps once, depending upon your talent for getting up; although I am sure I should feel very sorry afterwards. I doubt however if you will still be in Paris in March when I return . . . You must believe me, my dear Smith, that this letter does not end on anything but a note of sincere and hearty contempt for you, your past, your present and your future.[51]

Smith, who claimed he never received this letter, went each afternoon to Café Deux Magots, expecting to face Hemingway – who actually returned to Paris for ten days at the end of February but kept to himself.[52] The two never again met, and some evidence indicates that Hemingway's response may not have been mailed. A postcard from Paul Mowrer said: "Hadley says to tell you somebody named Chard Smith is a good friend of hers and worth preserving – also be careful of him on your own account."[53] Often enough his better sense kept him from mailing such letters, but just as often he did mail them, to his later regret.[54]

Regret, of course, was an Oak Park response. Had he been as free as Harry Crosby there would have been no regrets, but the cost of that freedom was to be as crazy as Harry, whom Ernest met for the first time at Gstaad. To look into Harry's eyes was, for Hemingway, to look into a cracked mirror. On the Piave, Hemingway lost a piece of his knee and his sense of immortality when the night mortar blast blew him out of himself. Harry Crosby lost his Norton-Harjes ambulance and a piece of his mind when an artillery shell landed in his lap. Ernest recovered most of his parts; Harry didn't bother. Ernest buried the fears deep and contemplated suicide when left too much alone; Harry forgot fear completely while systematically planning his suicide: he and his wife, Caresse, would dive together out of an airplane and mystically enter into the sun. Frequently dressed in black and sporting an ever-present black boutonniere, Harry Crosby turned heads with his bizarre acts. He wore his long fur coat in all seasons, wrote ethereal, disturbing poetry, and was apt to do the most unexpected most of the time: the man who let loose the bag of snakes at the Four Arts Ball, that Harry Crosby. A nephew of the Morgan banks, he lived beyond his means, enjoyed beautiful women, strong drink, most drugs, and all his appetites.

His first encounter with Hemingway was brief. Ernest had only just arrived at Gstaad when Harry was packing to return to Paris, leaving Caresse in tears and her children engaged in a game of throwing ink on the Hotel Palace's main lounge carpet.[55] Crosby's last night at Gstaad was spent drinking with Ernest and Archie, both of whom got a little tight and began telling stories that were almost true. In his journal, Harry Crosby wrote:

And with M[acLeish] and H[emingway] to a hof bar where we drink new wine. H the realist and M the dreamer. And there was potato salad. And they both know Joyce and go to his readings. And they said he spent 1,000 hours on the last chapter of Ulysses. And I asked them what they thought of Cummings and they both like The Enormous Room best and I haven't read it. And they both think Cocteau is an ass and so do I and all three of us despise the English. And M said to read Anabase (Perse) and H said he wrote the story about the Wind Blows ["Three Day Blow"] (the best damn story in the book) in half an hour. And M is quieter but they both have charm – rare in anyone, especially men – nowadays. And M said he read very little. And H had been to the cock fighting in Seville. And we drank. And H could drink us under the table. And everyone wanted to pay for the wine. And M won (that is he paid). And out into the cold and a hard walk up hill.[56]

GSTAAD AND THE WORLD: FEBRUARY 1927

A few days after getting his mother's letter, he forced himself to answer it. Yes, he was pleased that her painting was going so well. (She said she was being paid $200 for her landscapes, fifty dollars more than he got from his last sale to *Scribner's Magazine*.) Some mothers lived for their children, basking in their deeds, but not his mother, not Grace Hall Hemingway as she signed her paintings. Never behaving like the mothers of his friends, she was always doing something different, dressing differently, marching for the vote, or making a scene somewhere with her wonderful contralto voice heard over everyone else's. Sometimes in Oak Park his performing mother had been an embarrassment to

1   Ernest and Hadley with Bumby at Schruns the winter of 1925–6, just
as their marriage was beginning to collapse. (John F. Kennedy Library,
by permission of the Hemingway Society.)

2 Passport photo of Pauline
Pfeiffer as she looked when
Hemingway first met her.
(John F. Kennedy Library.)

3 Skiing up on the Silvretta, March 1926: left to right, ski instructor,
Hemingway, John Dos Passos, Gerald Murphy. (John F. Kennedy Library.)

4 Marie Rohrbach and her
husband, Ton Ton, holding
Bumby, whom they were
keeping in Brittany during July
1926 while the Hemingway
marriage was coming apart.
(John F. Kennedy Library.)

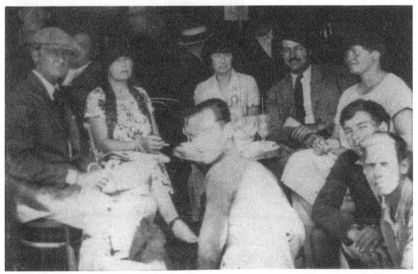

5 Gerald and Sara Murphy, Pauline Pfeiffer, Ernest and Hadley Hemingway in
Pamplona during summer 1926. A month later Ernest and Hadley separated.
(John F. Kennedy Library.)

6 At the morning *amateurs* in the Pamplona bull ring, the men try their nerve against the padded horns of a cow. (John F. Kennedy Library.)

7 Archibald MacLeish, poet and friend of Hemingway's, whose moral and critical support helped him through his separation and divorce. (Library of Congress.)

8 Ernest and Pauline in a photo taken either on their wedding day or shortly
thereafter. (John F. Kennedy Library.)

9 Ernest and Pauline on the
beach at Hendaye in
September 1927.
(John F. Kennedy Library.)

10 Virginia Pfeiffer at Gstaad during the winter of 1927–8. (John F. Kennedy Library.)

11 Key West (ca. 1930). In the foreground are the ferry slips adjoining the rail lines to New York. The afternoon ferry from Havana has arrived next to the waiting train. At the upper right is the US Navy base with its submarine slips. The large building in the center of town is the La Concha Hotel. (Monroe County Library.)

12 John Dos Passos, the "old mutton fish" as Hemingway called him, displaying his tarpon catch in Key West, ca. 1928. (John F. Kennedy Library, by permission of the Hemingway Society.)

13 Uncle Willoughby Hemingway (far left), visiting from missionary work in China, with Ernest, his mother Grace, and Pauline standing against the Hemingways' new Model T Ford roadster. Pauline is seven months pregnant. (John F. Kennedy Library.)

14 Father and son, Clarence and Ernest Hemingway, meeting for the first time in over five years. Place: Key West. Date: April 10, 1928. Eight months later Clarence committed suicide. (John F. Kennedy Library.)

him; sometimes her impossible way of professing joy in the least likely circumstances was enough to anger anyone. She was a big woman with a big voice who never doubted her own worth. When her voice began to fail and voice lessons were no longer lucrative, she taught herself to paint with a little help from the Chicago Art Institute. "Did I tell you," she wrote, "I had been voted into the Chicago Society of Artists. I am also a member of the 'All Illinois' and the Modernist group. . . . The teachers at the Art Institute say I have instinctive design."[57] In the enclosed Marshall Field catalog he found her *Blacksmith Shop* which even in miniature he recognized immediately as coming from Horton Bay. He had used the same shop in "Up in Michigan," his story about Jim Gilmore, the blacksmith, and Liz Coates. She ended the letter, "Thought you would rejoice in my success," and enclosed, without comment, a piece from the *Tribune* praising his drunken dialogue in *The Sun Also Rises*. From anyone else he would have been pleased with the clipping, but he knew that she meant it to say, "I told you so."

Trying to keep his hurt under control, he wrote the letter as evenly as he could, saying that it was natural for her not to like his novel and that he regretted her reading "any book that causes you pain or disgust. . . . I am sure the book is unpleasant. But it is not *all* unpleasant and I am sure is no more unpleasant than the real inner lives of some of our best Oak Park families. . . . in such a book all the worst of the people's lives is displayed while at home there is a very lovely side for the public and the sort of thing of which I have had some experience in observing behind closed doors. Besides you, as an artist, know that a writer should not be forced to defend his choice of a subject." That should be plain enough for her to read clearly because God knew, he had seen enough public faces and private disgraces in their family home to fill two novels. There was Uncle Tyley, the happy drunk, chasing the maids, and Uncle Leicester, self-exiled in California for some dark deed. And he could not forget parental arguments in the kitchen, and the terrible way his father retreated afterwards into himself, refusing to face his mother and growing more and more "nervous" as his sisters called it. He could have given her chapter and verse on the lovely unpleasantness inside her front door.

"As for Hadley, Bumby and myself," he said, "altho Hadley and I have not been living together in the same house for some time (we have lived apart since last Sept. and by now Hadley may have divorced me) we are the very best of friends." Leaving his marriage behind in that single sentence, he changed the subject to the sales of *The Sun Also Rises* and rumors about his life. No matter what they heard, he promised that he was not always drunk, having only wine or beer with his meals while leading a "monastic life." As for his writing, maybe they would never like it, but then, if they stuck with him, they might one day find something they liked a lot. "Dad has been very loyal and while you, mother, have not been loyal at all I absolutely understand that it is because you believed you owed it to yourself to correct me in a path which seemed to you disastrous." He closed the letter with best love to them both and signed it "Ernie."[58] Two days later in Detroit, his older sister Marcelline, after reading the premature news of his divorce in the *Free Press*, wrote to say she was surprised, but that life was "so perplexing . . . one should never be surprised."[59]

No sooner was his letter in the mail than Hemingway received one from his father, telling about the visit of Ford Madox Ford to Oak Park. "He called on time," his father noted, "and made a very charming guest," who declared Ernest to have a great future.[60] He could imagine Ford's cultured English accent thrilling his mother, who delighted in all things British – except, of course, of his depiction of two British drunks in *The Sun Also Rises*. What with Ford parading about the States saying God knew what about him and everyone else he knew reading about him in the newspaper or on the dustjacket of the novel, his life was not his own. When Sylvia Beach sent him the January *Vanity Fair*, he found Dorothy Parker using him in her Paris essay like a fictional character. "There is . . . no more than a thin line of moss," she wrote, "to stamp the spot where Robert Benchley and Ernest Hemingway had that big philosophical discussion about the meaning of life. Yes, it was right here that the trenchant Benchley cleaned up the whole matter forever. 'No, but really,' said he, for posterity, 'life is a pretty funny thing.' "[61] The more he learned about himself from the media, the funnier his life became. This other Ernest, concocted by his publisher, had two children to his one, had been a walloping war hero and afterwards worked his way through college as a boxing instructor. He asked Perkins to stop the Scribner publicity people from putting out such tall tales, insisting that he was with the Italian infantry as "a very minor sort of camp follower," was never a high-school football hero, had only one child, and had never been to college, much less earned his way as a boxing instructor. He was wounded and had four medals, but they were given not for valor but for being an American in Italy. One was given mistakenly for action on Monte Maggio when he was "300 kilometers away in the hospital at the time." "So it would be a great favor to me if we could lay off the

Biography . . . anything we put out ought to be true. And anytime I break a leg or have my jewels stolen or get elected to the Academie Française or killed in the bull ring or drink myself to death I'll inform you officially."[62]

Because he was a storyteller by both trade and inclination, Hemingway often embellished his life for old friends and chance acquaintances, or improved upon it in letters when he wanted to amuse. Before it was over, he was as much to blame as the media for creating the larger-than-life Hemingway who prospered outrageously on paper. That the public myth so prospered was, of course, a function of America's need for such a man.[63] Despite his efforts to stop the Scribner publicity mill, *Time* magazine, in its review of his next book, reported that

Author Hemingway was a football star and boxer at school. In the War he was severely wounded serving with the Italian Arditi, of whom he was almost the youngest member.[64]

Nothing in his next collection of stories would deflate or detract from the myth-making process now well under way.

On February 14, he sent Max Perkins the line-up for the book he was now calling *Men Without Women*. In all the stories, he said, "the softening feminine influence through training, discipline, death or other causes" was absent. The characters were a lovely bunch: an aged-out and dying bullfighter, hired killers, a double-crossed prizefighter, a drug addict, a homosexual army officer, dead wives, and lonely men. Somewhat illogically included was the Liz Coates seduction story, "Up in Michigan," which Hemingway had been trying to get back into print since its obscure 1923 publication.[65]

A few days earlier, he sent a copy of "A Pursuit Race" to MacLeish back in Paris seeking his critical opinion and asking him to take the story to Marguerite di Bassiano for possible publication in *Commerce*. "A Pursuit Race," centering on a drug addict with a drinking problem who was stalled out in a Kansas City hotel, was an unlikely story for any European magazine. MacLeish said he would forward the story but without "expressions of opinion. I can't do it without being either your agent or a lady editor. And I don't want to be either."[66] Hemingway, misreading MacLeish's comments and imagining a literary insult in them, responded hurt and angry, demanding an opinion on the story. Archie quite candidly said that he did not like the story, which took him "all wrong." The opening paragraph sounded "like a parody of your stuff

107

and had nothing honest to do with the story. And I thought the story itself missed fire by that narrow fraction of an inch which is the difference between failure and success in work as close to the bone as yours."[67]

MacLeish, however, liked "A Simple Enquiry," "a fine, cool, clear piece of work" he called it. But it was a story about a homosexual proposition which no American magazine was likely to publish, not when New York was closing Broadway shows for corrupting the public morals.[68] Hemingway had begun the story in November, when the Italian war was much on his mind, and rewritten it in Gstaad. Archie saw how it worked immediately: "Ten things 'said' for every word written. Full of sound like a coiled shell." In the mountain hut the Italian major lay on his bunk when the young soldier came in with the firewood as ordered. All the major asked him was if he had ever been in love with a girl. The soldier insisted that there was a girl whom he did not write, but yes, he was in love. He was quite sure. The major asked him if he was corrupt. "I don't know what you mean, corrupt," he replied. The major was relieved. "Life in the army was too complicated," he thought. Still he kept the boy on as his servant where he would have less chance of being killed. The story ended with the boy walking "awkwardly across the room and out the door." He was flushed and "moved differently" from when he arrived. Using no offensive words, the proposition was never stated directly, but it was there. Let the reader figure it out for himself, and if he knew what the "simple enquiry" was about then his mind supplied the details. It was better than shorthand, better than trick endings, and nothing happened, absolutely nothing. It was pure story where repetitions were natural, and the adjutant smiling at the end said everything. The major was left alone on his bunk. "The little devil, he thought, I wonder if he lied to me."[69]

The major was probably a fascist now in Mussolini's Italy where the unsinkable Ezra seemed to be doing quite well in the land of castor oil and blackshirts. In late January, Guy Hickok wrote that he was thinking about taking an Italian trip to write "some silly stuff about Fascism."[70] A week later Hickok proposed that Hemingway join him on the March trip. "Fix up a bag and take the other seat in my Henry assuming he [the auto] hasn't fallen apart by then, and we'll splutter down to Rimini and sizzle and spit up to San Remo."[71] It was exactly the invitation Ernest needed, for two months in the mountains with none of the men visiting and only Pauline and Jinny for companionship had left him restless among so many British tourists. During the Chamby and Schruns winters, there was a group of winter people, an audience to play to and joke with. His love for Pauline had not ebbed in the least, and their nights were lovely with the blue light off the snow coming through their window, but he had been a long time without male company. By 18 February, when he returned to Paris to bring Bumby back to Switzerland for a holiday, Pauline had already agreed to his making the trip with Guy.

Ernest wrote Hickok that he remembered enough of his Italian to keep the car in gas and oil and probably get them two beds at night. They could stop off in Rapallo to see Ezra who had written to say he would be "most deelighted to receive you and Le Sieur Hickok on you[r] prox. visit to the Kingdom of Italy." Guy replied that they could "revisit your old front. I know how all the soldier boys love their old fronts. We could do anything you please as long as San Marino was on the way."[72] But Ernest was not interested in his old front. Not this time. He remembered taking Hadley back to the Piave and how badly that turned out. The trip would be more like a bachelor party and an Italian farewell, for he did not think he would see Italy or Ezra again soon. Pauline was talking seriously about returning to the States, not this year but next, and after that nothing was clear. With the dollar beginning to fall against European currencies, no one could say what the future was for Americans in Europe.

Chapter Eight

RITUAL ACTS

Across the room from Ezra, listening and watching, the journalist and the author sat on a hard bench near the window, their wine catching the weak afternoon sunlight. It was cold in Rapallo, and it had been cold along the coast all that day. Covered with dust from gravel roads, the two travelers were four days out of Paris on their way to Rimini. It was a long trip to make by auto and a chancy one with the possibility for breakdowns and Fascist interference. That was the author's euphemism, interference. *The journalist did not want to be interfered with by any goddamn Fascist. If they were polite, Ezra kept saying, they would not have to worry about the castor oil treatment. Fascists did not waste castor oil on tourists. On the table were newspaper clippings of Olga Rudge's private violin concert for Mussolini. Benito, it was said, greatly admired Olga's technique which he found so rare in a woman. There were many rare things in Italy that year, much rare violence and some rare murders. According to Ezra, Il Duce, every afternoon, picked up the rarest of his five violins to work on his technique.*

PARIS AND ITALY: MARCH 1927

As Hadley kept explaining to him, a French divorce was quick but it was not simple, even when the charge was desertion on his part. First there were judgments and then secondary hearings and more legal confusions to be paid for. On March 10, there were almost final papers to sign that would make the decree absolutely final on April 14. Hadley had booked a passage to the States on April 16, taking Bumby with her for an extended visit.[1] "But you are not free to remarry," she told him, "until between the 20th & 30th of April – on account of Burkhardt having to put things right *after* the decree with the *mairie* of our district."[2] All Ernest had to do was pay the lawyer's bills and the court costs. And as Pauline explained to him, a Catholic marriage was not simple to arrange but it would be quick once they completed the paperwork.[3] The lawyer, the judge, the priest, and the mayor all were party to the ritual. Caught between the decorum of French law and the implacability of Church law, Ernest was pleased to be going to Italy with Guy Hickok.

He, Pauline, Jinny, and Bumby returned to Paris on March 10 in time for him to sign the last of the divorce papers and return his son to Hadley, who looked more stylish and less dowdy than he remembered, due in part to her new clothes bought and borrowed for her trip home. He, too, was better dressed, wearing the tailored suit that Pauline paid for. They were polite, smiling awkwardly in front of the judge, Hadley supported by Winifred Mowrer, with whom she was leaving the next day for Chartres to celebrate the divorce. As he watched the two women walk out together, Hemingway might have wondered who had been set free, himself or Hadley. With Winifred on her arm, she looked and acted that day like a new woman with inner resources Ernest had not suspected, a woman relieved to be on her own.[4]

In the next day's *Herald*, all the world could read about his no-longer marriage, an event which Guy had warned him was being closely followed by journalists who remembered him from his Anglo-American Press Club days.

> One of the four divorces granted Americans in Paris yesterday was given to Mrs. Hadley Richardson Hemingway, 35 rue de Fleurus, whose husband Mr. Ernest M. Hemingway is the author of the recently published "The Sun Also Rises," a novel of life in the Latin Quarter of Paris. The son of a doctor, Mr. Hemingway lived much of his life in Northern Michigan, later coming to the French capital where he made his residence.[5]

The *Tribune* made further comment:

> Certain American literary circles in Paris were not surprised yesterday to learn of the divorce decree which a Paris court has just granted to Mrs. Ernest M. Hemingway, wife of the well-known writer, who has made his headquarters here for the past several

years. To the large following which the young author attracted on the Continent, however, the news comes as a decided shock since the couple were believed to have been living happily together.[6]

It was not the sort of publicity that encouraged him to spend time in the cafés or to look up old friends, but that Saturday he did go by Shakespeare and Co. to return *The Spanish Journey* and check out the latest David Garnett novel.[7] He told Sylvia to watch the *Atlantic Monthly* for the publication of "Fifty Grand." He did not know when it would appear because the Perkins telegram only said "ATLANTIC TAKES FIFTY GRAND."[8] In the bookshop's magazine rack he looked over the first issue of *transition* featuring Joyce's "Work in Progress," Stein's "An Elucidation," and poems by old friends Evan Shipman and MacLeish. Beside *transition* was the first issue of Ezra's *Exile*, which, he noted, managed to misprint his "Neothomist Poem" as "Nothoemist Poem." Inside was Ezra's flyer, announcing that *Exile* would appear three times a year until Pound got "bored with producing it." The first issue "contains writing by Guy Hickok, John Rodker, E.W. Hemingway and yours as circumstances permit, EZRA POUND, editor." So now he was E. W. Hemingway. At least Ezra spelled the last name right. Two days later came the postcard: "As the error does NOT occur in the proofs. I suppose some G.D. NEOcroyant in the print shop has been abaht his MASTER'z bizniz. Holding proofs here to prove it teh yuh, w'en youse kums."[9]

In London, Hemingway's corrections to page proofs for *Fiesta*, as *The Sun Also Rises* would be called in England, were being made at Jonathan Cape's publishing house. In New York, Max Perkins was waiting for the typescript for *Men Without Women*; Oxford University Press wanted a collection of essays and *Harper's* wanted to serialize his next novel.[10] In Paris, Pauline and Jinny were hunting for a new and larger apartment. There were plenty of problems about their marriage but nothing that Pauline could not solve. Hadley had taken care of the divorce; Pauline could handle the wedding. At dinner the night before the travelers departed, Pauline made good an earlier promise to Hadley when she signed her new will, leaving $10,000 to Bumby and the rest to Ernest. Guy and Mary Hickok witnessed the simple document.[11] Early the next morning, Ernest and Guy cranked up Hickok's old Ford coupé with its cracked windshield and were on the road to Italy.

It was an intense, grueling trip with no time to dwell on vistas or explore the country. In eleven days Guy drove 3,000 kilometers while

Ernest navigated over muddy, narrow roads on which they seldom got the Ford up to speed. Leaving Paris on March 15, they followed the right bank of the Rhône south, not reaching the Italian border until 18 March.[12] That night in Rapallo, after supper with Ezra and Dorothy Pound, they added up the mileage: 1,300 kilometers in four long days. They were seeing plenty of country but none of it for long. Guy, who had some idea of writing features for his *Brooklyn Eagle* on Fascism, could not speak the language and spent most of his time concentrating on the road. It was slow going at fifteen or twenty miles an hour and frequently slower on hills and through small villages strung out like beads on the road.

From Rapallo they followed the coast south and east on a road that rose and fell, twisted and turned toward La Spezia. For the last twenty kilometers, they gave a lift to a young Italian who stood on the running-board and leaned out on the turns. Grinding up the hills, the old Ford seldom got out of first gear, its radiator boiling muddy water.[13] They were following a set itinerary on a circle tour: Genova, Rapallo, La Spezia, Pisa, Firenze, Rimini, Bologna, Parma, and back to Genova. Along the way, Ernest received daily mail from Pauline, who learned during the Hundred Days how dependent her husband-to-be was upon her letters. Her first letter, written the afternoon of Hemingway's departure, allowed that this "Italian tour for the promotion of masculine society" would have to last him a long time, "for I'm very sure your wife is going to be opposed to them."[14]

While Ernest and Guy puttered on across the Romagna and into Rimini with a glance at San Marino, Pauline was efficiently arranging their Paris future. With the help of Ada MacLeish, she found a Left Bank apartment at 6 rue Férou, a quiet, cobbled street of religious shops that joined the church of St. Sulpice with the Luxembourg Gardens. The three-year lease was only 9,000 francs a year, but there were some other fees, including a large one to the present tenant, which Pauline was certain Uncle Gus would provide in a pinch. Further from the heart of Montparnasse, the apartment cost only 50 francs a month more than Hemingway's cold-water flat on Notre-Dame-des-Champs. With the franc stabilized at twenty-five to the dollar, a month's rent on rue Férou came to $30. For this price, they got a garden courtyard, a large master bedroom and salon, dining room, kitchen, two small rooms – "that could be one for you and one a little bedroom for maid or guest or infant or storage" – two toilets ("one for each clipping book"), a bathroom and kitchen. Open front and back, the rooms got morning and afternoon

113

sunlight. Compared to his old flat, the rue Férou apartment had more room, more comfort, and more heat. For Pauline, the apartment was exactly what she wanted: Left-Bank enough to satisfy Ernest; comfortable enough and far enough away from noisy summer tourists on Montparnasse to please her.[15]

Pauline was also leaving nothing to chance or Ernest's efforts with regard to the marriage. Father MacDarby, her old friend, gave her sound advice as did the local French priest. They needed baptism certificates (hers was in hand) and proof that Hemingway's first marriage was outside the Church. The hard part was finding a baptism certificate for Ernest, which probably did not exist. "As you are in Italy can't you make enquiries?" Pauline asked. "The priest says all baptisms in hospitals are registered. Or maybe you could find the priest who baptized you. What they want is conclusive proof of baptism. If you can get this then things will begin to march, but nothing can be done until these documents are handed in." They also had to have lived three months in parish residence before the wedding could take place. "The simplest thing seems to be married in the church at Victor Hugo. Then I suppose the civil ceremony must take place before that – but you can find out about that."[16]

When she wasn't apartment-hunting or priest-probing, Pauline, with Jinny's help, did her best to clean up Gerald Murphy's studio, which Ernest in seven months had turned into a litter bin. First she had to warm the place up, pick up his clothes, and send sweaters to the cleaners before she could throw out the trash. The hard part was recognizing what was trash. "Awful lot of papers," she told him. "I may just develop a firm platform about papers. And then, of course, I may not. But you got a lot of papers."[17] Reminded by the task of how little she enjoyed housework, Pauline also set about looking for a permanent maid. Walking through the Luxembourg Gardens, she and Jinny ran into the Hemingways' maid, Marie Rohrbach, with Bumby in tow. "Marie," Pauline wrote, "is cockeyed to come to work for us." That idea lasted only as long as it took Hadley to write the letter to Pauline pointing out that Marie was not joint property and was in no way part of the divorce settlement. Pauline, who was in most cases sympathetic to Hadley's situation, quickly realized her mistake. "I was so pleased about getting a good cook," she wrote Ernest, "that I didn't consider the ramifications. You can't build an old house with new bricks or the other way around, can you?"[18]

In Italy the young men were wearing Fascist armbands and acting very superior. All along the Yugoslavian border, Italian artillery was gathering in support of Albania, but no one thought there would be a war. Not this time. Whatever Hemingway went to find in Italy, he could not miss the handwriting on the brick walls of Imola, Modena, and Parma, where Mussolini's pop-eyed portrait was stenciled along with hand-painted *vivas*. Ernest and Guy were both disgusted: too many superior young men on the roads and too many whores now working the restaurants. By driving two hours in the dark along the coast road past Imperia and San Remo, they arrived tired, hungry, but safe in the French town of Menton in the evening of 24 March. As he wrote soon afterwards, "The whole trip had taken only ten days. Naturally, in such a short trip, we had no opportunity to see how things were with the country or the people."[19] Guy Hickok's sentiments were more pointed. "The Italians are such an unpleasant subject," he said, "that I hate to spend time thinking or writing about them." Two days later and less than a half-day's drive from Paris, Hickok's Ford broke down beyond quick repair. Once they hauled it into Dijon and found a mechanic, Hemingway left Guy with the repairs and caught the first train into Paris, four hours away. Tired, rumpled, and unexpected, he arrived to kiss Pauline and hug Jinny, ready to begin his new life.[20]

PARIS: MARCH 31, 1927

Back in Gerald Murphy's studio, he sat at the makeshift table where his new portable typewriter was surrounded by neat stacks of paper and incoming mail. He could see that this new life, through no particular effort on his part, was going to be better organized than his old one. In one stack, Pauline had piled up magazines – *Field and Stream, Toreros, The Ring, Auto, Exile, transition, Saturday Review* and *Scribner's*. On top of the magazines was an envelope with tickets to the six-day bike races.[21] On all sides and continuing on to the floor were discrete stacks of his life's residue. As Pauline had noted, there was a lot of paper in his life – manuscripts and carbons, letters, newspapers, magazines, programs to almost forgotten boxing matches, bull fight tickets from summers past, overdue books and paid bills, half-filled note books, and to-do lists long since done. There were old passports, new divorce papers, dead leases, dated book reviews, and aging photographs.

It was his old life laid out upon the table, the one he had come to Paris to create. They arrived in town on Hadley's money and his journalism, made their marks and lived their lives, climbed the stairs, bore the child, paid the bills, and wrote the books. All those names and places, all the old hotels and half-written stories, surrounded him now in these neat piles. In five-and-a half years he had become a name and face well known along the Left Bank, a friend to the great writers of his time, an item in the Paris papers and New York reviews, and a writer whose best-seller was not bringing him a penny. This new life could not be a completely fresh start, for one always carried old baggage on one's back, but he was traveling as lightly as possible into uncharted country. He took with him his thousand-dollar debt to Scribner's for advances, three changes of clothes, one new suit, an old camera, a decent touring bike, the new Corona portable, one pair of old skies, a bamboo fly-rod, and a lot of books. His dead paper, old letters, and yellowing magazines could be trunked and buried, the way pirates laid down treasure against their dotage.

Reading through the letters that arrived while he was gone, he could not bring himself to answer many of them. Virgil Thompson wanted a story for his new magazine, *Lazrus*, which would pay 33 cents for every 100 words.[22] At that rate "A Simple Enquiry" was worth $3.96. Forget *Lazrus*. The two letters from his father were about what he expected. As long as the divorce was not in the Chicago paper, the Doctor could say that it was fortunate for the family that the wire service said Ernest came from Toronto. But when the *Tribune* carried the story, he wrote, "Do tell me the truth! To break a Life contract is so serious a matter, there must have been some cause. Wish I could send you some encouragement."[23] A month earlier, his mother completely surprised him, writing "I'm sorry to hear your marriage has gone on the rocks. But most marriages ought to. I hold very modern and heretical views on marriage – but keep them under my hat."[24] As one of Grace's friends said, "So many people fail to look behind the artist Ernest has become to the home and parents."[25]

Another unexpected Oak Park response came from Bruce Barton, son of the village minister and now a New York ad-man boosting American business. In his last letter, Max had included the proof of a Barton review of *The Sun Also Rises* written for the April *Atlantic Monthly*. Barton announced that "A writer named Hemingway has arisen, who writes as if he had never read anybody's writing, as if he had fashioned the art of writing himself." His characters, Barton said, without morals, ideals, or religion, drank too much, but they had courage and friendship. "And they are *alive*. Amazingly real and alive." Proving that he still had one foot in Oak Park, Barton, like Grace Hemingway, also hoped that Ernest would one day write a book "about more respectable people."[26] Max said the review, however misguided, was "all to the good," meaning that it would help sales. Ernest got off a quick note to Perkins, saying that he did not yet have the *Men Without Women* material ready to send. "I had, unexpectedly, to make a trip down to Italy after some stuff, which I couldn't get, and it knocked out my entire schedule of work."[27]

Now that his old routines were broken, nothing, it seemed, was going *expectedly* in his life. He had seen more of Pauline before his separation from Hadley than he had recently. The Italian trip was his own choice, but even now they could not live together until after the marriage, for until the end of April, her fabled and wealthy Uncle Gus was in Paris to open a new Richard Hudnut salon on the glitzy rue de la Paix.[28] With family decorum and a good deal more at stake, Ernest and Pauline were circumspect and almost innocent around her uncle, who knew Paris quite well, picking good restaurants and paying all the bills. Augustus G. Pfeiffer, majority stockholder in the Richard Hudnut cosmetics enterprise, was a practiced European traveler who enjoyed good food, while collecting rare chess sets and small companies the way some men acquire new shoes.[29] He was thin, sharp-nosed, and canny, with an eye always on the main chance. It was Ernest's great luck that this new-found uncle, who was childless, doted on Pauline, for Uncle Gus would become Hemingway's surrogate father and benefactor for the next ten years. More immediately, Gus put up all the money needed for Pauline's rue Férou apartment.

Of all the letters on the table, the only ones he could bring himself to answer were two from Scott Fitzgerald, who was back on the east coast after a month in Hollywood. The letterhead was from the Roosevelt Hotel in Washington, D.C., which Scott said Ernest could have if he would only send for it. "It was formerly the warehouse where Theodore Roosevelt kept his jock straps – you remember, of course, how balls kept growing on him after the Spanish-American war until – poor wounded heart – he scarcely knew where to turn."[30] In the second letter, Fitzgerald reported on his lunch with H. L. Mencken, whom Hemingway had never forgiven for his dismissal of *In our time*: "The sort of brave, bold stuff that all atheistic young newspaper reporters write."[31] Fitzgerald promised that Mencken was reading *The Sun Also Rises* and would now be interested if Hemingway would send him some fiction.[32] Scott's ceaseless boosting of his career may have puzzled Hemingway, who occasionally recommended a writer to a publisher but never spent as much effort doing it as Scott did for him. Fitzgerald, already astride fame's pinnacle, seemed determined to pull Ernest to the same height.

Before he could answer either letter, Scott's telegram arrived: VANITY FAIR OFFERS TWO HUNDRED DEFINITELY FOR ARTICLES WHY SPANIARDS ARE SWELL OR THAT IDEA.[33] Fitzgerald's enthusiasm pushed Hemingway back to his typewriter. He did not want to write stories to order, he told Scott, "but you thought up a swell subject that wouldn't be any form of jacking off for me to write on at all . . . Wrote something for them yest. morning in bed. Will look at it tomorrow and then fix it up and send it on. Some crap about bull fights." He told Fitzgerald that Hadley was in love, he was broke, and that characters out of *The Sun Also Rises* were reportedly after him with weapons. "So I sent word around that I would be found unarmed sitting in front of Lipp's brasserie from two to four on Saturday and Sunday afternoon and everybody who wished to shoot me was to come and do it then or else for christ sake to stop talking about it." Of course, it was a joke started by Guy Hickok, but a joke worth repeating. He, Ernest, was leading a simple life, staying away from the Quarter and missing Fitz, who was "the best damn friend" he had.[34]

After he put his Fitzgerald letter into the mail, he returned to the typed and untitled piece he'd written for *Vanity Fair*, where his comedic friends, Bob Benchley and Dorothy Parker, were regular contributors. Ever since his high-school newspaper days, Hemingway took pride in his ability at humorous satire, particularly when it involved style as it did in *Torrents of Spring* or in the piece he recently sold to *The New Yorker*. His "Letters" for Ford's *transatlantic review* had been a variation on that mode, and in *The Sun Also Rises* he did the humor, he thought, quite well in the different voices. But reading back through what seemed funny only yesterday, he could not believe that he had written it. Satire was a mistake with *Vanity Fair*, where spoofing their typically exaggerated style and trendy humor sounded simply inane. He scanned the pages where his running joke about how many words he had written and when the piece would be long enough for the format fell flat on its face. "If the reader doesn't like me to write this way I can write a lot of other ways," he wrote, "but I have not seen a copy of Vanity Fair for a long time and I am just trying to write the way I remember it used to sound when I read it."

Tired, edgy, and out of tune with his talent, Hemingway discovered there was nothing he wanted to share with *Vanity Fair* about Spain, for the country meant too much to him to throw away as a joke. As a result the words were nothing more than an exercise in filling up pages. "The country itself is called Spain after an old Iberian word meaning spain." Then he told them "Juan Gris is a gris is a gris is a gris. Is a Gris? I learned to write this way about painters from Gertrude Stein." Later he stuck in the boxing joke from "Fifty Grand" which he once cut on Scott's advice and which he still thought was a great joke even if it had nothing to do with Spain. More comments on how many pages to fill his quota and then a parody of Dorothy Parker followed by more remarks to the reader: "Do you like this so far, reader? I'm afraid you don't. But, reader, be a sport. I don't like it either. I can't seem to get that real Spanish feeling into it. . . . It simply has not got it, reader. I don't know what I can do about it."

Then an anecdote about Picasso's paintings blowing off the top of his car shifted without logic to remembering a trip to Madrid traveling third class with a wine salesman who shared all his samples. That too was a recycled piece, but it led him to remember going to Madrid with Hadley and staying at the bullfighters' pensione. That's where his thin humor stopped and memories of Spain flooded in until finally he had to say it: "I love it very much and if I do not write about it that is because it is too good to write about." *It* was Spain, was Hadley, was the bull fights, was the end of the line. After a moment's pause, he tore the eight typed pages roughly in half, dropping the pieces into the stack of old manuscripts marked for storage.[35] *Vanity Fair*'s readers would have to do without their dose of Hemingway, which, as he liked to say, was no worse than a bad cold.

He turned instead to his notebooks from the Italian trip where wind was blowing down the dirt roads. Once his journalism had shaped his fiction; now he let his fiction shape the essay. Within a few days he reduced the ten-day excursion to three representative scenes: the village hitchhiker who barely thanked them for the ride; the whores doing their best to detain them in the café at La Spezia; and the Fascist on the bicycle who over-fined them for a dirty license plate. He wrote it out quickly in two different notebooks, holding it all together with the road, the weather, false smiles, and crisp dialogue.[36] After all the kidding he had taken from Hickok about using real people in his fiction, he thought it amusing to use Guy in the story and even more amusing to do a variation on Guy's article in the first issue of *The Exile*. There Hickok described his recent American visit and the voyage back to France where he was shocked by the behavior of American college girls.

I wished that the girls would not feel that it was obligatory to cross their knees in such a way as to show the steward their underwear. They spent hours trying to see who could tell the roughest stories . . . I showed some curiosity about what they called "necking" in the States. The Vassar girl said she would show me. She smeared wet lip rouge perfumed with Scotch from my chin to my ear and when I laughed she was angry.[37]

At La Spezia the whore with the nice breasts was all over Guy who was saying, "Tell her we have to go. Tell her we are very ill, and have no money."[38]

PARIS: MAY 4, 1927

All of April he stayed away from Montparnasse where sidewalk cafés were crowded noon and midnight with American tourists, some looking for a glimpse of characters out of his novel, others behaving as if they were auditioning for the parts. Left Bank gossip columnists, who had nothing to report on him, were reduced to using him as a point of comparison:

Becan . . . has come back from the land of the Basques with ideas and materials aplenty. Like Ernest Hemingway who goes down and fights bulls so that he can come home and write about his experiences in "This Quarter" and in "The Sun Also Rises."[39]

For a man who continually told inflated stories about himself, Hemingway was unnaturally reticent about his divorce and said almost nothing about his pending marriage. Early in April, he and Pauline spent four nights at the Velodrome watching the six-day bike races where they saw Guy Hickok but almost no one else they knew. Few of his old friends were in town, and for those he had little time, although he did spend one drunken evening with painter Waldo Peirce, a huge man with flowing beard, a big laugh, and a lovely wife. "He's a remarkable cuss," Guy Fangel wrote Ernest after pouring Peirce on to his night train, "Rabelaisian without and, I understand, puritanical within; one of those combinations bound to sprout occasionally in our New England environment."[40]

120

Two days after his divorce was final, Hemingway checked out a history of the Spanish Inquisition at Sylvia's but did not linger, for he was trying to get *Men Without Women* completed for fall publication.[41] The world, despite his best efforts to prevent it, continued to intrude, and the month had passed with almost nothing to show for his time. Each day there was the possibility that he would have to vacate Gerald's studio on a moment's notice. Murphy had written from Berlin that some time in May, he and Fernand Léger were going to use the studio as the stage for an experimental film.[42] Each day there was Uncle Gus to tend to or something else to be done about the wedding. Having testified that he had been baptized during the war in Italy and that his first marriage was outside the Church, Hemingway received, on April 25, the necessary dispensation from the Archbishop of Paris which removed the last obstacle to the ceremony. The penultimate formality was the publication of the banns, which began Sunday (May 1) in the parish churches of St. Honoré (Pauline's) and St. Pierre-de-Montrouge (Ernest's), and continued on the following Sunday.[43] Of course there were priests to be seen, confessions to be made, papers to be signed and returned, a ring to be bought – all a far cry from the simplicity of his first marriage at Horton Bay.[44]

If it wasn't the Church, there was always the new apartment to take up time – agreements to be signed, delivered, and made right with hard francs, deposits to be made on electricity – and the old flat to be tended to. To negotiate the new apartment lease he first hired a lawyer, Albert Legrand, to deal with the rent controls. He and Pauline, backed by Uncle Gus, agreed not only to pay the back taxes on the apartment for the first three months of the year but also to pay C. Thomas Bailey, from whom they were subleasing, a full year's rent (9,000 francs) as a privilege fee as well as three months' advance rent starting on the first of April.[45] For a man without a home, Hemingway was strangely rich in Paris apartments. Pauline, from her sense of propriety, was still living in her apartment on rue Picot. He was still paying rent on the Notre-Dame-des-Champs flat although neither he nor Hadley had lived there for nine months.[46] With Gus Pfeiffer covering their most immediate expenses, money was not a pressing problem for Ernest and Pauline, although he continued to tell friends like Fitzgerald how broke he was. It was a bit embarrassing when Scott sent him a $100 check, saying "I hate to think of your being hard up. Please use this if it would help."[47]

Compared to Scott, Ernest was broke and in debt, but only if he did not consider Pauline's $3,600 a year income from her well-managed trust

121

funds. Added to that secure money were the one-time wedding checks arriving from the States. Thousand-dollar checks were sent by Pauline's parents in Piggott and her Uncle Henry in New York. Aunts Kate and Eunice also sent checks, as did Uncle Gus and Cousin Delight.[48] By the time the checks were totaled, Ernest and Pauline had enough money to live a year in Europe without income. Thus when the Boni & Liveright representative came around with a contract promising a $3,000 advance on his next novel, Ernest was able to turn it down without too much thought.[49] And when his younger sister, Madelaine, suggested that she visit him in Paris, he encouraged her, saying that she could live with Jinny and travel with himself and Pauline. When Madelaine said she could not afford the expenses, Ernest wired her: PLAN TO ARRIVE MIDDLE OF JUNE STAY WITH ME PARIS THEN PAMPLONA TOGETHER EARLY JULY ALL EXPENSES PAID COUNTING ON YOU ABSOLUTELY ERNIE.[50] Such largesse did not speak of a man much worried about money.

On Holy Saturday, he put Hadley and Bumby on the boat train for the coast and on to the States, and five days later the French legal system said he was finally free to remarry.[51] While tourists lapped up champagne at Zelli's and Josephine Baker's place in Montmartre, he and Pauline made a private Paris for themselves, keeping away from familiar places. College girls were shaking it out to the Black Bottom, and Brick Top was singing "*You got the right key but the wrong key hole*," but that was someone else's life, not theirs. Avoiding all the old familiar places without making the effort into an effort, the two lovers were creating new routines in a city half haunted with memories. Never go back to your old front, he once told his newspaper readers. It was good advice for old soldiers and newly divorced men. He needed a new café, a fresh bakery, a different news stand – all easily discovered by moving closer to the river. But all of Europe was smaller now, for they could never return to the special places he and Hadley once discovered together, not to the Taube at Schruns, not to Cortina, Chamby, or the bull fighters' pensione in Madrid.

On May 4, clearing out one segment of the old life, he sent Max Perkins six stories for *Men Without Women* to go along with the three being published in *Scribner's Magazine*. As soon as he found a copy of "A Banal Story," he would send it along. Without saying anything to Max about his imminent marriage, Ernest promised that two more stories – "Italy 1927" and "After the Fourth" – would be in the mail within three weeks. By the middle of June, he hoped to have at least three new stories written. A long bull fight story that he was rewriting, "A Lack of Passion," was a possibility, but "Up in Michigan" he would probably hold out, for it did not seem right for the collection. "I want the book to be a full $2.00 size," Hemingway said, "but there is no use sending stories that would just be filler. Though I need some quiet ones to come in between the others. Hope to have something good next month." Max would have to look closely at the words; there were a couple in "A Pursuit Race" that might be offensive. Any suggestions Max had for the order of the stories would be appreciated.[52] As he put the letter into the overseas mail, aviators on both sides of the ocean were preparing themselves and their aircraft to be the first to fly the Atlantic non-stop. A new age was about to be born.

PARIS AND THE CAMARGUE: MAY 1927

Like all Catholic couples in France, Ernest and Pauline were married twice, once in civil ceremony at the *mairie*'s office and once in the church. What started as an orderly progression in Hemingway's notebook turned into a rush before the marriage was final. Ernest made careful notes about the civil ceremony, the confession billet, buying the ring, finding witnesses, and collecting the various receipts needed. The Saturday before the wedding (May 7), he planned to pack up at Murphy's studio, deposit Scott's check, and have dinner that night at rue Férou. Sunday after church, he would pack more of his things from the Notre-Dame-des-Champs flat and answer letters. Monday there would be time to pick up the bicycles, tell Mike Ward (his male witness) where to appear, and also decide where to honeymoon. Tuesday (May 10) he would meet Pauline at the church at 9.30 to fill out more papers and then pick up train tickets. "Advise Ada and Archie," he noted. On Wednesday they would marry in the civil ceremony at the *mairie*, and on Thursday (May 12) at 11.00 a.m. at the Catholic church.[53] Then, for reasons no one remembers, both the civil and church ceremonies were rescheduled for Tuesday (May 10), back to back.

On Tuesday morning someone reminded Ernest that to be married at all they first needed to renew their Ville de Paris identity cards, which forced a quick taxi stop on the way to the *mairie*. Ernest listed his profession as *journaliste*.[54] Late that Tuesday morning, Ernest in his tweeds, Pauline in her pearls, accompanied by their two witnesses –

Virginia Pfeiffer, and Mike Ward from the Guaranty Bank – arrived finally at Place de Montrouge, passed by the statue of the burned heretic and through the gardens to the *mairie* of the fourteenth arrondissement. In the garden a bronze horse was being attacked by a lion.[55] At 11.30 a.m. the brief ceremony was completed and all papers signed. In the Name of the Law and in the presence of adult witnesses, he, Ernest Hemingway, divorced of Hadley Richardson since the 21st of April, was now joined in matrimony with Pauline Pfeiffer. He gave his age as twenty-seven and his year of birth as 1899; Pauline was recorded as thirty-one years old, born in 1895. Georges Cahen, *mairie*, affixed his signature to complete the ritual.[56] With their certificate in hand, the couple and their witnesses had barely enough time to recross the river into the sixth arrondissement where, at Place Victor Hugo, Pauline's priest was waiting for them in the side chapel of St. Honoré d'Eylau.[57]

Having been stamped as valid, signed, and sealed, and doubly married, the Hemingways repaired to 44 rue du Bac where Ada MacLeish prepared a light lunch for the wedding party. Later Ada said that she and Archie had not attended the wedding because she "was completely disgusted with Ernest's efforts to persuade the Catholic Church that he had been baptized by a priest who walked between aisles of wounded men in an Italian hospital – therefore Ernest was a Catholic and Hadley never had been his wife and Bumby was a bastard. To see this farce solemnized by the Catholic Church was more than we could take."[58] What she did not remember to say was that she was completely exhausted from her Conservatoire de Musique debut concert the previous night, and could not possibly have been up and dressed early enough to have rushed about Paris with the wedding party and also to have prepared lunch.[59]

By the following àfternoon, Ernest and Pauline, baggage and bicycles in tow, were aboard the *rapide* to Avignon where they picked up the local P.L.&M. railway to take them as far as Aigues-Mortes, the old, walled crusaders' city. That day the newlyweds did not pause to walk the ramparts but continued on by hired car another six kilometers to the even more remote fishing village of Le Grau-du-Roi where they found rooms in a small pension. At the mouth of the flat Rhône delta, the village was cupped by open, empty beaches. Behind it stretched the hot plains and bays of the Camargue, a land of shallow estuaries, salt marshes, and low swamps where wild bulls and African flamingos dotted the terrain.[60]

The sun rose next morning to creaking sails and noisy gulls, strong coffee and hard rolls with local jam on a bare table. Paris time and most of its world disappeared. As they woke to their new life, Juan Gris was being buried in the old cemetery at Boulogne, and Charles Lindbergh was landing his *Spirit of St. Louis* at Le Bourget. But there in sunlit Le Grau-du-Roi, only the essential elements remained: the fishing fleet in its harbor, the simple rhythms of village life, and open beaches where a man and his wife could bathe as naked as they wished. For the first time Ernest and Pauline were perfectly alone. Flat dirt roads carried them by bike across still lagoons and open pasture back to Aigues-Mortes, its stone walls rising up out of the salt marshes like an ancient mirage. The town itself was cramped and rather uninteresting, but from the walls, the unobstructed view out across the Camargue was worth the climb. Once the debarkation point for crusaders, the port had long since silted up, its sailing days not even a memory. Here and there among the marshes to the shore side, canals were being dug to drain the land for vineyards. Ernest and Pauline walked the ramparts and crossed the green moat into the Tower of Constance, with its twenty-foot-thick stone walls.[61]

Twelve days after they arrived in Le Grau-du-Roi, the great spring festival and Gypsy pilgrimage began forty kilometers away at Les Saintes-Maries-de-la-Mer. Years later one of their sons said that Ernest and Pauline went to the festival with faces darkened by berry juice and disguised as Gypsies, but disguises were unnecessary for this was not a private event. If they went in costume, as they may well have, it was for their own delight and not from necessity.[62] If they went by bicycle, as their son also said, they had a long day of it, twenty-five miles of dirt roads and no place to stay at Les Saintes-Maries where every room was booked weeks in advance. Along the way the road was jammed with painted Gypsy wagons, sputtering autos, locals on horseback, and pilgrims afoot, all intent on witnessing the relics of the sainted Maries – Mary Jacoby and Mary Salome – themselves the mothers of saints and set adrift in an open boat, as the legend tells, with Mary Magdalene, Martha, Lazarus, and St. Maximinius. Their wooden boat was said to have come ashore at what was now Les Saintes-Maries, and each year on May 25, two wooden Maries, more busty than one might expect, were carried in a small boat through the village and back to the sea with great ceremony. The priests and archbishop first lowered the ancient reliquary from the church ceiling, removing the silver arm containing holy ashes and bones of the two women. Surrounded by Gypsies, rich incense smoke, *guardiens* on white horses, and religious tourists like Ernest and Pauline, the archbishop carried the reliquary to the shore where he raised it aloft as the bark touched water. In the night crypt beneath the fortress-like chapel, the Gypsies paid special homage to the blackened figure and preserved bones of their patron saint, Sarah the Egyptian.[63]

During those three weeks of his second honeymoon, Hemingway never stopped writing, for he had a book of stories to publish in the fall. At Le Grau-du-Roi, he found the right ending for the story about Nick's broken heart which he titled "Ten Indians." His first notebook draft, dating back to September of 1925, had been revised in a cold Madrid May of 1926. He had most of the story right, understated and taut; the generation for whom "sex appeal" was a new and daring term did not need to be told what Prudie was doing "threshing around" in the woods with Frank Washburn. And the next year the college girls were humming, "*I wanna be bad. I wanna blow a fuse. I wanna make big deal with my sex appeal. I wanna be in the news.*" With the waves breaking on the French beach, Ernest saw that having Prudie come to Nick in the night was not as effective as Nick alone, waking the next morning with the "big wind blowing and the waves were running high up on the beach and he was awake a long time before he remembered that his heart was broken."[64]

That was one story, but he needed another to bring the collection up to his expectations. After trying to revise "Up in Michigan," he decided to put it aside along with "A Lack of Passion," his story of a potentially homosexual bullfighter. Among the manuscript fragments he took with him to Le Grau-du-Roi was a two-year-old sketch that began with the narrator and Hadley on a Spanish train as it stopped at Caseta on the Ebro river. "*Look* at those god-dam white mountains," the narrator says. Hadley replies that they are "the most mysterious things I have ever seen."

They were white mountains, not white with snow or any artificial aid but white themselves furrowed and wrinkled by the rains . . . On a cloudy day they might have been gray as a white elephant is gray in a circus tent; but in the heat they shown white as white elephants in the sun.[65]

Without any obvious destination, the sketch stalled on the sixth page where Hemingway returned to it that morning when Pauline was watching the fishermen mend their nets and the morning light was still cool in their rented room. All he needed was the setting and those white hills and a little heat to start a story he had been thinking about for some

126

time. a pregnant woman and her lover, maybe her husband, discussing an abortion. Eliot's gossiping *Waste Land* women said it:

> It's them pills I took, to bring it off, she
>   said.
> (She's had five already, and nearly died of
>   Young George.)
> The chemist said it would be all right, but
> I've never been the same.
> You are a proper fool, I said.
> Well, if Albert won't leave you alone, there
>   it is, I said,
> What you get married for if you don't want
>   children?[66]

Like Eliot, Hemingway wanted to write the story without ever using the word, abortion.

It opened at the way-station on the Ebro waiting for their train to come in, waiting to connect, and at the end they were still waiting, the American man and woman. Jig was her strange name, and she was pregnant. The argument started while they were drinking their beers, large, cold ones, and Jig was looking through the trees at the hills beyond.

> "They look like white elephants," she said.
> "I've never seen one," the man drank his beer.
> "No, you wouldn't have."[67]

Then they argued about the drinks and how the things they waited to taste all came out licorice, but that wasn't really the issue. The issue was the baby growing in Jig's womb as they sat there in the Spanish heat a long way from home.

As one argument subsided and more beer was served, the conversation, which was the story, turned to the real problem:

> "It's really an awfully simple operation," the man said. "It's not really an operation at all."
> The girl looked away at the ground the table legs rested on.
> "I know you wouldn't mind it, Jig. It's really not anything. It's just to let the air in."

127

It went on like that with Jig wanting to know how they would be afterwards, would he love her still and would he be nice when she said something looked like a white elephant? He kept insisting the operation was perfectly simple and that he always loved her and there was nothing to worry about. It was perfectly safe. But he said it too often, and the reader knew the man didn't mean it and Jig knew it too.

Seventeen days after his marriage to Pauline, Hemingway put typescripts for "Hills Like White Elephants" and "Ten Indians" in the mail to Max Perkins, suggesting that they might also include "Italy 1927" under a different title. Thanking Max for the $750 advance on *Men Without Women*, he said he would be in Paris for the next month and then to Spain for as long as the advance money held out. "Am healthy and working well and it ought to be a good summer."[68]

Chapter Nine

PILGRIM'S PROGRESS

When 10,000 protesters gathered in the Cirque de Hiver, the couple were in Valencia for the feria. *When bombs went off in New York and Baltimore, he was fishing for mountain trout above La Coruña. While 50,000 communists, anarchists, Frenchmen, American tourists, and visiting Italians staged, in the Bois des Vincennes, their protest against the American court's decision, it was softly raining in the cobbled streets of La Coruña where land's end stretched out into the grey Atlantic. He and his wife were lost in Spain when they threw the switch in Boston, electrocuting Sacco and Vanzetti. After all the marches, petitions, and hearings, all the stately reconsiderations, the answer was death. "What about this goddamn human race anyway?" Dos Passos asked. And Archie, who was living that summer on a Massachusetts farm, said, "The fight has gone out of these people. Me for instance. I was wild about it. So I argued a long time with some Boston lawyers and then changed the subject. A great race. Stink. Spew them out. And perhaps the boys were really guilty. O hell!" At the old pilgrimage site of Santiago de Compostela, the couple did not need a weatherman to know which way winds were blowing.*

PARIS: JUNE 7, 1927

The honeymooners waited until the Memorial Day crowd thinned out before returning by train to Paris. After quiet days in Le Grau-du-Roi, Paris seemed more frenetic and more crowded than usual with summer

129

tourists. Everyone was breathless over something, the next parade, the next extravagance, the next transatlantic pilot to fall out of the air. Not a newspaper could be printed without Lindbergh's name on the front page. On both sides of the Atlantic, other fliers, eager for fame, were waiting in airdromes for weather to clear. Last summer it had been channel swimmers. This summer it was ocean pilots soaring into glory or oblivion. A few made it safely; most did not. Within a few months' time, twenty-seven men and one woman, along with their flying machines, disappeared into various oceans. Trying to ignore Americans clutching Paris guidebooks and fumbling with street maps, Ernest made his rounds quickly, picking up mail at the bank, at the Murphy studio, and at Sylvia's bookshop where he checked out a biography of Parnell, the betrayed Irish leader about whom Joyce loved to write.[1]

Sitting at the table in their new apartment on rue Férou with sunlight flooding the room, Hemingway opened the letters, starting with the easy ones. The Murphys, in town for a week looking for company, had come and gone. Gerald said, "*Thank God* that somebody like Lindbergh does something like what he's just done some of the time. It tightens the main-spring."[2] The letter from his sister, Madelaine (called Sunny) said she could not come to Pamplona with him and Pauline. If only they were going to see cathedrals rather than a fiesta, Doctor Hemingway and his wife might have supported the trip. "They have a horror for Fiestas and Spain in general – ever since your books. They can't believe that I would become anything but a prostitute if I ever visited such a place."[3] Then there was Guy Hickok's touch of humor to balance the scale. Now that "Italy – 1927" was published in the States, Guy said he understood "why everybody you use in your stuff goes out and gets a gun." He felt like Duff Twysden, who was reported to have said that she had never slept with the bull fighter. Referring to the girls in the Italian café, Guy said, "She didn't put her damned arm around my neck. If she had I shouldn't have minded."[4]

The several letters from Hadley he saved for last, arranging them by postmark and reading them slowly. In New York she found over $5,000 accumulated in *The Sun Also Rises* royalty account, from which she drew $1,000. The money was grand but nothing could help with Bumby except a day and night nurse trained in his strange patois of Breton French and curious English. Bumby, she said, "still insists that you are in Italy and prays for you at night."[5] Her life was easier in St. Louis where her sister Fonnie's kids and maid looked after the boy. "Will slip up to Chicago sometime during this visit," Hadley said, "and believe me that is devotion, Tatie, because it's not only emotionally trying but hard work with Bumbi alone."[6] Having always had a nursemaid for the boy, Hadley was ill prepared for single parenthood. Her last letter, which had barely arrived, spoke of occasional bad dreams, "but I think I'll pull through alright. I imagine you are blissfully wedded by now . . . Give my hulloo to the Archies and the Murphs – their clothes are *grand* – people love my clothes." (He might be remarried, but she could still remind him that he never let her buy new clothes.) "I sure have luck," Hadley said bravely, talking to herself.[7]

Now, in the warm streets of summer, Paris was less lovely for Ernest than she had ever been in winter rain. Five years earlier, he and Hadley, unknown and in love, delighted in discovering the city. Every street was such a new street, every corner filled with possibility – book stalls along the river, tiny galleries around the Ecole des Beaux Arts, old men in the Tuileries, artist models on the terrasse. When the franc was at twelve to the dollar, they were tourists; as it rose to eighteen, they became old hands in the neighborhood, recognized at the Dôme by painters and writers. Now with the franc at twenty-five, Hadley was in California and he, having become legendary along Montparnasse, took no joy on the boulevard. The gossip columnists missed his presence:

> on the tranquil and shaded terrasse of the Closerie des Lilas . . .
> Ford Madox Ford . . . and Sisley Huddleston [meet] in the grove
> where Lisle Bell, Manuel Komroff and Ernest Hemingway used to
> meet with their friends for breakfast last season.[8]

All the boozy evenings on Montmartre with McAlmon and Ezra, all the afternoons at Gertrude's, all of that was now Hemingway's past. McAlmon was unspeakable, Ezra in Italian exile, and with Gertrude there was nothing left to say. Everywhere he turned there was another young writer or painter beating his drum, cadging a drink. Ideas and styles that were once private and exciting had quickly become public domain. As Art Moss put it:

> There's a new type of Hobohemian on the South side of the Seine.
> Off hand, I should say it has evolved out of the long succession
> of the highbrowed journals that commenced with Gargoyle and
> has now arrived at the Transition stage. It talks like a page out of
> Joyce, crossed with five hundred words of Stein, seasoned with an
> ounce of Pound.[9]

131

Between these newly resident intellectuals and the burgeoning tourists, the Left Bank was losing its charm. Evenings in the café with the light beginning to fail and saucers piling up, those evenings were becoming impossible. At Diaghilev's Ballets Russes, he and Pauline suffered through Stravinsky's *Oedipus Rex* which Ernest found to be too Arty for words.[10] Wherever he looked the pretentious abounded. The latest guidebook to Paris "with the lid lifted" assured its readers that at Deux Magots one could hear "more dirty stories and advice as to where to buy 'adorable dresses' all in English than anywhere else in Paris." The Select, one read, was filled with "gentlemen with long, wavy hair and long, painted fingernails and other gentlemen who, when they walk, walk 'Falsetto,' toss their hips and lift their brows." And for "a big kick" one should dine at the Café des Mariniers, "a gala place this, a corking novelty."[11] That first weekend the Hemingways were back from the Camargue, three thousand American Rotarians stormed into Ostend, planning to invade Paris next. Gathering at embarkation points all across America, thousands of war veterans prepared for their late June return to Europe. It was just as well that Ernest and Pauline, staying pretty much out of everyone's sight, were in town only until the end of June when they would escape, as Ernest usually did, to Spain for the summer. But even Pamplona was under threat of American invasion. Gerald Murphy wrote that "Harpo Marx wants to go to Pamplona. Would you be good enough to write Sara the date thereof, so that she can do as she feels best about it."[12]

On Tuesday, June 7, as Pentecost weekenders left Paris and locals returned, Hemingway woke to the *Herald* headline:

Bellanca Ship Sets New Non-Stop Mark of 3,905 Miles in 46½ Flying Hours; Forced to Land 50 Miles From Berlin

Chamberlin, the pilot, and Charles Levine, the millionaire passenger, had outflown Lindbergh – but two weeks too late to be long remembered. Before the end of June, the *Herald* was running a serial biography of Lucky Lindy, the Lone Eagle. Somewhere over Newfoundland, Nunguesser and his "White Bird" disappeared from sight and shortly there after from the front page. At Antibes, Gerald Murphy was preparing his sloop for racing action in the Mediterranean. In a fragment of poetry Ernest mused:

The rail ends do not meet
The sun goes down

SANTIAGO DE COMPOSTELA: AUGUST 1927

And only rivers run no race
Nor does still water run so deep
Levine, Levine the Hebrew ace
Mackerel skies at night are the sailor's delight
Or they break the sailor's heart
A sailor's life is the life for me
The ground rolls green
As green as the sea.[13]

That afternoon he enclosed a check for 700 francs in his last letter to the landlord of 113 Notre-Dames-des-Champs. "Because I am leaving Paris," he said, "I shall not keep the apartment any longer. You may rent it immediately if you wish."[14] In a part of his heart, he had already left Paris; his actual departure was only a matter of time.

SANTIAGO DE COMPOSTELA: AUGUST 1927

Ernest and Pauline kept to the rail lines in Spain, following the bull-fights. After seven days at the Pamplona *feria* and another seven recovering on the San Sebastian beach, they watched the matadors in their ritual at Valencia and Madrid. From there, they went on to La Coruña where the country "was a lot like Newfoundland and it only clears between rains but the rain is natural and you don't seem to get wet."[15] With Pauline lovely and lithe, her hair cut as short as his own, Ernest could not have been happier or more in love. As they entered Santiago de Compostela, granite walls and cobbled streets glistened with recent rain, and the grey mountains cupping the plateau were vague in afternoon mist. Had they come the old pilgrim route, "the Milky Way" south from Pamplona, they might have counted medieval crosses and ruined statuary, crossed themselves at Burgos and León, arriving finally here for the great feast of St. James. They could have, but they did not. Three weeks earlier, the small medieval town would have been bursting with color and crowded with true believers. But they chose instead to arrive when the July pilgrims were departed, their promises fulfilled.

Arriving in the lull and quiet of the aftermath, Ernest came to Santiago on his own terms, making his private pilgrimage. From La Coruña he brought with him the corrected galleys for *Men Without Women*, which he mailed from Santiago on August 17. It was less than a

133

religious act, but not without significance, for to this ancient pilgrimage site the pious brought stranger wishes than Ernest's for a best-seller. The collection of stories was at this stage dedicated to Virginia Pfeiffer, "after a hard winter," a dedication not without irony, for Jinny was a woman without men. In June, Ernest wrote his newly acquired mother-in-law that he was doing his best to introduce Jinny to eligible men, but Clara (Jinny's companion) "will kill all that in a week" with "her constant propaganda" against "all marriage and all men." "Marriage is one thing that Clara is determined shall never happen." He could not directly say that Jinny was uninterested in men, but the message was there. He assured Paul and Mary Pfeiffer that Jinny "goes to mass on Sunday, [and] also keeps ember days."[16]

For two wet weeks he and Pauline lived within the shadow of the great Cathedral of Santiago, attending Mass and walking the narrow stone streets where the scallop shells of St. James were carved in profusion on every wall. In Santiago it was easy to be Catholic when the old town reeked of religion, every corner turning on to another pilgrim's reach. Mornings they woke to the peal of cathedral bells, and the evening air carried vespers from numerous convents and monasteries. As devout as any Catholic couple, Ernest and Pauline walked up the double stairway to wonder at the Gate of Glory where the enthroned Christ presided, surrounded by prophets and apostles with angels rampant. At his feet rested St. James the Apostle, leaning on his staff, the pilgrim's pilgrim. Seated about the perimeter of Our Lord was the Divine Orchestra of twenty-four Ancients, instruments at hand – citola, sinfonia, and harps – celestial music in waiting. Not far away, to remind the faithful of their alternative, into two of the archivolts were carved hideous devils with the damned caught up in their teeth. The two pilgrims stopped at the Tree of Jesse where five time-worn hollows exactly fit their fingers and where traditionally five Aves were recited. Inside the cathedral, St. James, dimly lit, presided over the main altar. His silver-gilt and bejeweled halo and collar caught the light of candles, reflecting onto his tawny, bearded face of enameled marble. Wide eyes and arched brows above almost pursed lips gave James the Moor Slayer a slightly surprised look as if caught unexpectedly by the pilgrims beneath him. Above his head, framing his glory, was a crown of gilded angels. Behind him, a rich darkness; before him, flickering candles. It was easy to believe, easy to be good, there in Compostela.[17]

There was also good food and wine throughout the town and trout fishing in the nearby mountain streams. "Caught four only but all big ones," Hemingway wrote MacLeish. "Two enormous bastards and had a fine time. These trout having been converted to Christianity by the Apostle St. James know a thing or two by now. They are pursued by dinamitors [sic], seiners, basket workers armed with pike poles and spears – to catch them on a dry fly you have to fool them."[18] He had fish in his creel but nothing in his writing poke; for two months he had been unable to write any new fiction. As he and Pauline lingered on longer than planned in the cool rains of Galicia, he tried not to think about his mornings of the empty page. In June, not knowing what would come next, he hinted to Max Perkins that he was planning a novel.[19] In Santiago, Max's enthusiastic reply caught up with him: "I was delighted to judge that you are actually writing a novel, too."[20]

Hemingway wasn't "actually" writing anything, but any day now something was bound to start. Unlike Fitzgerald, Hemingway refused to plan his fiction with elaborate diagrams, for he was sure that if he thought the story through to its conclusion, it would lose its spontaneity, and he would lose the joy of living inside the story while it developed. As a method, this untrammeled approach worked well for him in *The Sun Also Rises*; it also worked to his advantage in the short stories when they came quickly to paper. But, on below average days, the method could lead to lots of dead ends, stories that never worked. As for starting a novel, it was a little like building a doorway without knowing if it opened into a house or a closet. From writing *The Sun Also Rises*, he learned that intense experience could produce vital fiction, but he could not count on life providing him with such experience on a regular basis. Nor could his next novel be anything like the last, for he was not going to repeat himself.

With his market expanding and potential sales arriving in the mail, Hemingway stood empty-handed and empty-headed. His last story – "Hills Like White Elephants" – he had given to *transition*, certain no American periodical would touch the abortion issue. In June the Hearst magazine people offered him a thousand dollars for the option to buy his next five stories at a thousand dollars each and twelve fifty for the next five, plus ten thousand for serial rights to his next novel with more gravy for screen options.[21] Hemingway negotiated seriously, pushing up the ante: he wanted twelve thousand for serial rights to the novel and thirty thousand for the motion picture rights. He got what he wanted. Mildred Temple sent him the contract which specified that "no changes shall be made to your copy without your consent . . . I think this covers every-thing we discussed, and I hope you will be willing now to sign your name on the dotted line. . . . I am enclosing a banker's draft for $1,000 in francs covering the option."[22]

As soon as Hemingway received the offer, he returned the contract, saying he was "disappointed not to be able to sign the paper," particu-larly as he had to turn down 25,000 francs option money. "You know how cheerful that makes you feel," he joked. "In some ways, for my own good, I think it would be better to write on the novel with no idea of eventual serialization in mind."[23] Had he not been married to Pauline with her assured income, he could not have afforded to turn down the Hearst offer. That same day he enclosed to Max Perkins a carbon of his rejection letter, saying, "I was pretty badly tempted as it was a splendid chance to sell stories but I really think the pressure would be too strong and too subtle in regard to the novel . . . now doesn't seem like the time to get in what seems to me to be the greased chutes."[24]

So there in Santiago, where small hawks hunted from the cathedral towers, Hemingway had much to be thankful for and much to request as pilgrims were wont to do. Two years had passed since he wrote *The Sun Also Rises*, and now he needed a new novel as good or better. Everyone, including himself, expected it of him; nothing less would do. From Boston, Buzz Henry enclosed a boost from his friend and revered American writer, Owen Wister, who found "The Killers" and *The Sun Also Rises* to be "perfectly extraordinary. I don't know any young writer whose style and gift seem to me to approach him. Were I thirty, that's the way I should wish to write. I hope he has a long career of develop-ment ahead and that he will become interested in more varieties of human nature. So far he reveals a somewhat limited field of selection."[25] Elsewhere, *Black Mask* magazine readers followed Dashiell Hammett's private detective "into a sitting-room on the second floor where Mrs. Gungen put down a copy of *The Sun Also Rises* and waved a cigarette at a nearby chair."[26]

Most mornings he sat down with his pencil in hand, but nothing came of it. Instead he typed letters, a sure indication that he was not writing fiction. He answered letters from Ezra, Dos Passos, Archie, Max Perkins, and Guy Hickok, telling them about the pleasures of Santiago; he wrote Uncle Gus Pfeiffer; he even wrote his aging Uncle Tyley Hancock, who eked out a living selling "rubber goods to anybody who will buy."[27] Archie was impressed that Ernest turned down the Hearst offer and equally impressed with "Fifty Grand" in the *Atlantic*. He wanted to know how well Mrs. Bill Bullitt knew Ernest, for she was in his living room "knowing ALL about Pappy which I dare say he doesn't know himself. . . . I wont have more than every other person I meet know ALL about Pappy. It gets monotonous."[28] Ernest replied: "As for Mrs. Bullet [*sic*] knowing all about me the bitch where in hell does she get that stuff. I went to their house once and refused many an invitation and didn't ask them to ours – and believe that is the best way to make half kikes know all about you. I did know when her hair was blonde but that was in Constantinople and besides the wench was surrounded by naval officers."[29]

The one letter that he did not answer came from his father, who, after some opening pleasantries, got down to the bone:

You wrote Sunny what we had never known and I wish all the "love pirates" were in Hell. Our family has never had such an incident before and trust you may still make your get-away from that individual who split your home. Oh Ernest how could you leave Hadley and Bumby? I fell in love with Bumby and am so proud of him and you his father. I rejoice in your talents and ability and success and shall continue to pray for you, that you may in some way reclaim your dear Hadley and Bumby. Put on the Armor of God and shun Evil companions. Had you answered any of my letters since last November and given me your confidence I would have been oh so happy and had less sleepless nights and fewer explanations, which I have been unable to make – for I knew not – only printed records of Divorce proceedings – Printed in Detroit, Boyne City & Chicago newspapers. – All clipped and sent to me! Your dear mother and I have been heart broken over your conduct. – Perhaps you have reformed – if so thank God & write & tell us. – Are you again married and to who? Let us know as at present we do not know what to say or think. God bless you dear boy, but remember – "What doth it profit a man if he gain the whole world & loose [*sic*] his own Soul!"[30]

Ernest had no ready answer for this added load of guilt. In the confessional the priest might absolve him before God, but who would absolve him with his father? He had never heard his father wish anyone into Hell before.

HENDAYE PLAGE: SEPTEMBER 15, 1927

They had been on the beach two weeks when the writing returned from beneath his consciousness. When he received an advance copy of the September *Boulevardier*, Art Moss's slick Right-Bank gossip and humor magazine, it carried a Louis Bromfield essay, "The Real Frenchman," in which he searched in vain through the French regions for this generic character. The piece ended:

A week later, as I turned the key in the door of my apartment, a wave of warm feeling came over me. I was returning to my own *real* French – to my cook Yvonne from Normandy, my chambermaid Helene from the Nièvre and my chauffeur Lucien whom comes from La Vilette. They are the salt of the earth and the realest of *real* French.[31]

Moss included a note asking Hemingway to write a companion piece on the "real Spaniard" for the October issue.

Hemingway's quick response was lightly satirical and slightly Dadaist, but it was also a dull knife in the side of Louis Bromfield, whom Ernest had every reason to like. Bromfield, an early supporter of Hemingway's fiction, encouraged Ernest to use *Torrents* to break with Liveright, and recommended him strongly to his publisher Alfred Harcourt.[32] In Paris, during the Hundred Days, Louis and his wife, Mary, gave Hemingway comfort and meals. In return, Hemingway wrote satiric letters about the Bromfields to Fitzgerald: "I went out there to dinner one night and they had a lot of vin ordinaire and cats kept jumping on the table and running off with what little fish there was and then shitting on the floor."[33]

Only three years older than Hemingway, Bromfield had three novels published in New York and a new play finished. His Victorian trilogy of an American family's vicissitudes was what middle-class America wanted to read in the Twenties. His second volume, *Possession*, was so successful that he and Mary were able to move into a large and expensive Passy apartment maintained with several servants. His third novel, *Early Autumn*, won the 1926 Pulitzer Prize for Fiction, although not every Left Banker admired the book. Elliot Paul, writer and co-editor of *transition*, could not stand him at any price: "Bromfield writes in cliches, uses words and phrases shamelessly which have been squeezed dry of all meaning, has all the faults of Dreiser with none of the latter's virtues. . . . *Early Autumn* shows no improvement."[34] From Hendaye, while working on his *Boulevardier* essay, Hemingway wrote Fitzgerald, "Did you see how Fanny Butcher the woman with the Veal Brains called Brommy the American Fielding. Jesus Christ. It was this that moved me to write again."[35]

The piece began:

With relation to Spain, Yanquis (as the Spanish call them) seem to be divided into three classes, i.e. (1) those who have been there like Alexander Moore and Washington Irving (2) those who have never been there but live in California (3) those who have read "Virgin Spain"; so until reading Bromfield in the September *Boulevardier* I had never thought whether Spaniards were real or not. Bromfield opened my eyes but there is no use my trying to write like him as in the above paragraph, as I haven't: (1) the education (2) the ease and social position.

I spent the European war in Spain it is true as an attaché to the Spanish army, sleeping often enough in dunghills and chateaux and the like, but to me the Spanish never seemed real. Somehow they didn't. They seemed like cathedrals. Perhaps I was youthful and romantic. Perhaps not. Perhaps they were cathedrals. I remember one night in the trenches a little way out of Madrid sleeping with a number of beautiful Spaniards in what, looking back on it now, must have been a dunghill. It may have been a dunghill. I remember thinking it was a dunghill and the war still being on, looking for Bromfield or Brommy as we called him then. He was not there and I remember the Ambassador was very upset and said, "Those aren't cathedrals, Hem. Those aren't cathedrals. Don't you know you're in a dunghill?"

As I recall I made no answer to His Excellency's remark beyond an abortive attempt to interest him in my search for the real Spaniard. The Ambassador was very much put out and said that I was no attaché despite the fact that I had my attaché's case with me and I recall him speaking of good old Brommy and saying, "By God if good old Brommy had been sent down here we'd have the boys out of the dunghills and into the chateaux by Christmas!"

All this literary gossip however has nothing to do with my search for the real Spaniard which has been carried out all over Spain.

What followed were three mildly amusing paragraphs in parody of Bromfield's French excursions in search of the real Frenchman. Ernest tries and fails to find the real Spaniard in Navarre, Galicia, and Madrid, where only local variations were discovered.

I must say I felt discouraged and was on the point of hiring me a parlor maid, a cook, and a chauffeur named Pilar, Concepcion and Isidoro respectively, to see if they would be the real thing like good old Brommy found, when, picking up the Heraldo de Madrid, I glanced over the *Telefonos y Telegrafos* and saw that thirty six people had been drowned by the falling into the sea of an autobus in Extramadura. Something told me that they were the real Spaniards and that they were all dead.

"Shall we go to Extramadura?" I asked my wife.

"Why, dear?"

"To find the real Spaniards," I said, for that autobus accident haunted me.

"Hell no, dear," my wife answered.

"Why the hell not, dear?"

"You are the real Spaniard," my wife said softly and as I looked into her eyes and saw the truth gleaming there, I knew that my search too, like that of good old Brommy for the real French, had ended in the home.[36]

Making fun of himself and his war experience, kidding Bromfield, the Dadaists, and *Boulevardier*, it was not a vicious parody, but it was part of a pattern. Almost always a counterpunch, a response to someone else's lead, his parodies usually said more about Hemingway's inner conflicts than they did about the object of his satire. No matter how much he belittled Bromfield's financially rewarding fiction and the classy apartment it brought him, there was a part of Hemingway that wanted those same rewards. After abandoning his cold-water flat on Notre-Dame-des-Champs, his residences and his lifestyle became not unlike Bromfield's. It would be another twenty-six years before Hemingway won a Pulitzer, but it was not because he did not want the prize. As he wrote Perkins shortly after completing "The Real Spaniard," "What about all these prizes? I am now writing a novel myself so I'm very interested."[37]

Whether it was necessary for him to write the satire in order to begin the fiction is not clear, but "Spaniard" was a warming-up exercise for something much more important — Hemingway's anticipated second novel. In that same letter to Perkins, he said: "You asked about the novel and as it seems that the more they are spoken of the slower they progress — except in the case of the gents who dictate them — I don't know anything to say except that 99 and 9/10ths remains to be written but I'm going on the six hour a day regime in Paris next week with nobody having the address." That same day he wrote Fitzgerald that he was "now going to write a swell novel," but he would not talk about it, for it was too easy to talk and not write.[38] That Hemingway was writing letters indicates that he had not yet started on the novel, but an idea was sufficiently formed that he could announce the project.

That same week, he answered his father's hurt letter sorrowing over his son's divorce. He had counted on Hadley making explanations when she visited Oak Park, but clearly she said little if anything about their divorce. He explained to his parents that he loved Hadley and Bumby now and always. "I did not desert her nor was I committing adultery with anyone. I was living in the apartment with Bumby — looking after him while Hadley was away on a trip and it was when she came back from this trip that she decided she wanted the definite divorce. . . . For over a year I had been in love with two people and had been absolutely faithful to Hadley. When Hadley decided that we had better get a divorce the girl with whom I was in love was in America. I had not heard from her in two months." Everything he said made the divorce sound like Hadley's fault, an impression he cemented by saying: "After we were divorced if Hadley would have wanted me I would have gone back to her. She said that things were better as they were and that we were both better off." He would never stop loving Hadley, he said, nor would he stop loving Pauline Pfeiffer to whom he was married. With no further explanation of his second marriage, he mailed the letter, a son's attempt to right himself in his father's eyes.[39]

141

Chapter Ten

THE NEW LIFE

At two in the cold morning, half asleep trying to close the broken skylight, he did not hear the cracked glass fall. That was his only luck. Had he looked up, even a little, he might have lost his left eye. Instead the falling shard caught his forehead, laying it open with the grace of a butcher's knife. His wife found him sitting on the toilet, cursing, blood streaming through his fingers and down his face to the floor. When hand pressure could not staunch the flow, they made a tourniquet from a kitchen towel, using a stick of kindling to twist it tight. His friend arrived by cab to find him waiting a bit giddy at the curb, one hand on the tourniquet, the other waving. They crossed the river with him talking light-headed and silly, circled Arc de Triomphe and whistled out along Boulevard de Neuilly. Before they reached the emergency room of the American Hospital where a young doctor was waiting, pain had set in and he was quiet. When blood again began to flow, sickly sweet, he said nothing, and again nothing when the doctor sutured the wound. There was no anaesthetic, but the sewing went quickly, three stitches to stop the bleeding and another six to seal the loose flesh back in place. Two hours after the glass fell, he was back at their apartment, his bandaged head looking like some trepanned veteran invalided home from the war.

PARIS: SEPTEMBER 1927

On 18 September, after watching the afternoon bullfights, Ernest and Pauline left San Sebastian on the night train for Paris to begin their home life together, the one they had promised themselves: new apartment, new bed, new clothes, new cafés. Old and cherished routines were broken: Pauline had no job to go to each morning, and without Bumby to bother him, Ernest had no excuse to leave home for a quiet café. In his closet, Ernest's new clothes hung neatly on their hangers: suit and slacks, fresh shirts, a distinguished overcoat. In their rack his new shoes were polished and waiting. Gone forever was his old mask of hungry writer living on the edge of poverty, and his new mask of successful Scribner author did not yet fit. On rue Férou the morning light was brighter than on Notre-Dame-des-Champs, and the street noises quieter than the old sawmill. It all took some getting used to, this new life.

Jinny, who always traveled light and lived on the wing, had shaped the apartment up quite nicely while the honeymooners were in Spain, and she now continued to live with them until she found a suitable hotel residence. After the long summer with Clara Dunn, Jinny's fine-boned face was almost gaunt. Ernest wrote his mother-in-law: "Virginia's summer with the Dunns brought her down to . . . 99 pounds and that is a little light for marrying off. . . . I don't think it was awfully healthy for her at 25 to be so much with Clara at 37 whose movements were in turn limited to those of Mrs. Dunn's, age 68. In the end it seemed Mrs. Dunn who became younger." He was going to dedicate *Men Without Women* to Jinny, but, he explained, the stories were so rough that it now seemed inappropriate.[1] He did not say how much he enjoyed living with the two women or how puzzling he found them. As a boy he grew up among a flock of sisters, all of whom doted on him, but this new arrangement was different and quite stimulating. Pauline and Jinny tolerated Ernest's patriarchal pronouncements with humor and teasing wit, for each sister, in different ways, was an independent woman. If Ernest wanted to play Papa, they allowed him his fetish.

From Piggott, Ernest received a letter from his new mother-in-law, Mary Pfeiffer, who said it was a joint letter to her daughters as well, for there was not enough going on in Piggott to support separate letters. She said she liked his writing style but some of his subject matter, like bull fights and boxing, was not to her taste. She was pleased that he was trying to get Virginia married, but warned him it would be difficult. She also hoped that he would bring Pauline home soon to visit.

> Now that it is all in the past I do not mind telling you that her last visit was anything but a pleasure to me. In fact it was the nearest thing to a nightmare that I have ever experienced in my waking moments, and I would like the remembrance erased from my mind

in as much as it is possible and feel that it can be done by another visit better than any other way.[2]

The letter was a peace offering which she signed "Mother Pfeiffer."

Her two daughters and her son-in-law made a country of three on rue Férou, keeping to themselves as Paris cooled into fall. It was not hard to remain invisible. The day Ernest and Pauline returned to town, twenty thousand American war veterans, with their wives and children, jammed into the heart of Paris – the second American Expeditionary Force as they called themselves. Organized by the American Legion, the great pilgrimage came ten years after their first invasion to save western civilization from the Huns. Now the Germans were back in the Midi, drinking the beer, while their war debt and how it would be paid remained unsettled. "Imagine Paris," the vets were told, "gala Paris with the streets bright and full of life . . . the cafes crowded and merry." And don't forget the cemeteries "where thousands of white crosses stand in the green sod, sweeping away in long rows – soil so sacred that the sight alone brings thoughts that cannot be spoken."[3] All that month and into the next at Cinéma Impérial, *What Price Glory* played to full houses. At Johnny's Bar, as Art Moss reported, "A number of round the towners who were more or less engaged in the late conflict have been . . . using it as a drill ground. Around about two o'clock every morning, they've started religiously going through the Manual of Arms."[4] The Great War, it seemed, was not yet over, nor would it be for another decade.

While thousands of aging doughboys marched in ragged step down the Champs Elysées, a smaller cortege accompanied the ashes of the once agile dancer, Isadora Duncan, to the Columbarium in Père Lachaise cemetery. On September 15, Isadora died grotesquely in Nice, "dragged under the wheels of an automobile which she was trying out before purchasing. . . . a long Spanish shawl which she was wearing became entangled in a wheel." With broken vertebrae and a badly mutilated face, her dead body lay several days uncremated while the authorities, after finding her Russian passport, had to clear papers with the Russian consulate. Her ashes were laid down beside those of her two children, surrounded then and later by several of the great female spirits of her age: Sarah Bernhardt, Colette, Loie Fuller, and Gertrude Stein.[5] Dead at forty-eight, Isadora had lingered on past her stop, refusing to admit that her ticket was used up. The Jazz Age babies on the boulevards had no time for Isadora's flowing togas or her pseudo-classic dancing. On rue Fontaine close to Pigalle, Josephine Baker, shaking it out to the Black

Bottom, did not miss a beat the day that Isadora died. Within a year Irving Berlin and Cole Porter were writing *Americans in Paris*, a sure sign that the party was over.

There were other, more violent signs pointing to political unrest across Europe, but traveling or expatriate Americans were not interested in the message unless it interfered with their private lives. Europe was a museum; Europe was vistas, visas, late nights of jazz and long afternoons on the terrasse amid a babble of languages. It was not politics. Taking a break from manipulating the stock market, Charley Mitchell, the brains behind National City Bank, discovered "little tension" visiting in Italy, and declared Mussolini to be much admired in the States.[6] Whenever possible, politics stayed home where there were only two questions: what did presidential incumbent Calvin Coolidge really mean when he said, "I do not choose to run," and who would the Republicans run against Al Smith, the Catholic New Yorker who threatened to dismantle Prohibition. So the college boys put on their golf caps, buttoned up their plus-fours, and tightened up their ties to spend "37 glorious days in congenial company, all expenses, afloat and ashore, only $385." It was two days in Holland ("You remember Holland"), Belgium lasted four ("small but swell in Bruges"), and quickly on to Paris ("All the nights are free in Paris"), then the long ride home.[7]

On the first of October, having spent the previous week entertaining another of Pauline's rich uncles, Ernest read back through the novel he started two weeks earlier. It was going "very well," he told Mary Pfeiffer. "I think [it] will keep me going every day until we will go to the mountains and ski and rinse out the head on the inside if possible and then start re-writing in a couple of months. Whether to go to America before or after that is finished is sort of a problem. You see when you are not working for anyone, but only in your head, and not writing down something that has happened but making it all up entirely, you get careful about going to new places while the work is going on because if one morning the head doesn't work and you can't make anything up, you are through."[8] Each morning he sat down in his new writing room, putting pencil to paper, creating what he first called "A New Slain Knight."

In March of the previous year, when he thought he would next write "a picaresque novel for America" about Red Ryan's escape from the Kingston prison, that was the title he chose. It was going to be a story of a "tough kid lucky for a long time and finally smashed by fate." In his notebook he told himself, "Criminals are not diseased men. We are all criminals. The criminal is simply a more normal, better coordinated man.

145

In the old days he was the professional fighter." Then in parentheses he reminded himself that "This is horseshit."[9] He still liked the "New Slain Knight" well enough to use it nineteen months later on his opening page, but he crossed that out early to call the new book simply:

A Novel
Chapter One
In Which Goodbye Is Said To The Old Places
in the First Person[10]

The story began at Walloon Lake, the heart of his first mature fiction and some of his best stories, began in the cottage where he lived every summer of his early years. Only now it was fall, when his father closed Windemere for the season, capping the chimney to keep out the squirrels, boarding up the windows for winter. After Grace took the summer children back to Oak Park for school, his father would spend a solitary week on the lake. Now, exactly when Clarence Hemingway was closing the Walloon cottage, Ernest was with him in his fiction, making it up lovingly, remembering all the sounds and smells of lake and woods, saying goodbye to a part of his life he missed deeply.

The invented story was of father and son, the best kind of story he knew, one he returned to frequently, trying to make up for his own father who disappeared from his summer life when Ernest most needed him. Dr. Hemingway's long and losing battle with his "nervous condition," as the children called it, began early, making him an increasingly moody and sometimes dark person, remote and demanding. By the time Ernest was twelve, the best days with his father were passed, leaving the son to wonder what had gone wrong and the father to wrestle with the demons of depression and paranoia.[11] In early October, when he received his father's latest letter, Hemingway must have smiled. His father, writing about Bumby's visit to Oak Park, said, "Surely hope you can bring him up with the love for Nature and fine ideals. How we would rejoice to have him with you at Windemere some summer."[12] There on the penciled pages, Hemingway let father and son say goodbye to the lake. Only the father was part of himself and so was the son, doubling up, then and now.

The imagined boy, Jimmy Crane, grew up on the lake, never having to go back to Chicago and never knowing much about his strange father or his missing mother. Now the boy was leaving the lake for a road life which he does not understand and which his father does not explain.

146

They close up the cottage, load their meager belongings into the motor boat, and push off from the dock with Jimmy running the boat. "When I looked back," he said, "the dock and the boat house were out of sight and there was only the point with three crows walking on the sand and an old log half covered in the sand and ahead the open lake."[13] That was the same point where Marge left Nick in "The End of Something," the same log Dick Boulton started to saw up in "The Doctor and the Doctor's Wife;" the crows were the same hungry three stropping their beaks in the "Twa Corbie," the source of his title:

> In behint yon auld fail dyke
> I wot there lies a new-slain knight
> And naebody kens that he lies there
> But his hawk, his hound, and his lady
> fair.
> His hound is to the hunting gane,
> His hawk to fetch the wild-fowl hame,
> His lady's ta'en anither mate,
> So we may mak our dinner sweet.[14]

That's the kind of story it was going to be, Jimmy's father against the world with no one but the boy for support, no hawk, no hound, no wife – a curious story for a newly remarried man to be writing.

As September ended, a tornado swept through St. Louis leaving eighty-seven dead among the ruins. In New York, Babe Ruth hit his sixtieth home run of the dying season. In Paris, Ernest Hemingway, waiting for his former wife to return from the States, sat down each day in his new writing room to be the author everyone said he was. It seemed to be working, this new life; he and Pauline did not talk about it, but she was pleased when he closed the door each morning. It was going to work. It had to.

PARIS: OCTOBER 1927

All that month Hemingway held to his routine, writing in the mornings, biking in the afternoons, and seeing almost no one. When the *Boulevardier* published his "Real Spaniard," Art Moss, the editor, cut out enough profanity for Ernest to protest in the *Tribune* that it was no longer his essay.

> I am always happy myself to have any little changes or alterations made in anything I write by either the editor or the publisher and, indeed, often solicit this. But as I am unable to afford to write for The Boulevardier – which solicits manuscripts through promising to pay its contributors the lowest rates in the world – this article was very kindly written for me by my wife.[15]

But no humorous letter to the editor could change the parody of Louis Bromfield, who, at that very moment, was in Oak Park lecturing to the ladies of the Nineteenth Century Club. Afterwards Hemingway's mother introduced herself to the author, asking him if he knew Ernest. "I should think I do," he told her. "He's one of my best friends." When Robert Cohn said the same about Jake Barnes in *The Sun Also Rises*, Jake thinks to himself "God help you."[16]

That October Ernest answered as few letters as possible, saving everything for his fiction. When Hadley and Bumby returned two weeks earlier than planned, he took a day off to meet them at the boat and moved Bumby into the spare bedroom until Hadley got her new apartment in shape.[17] Despite this interruption, by October 20 he claimed to have 30,000 words written on his novel.[18] Like the summer of *The Sun Also Rises*, pages piled up so easily that his moments of self-doubt seemed foolish. A few name changes as usual, a blotted line or two, but he made no substantive revisions as the story line followed the train tracks from northern Michigan to Chicago to New York. It was a story of double focus: the education of the young boy, Jimmy Crane, who knew little of the urban world, and the survival of his father, a professional revolutionist of such repute that the State Department would no longer allow him an American passport. Jimmy, the tyro, narrated the story while his father and other male tutors taught him rules of the road.

Mostly his father taught him to pay attention to significant details. "Notice everything you can," he tells his son. "Remember everything you see. Draw any conclusion you want. But never know anything when a thing is going on."[19] On the train to Chicago there were two detectives, each with a criminal handcuffed to his wrist. Jimmy watched them carefully, but at the Cadillac lunch stop, he missed the real action completely. When the one prisoner irritated his captor enough that the detective began to cuff him about the face, Jimmy did not keep his eye on the criminal's hands.

"Well," my father said. "While the sergeant hit him in the face with the handcuff on his right hand he picked up a steel-bladed knife off the table with his left hand and put it in his pocket."

"I didn't see."

"No," my father said. "Every man has two hands, Jimmy. At least to start with. You ought to watch them both if you're going to see things."[20]

When the prisoner knifes his captor in the men's room and escapes through the window, Jimmy says he doesn't know what to think about their silence. His father replies, "Neither do I."

Jimmy and the reader do not know what to think about a father who feels more akin to criminals than the police, a father who regularly and religiously drinks too much, a father who cannot tell his son the complete truth. Jimmy thinks they are going to Canada, but instead it's New York via Chicago. In Chicago his father tells the cab driver they are going to Europe, which is news to Jimmy. His father also says they are going to a hotel but instead they arrive at the butler-attended house of a rich aunt. "It's a hotel in the French sense," his father tells him. "Hotel de Crane." From his Aunt Ruth and his father, Jimmy learns that he was born in Paris and that his mother still lives there: curious information for a fourteen-year-old not to know about himself. His father, carefully and at regular intervals decanting his apparently bottomless bottle of Scotch into a pocket flask, sips his way through the afternoons and evenings, a man with a murky past and vague future. Having lived too long on the losing side of revolutions, he trusts no one, not even his son. He explains to Jimmy that he does not tell him more "because someone might question you sometime in a very nasty way they have of questioning people and what you don't know you can't tell."[21]

The father is full of advice, some of it less than helpful. "Thinking," he tells his son, "ruins a boy. Thinking and masturbation." Jimmy, again somewhat strangely, does not know what masturbation is. "It's something like thinking," his father tells him. When his father finds Jimmy kissing the secretary in the family lawyer's office where he has gone to raise money, he becomes angry, forgetting he told his son that he had to learn more about women. "If you want to please me don't kiss anybody at all for a while yet," the father says. Three days later when Jimmy tries to kiss his aunt's maid, she slaps his face.[22] The further Hemingway developed the story, the more Jimmy began to age, until he finally sounded more like a teenager and less like Bumby, but something remained fundamentally wrong about his voice and the naïve questions he asked. Reading back over the first eight chapters, Hemingway wrote himself a note: "Re-write all Chicago stuff after arrival – eliminate all the shit."[23] The next day he wrote Archie MacLeish:

Papa has been working like a son of a bitch and has nine – count them but don't read them – chapters done. Is going well, reaping the results of the long layoff. Been back three weeks or so, haven't been in bed later than 10 o'clock – seen nobody – working all the time.[24]

That he was writing was more important than any flaws in the fiction, and unlike *The Sun Also Rises*, he was making it all up. Jimmy and his dad were living the secret, male roadlife that Ernest, at fourteen, never had with his own father. Here he was able to imagine both fictive father and son, creating his revolutionist from his reading and his acquaintance with Charles Sweeney, a soldier of fortune for whom war and revolution were money in the bank. Hemingway's fictional father was a homeless road man, on the move and unencumbered by wife, property, or conventional morals, a man without fixed political allegiance who could accept family money from the lawyer without accepting the system that produced the money.

Mr. Crane, still without a first name, was a recognizable product of his creator's penchants and the political times. All his life, Ernest read about and admired secret codes, clandestine operations, and clever spies. He lived in the age of the provocateur, when it took only three to make a Russian revolution, one to light a fuse. In Spain, while touring bull rings and cathedrals, Hemingway could not avoid talk of revolution, which reappeared in the *Herald*'s October 3 headlines:

POLITICAL COUP FAILS IN SPAIN

Two Army Officers Charged With
Launching Attack on De Rivera

Within the next week, bungled revolutions appeared daily in the *Herald*.

October 5

BULLETS HALT MEXICAN COUP

General Sarrano and Fifteen Followers
Shot by Federal Firing Squad

October 8

Bulgarian Bands Attack Several Serbian Villages

Soviet Spy Plot Bared In Vienna As Doctor Is Held

In Nicaragua, American marines relentlessly pursued General Sandino's guerrillas, the Sandinistas, who opposed the conservative, pro-American government. By 1927 the twentieth-century agenda between haves and have-nots was well in place. With graffiti obvious on broken walls throughout the hemisphere and political unrest increasing, Hemingway's revolutionist was an astute choice for his fiction. But could he imagine the fugitive life fully enough to make it plausible?

The day after he wrote MacLeish, Hemingway took Mr. Crane and Jimmy to a west side Chicago kitchen where six Italian men are eating pasta and drinking Chianti. Jimmy learns to roll his pasta on his fork and listens to the men discuss the safest way for his father to re-enter Italy. One says to go by way of Modena. Another says there is less risk coming down the lake by boat from Switzerland. Finally they ask Mr. Crane if he wants to see "the old man," which he does. Jimmy follows his father into a bedroom where a white-haired old man with dark skin and "a purple bulge like a small grape" on one side of his nose is lying in bed. Crane apologizes for Jimmy's stare, telling the *capo* that he has taught his son to be observant. "You're not going to Italy are you?" the old man asks. Crane says he isn't. "It's a country I no longer care about." But when asked where he will go, Crane is noncommittal. "Quite right," the old man tells him. "I wouldn't mention it in your place. I only asked from curiosity." When asked how many revolutions he has seen, Crane says "Twelve." At conversation's end, Crane gives the old man $100 cash for a false passport. As he and Jimmy leave, the old man says, "I hope you have a long life, settle down and stop all this nonsense."[25]

For six weeks the story covered ground Hemingway remembered from earlier train trips to New York. After the summer dry spell, it felt good to be on top of his game again. Cornered one day at Sylvia Beach's bookshop by Alex Small, the *Tribune* gossip columnist, Hemingway was asked what he thought of Glenway Wescott's new novel, *Grandmothers*.

151

"There are only two troubles with that book," he replied. "One is that every word of it was written for immortality." Small concluded, "Here, alas, I must stop, truncate Mr. H's aphorism, and leave you gaping in wonder."[26] Two days later in New York, *Men Without Women* was published with a black silhouette of a virile bull on its cover, and before the month was out Pauline was pregnant. When his writing went well, the world went well with it.

PARIS AND BERLIN: LATE FALL 1927

Then one morning the story began to lose its energy. Several weeks passed before he completely lost its pulse, but looking back over the pages, he could see it turning away from the central issue of Crane the revolutionist. "Cut out all the shit in these last two or three chapters," he told himself in the margin.[27] Changing the name from Crane to House did not help. Each day he went into his surgery, trying to save the novel, and each day the patient grew worse. There was too much talk and not enough action as the narrative weight fell more and more on the boy, whose sometimes precocious remarks were wearing thin. On the New York train Ernest had the night porter and the dining car chef do a little minstrel show routine, a little buck and wing, ending with slapstick echoes from Hamlet. "But my God, Jimmy," the porter told Jimmy, "the only thing that saves a man is to have a view point."[28]

Two days after *Men Without Women* was published, Hemingway telegrammed Uncle Gus:

WOULD APPRECIATE NOT SENDING FAMILY BOOKS UNTIL YOUVE READ YOURSELF AS SOME STORIES POSSIBLY DISPLEASING[29]

By the first of November, when the New York reviews began to appear in Paris, Ernest's writing had come to a halt. Dorothy Parker loved the new book, as did *Time* magazine,[30] but others did not see what he was doing or did not appreciate it if they did. Krutch could not forgive him for being an expatriate writing about inarticulate characters: "sordid little catastrophes in the lives of very vulgar people."[31] The *Saturday Review*, with a headline reading "Simple Annals of the Callous," decided he was neither Shakespeare nor Tolstoy.[32] And Virginia Woolf found his dialogue excessive, lacking proportion; he was "candid" and "highly skilled" with "moments of bare and nervous beauty," but he was "modern in manner" only, "self-consciously virile," and his stories "a little dry and sterile."[33] Hemingway wrote Fitzgerald that he had seen the reviews of Burton Rascoe and Woolf and a couple of others. "These goddamn reviews are sent to me by my 'friends', any review saying the stuff is a pile of shit I get at least 2000 copies of. . . . Am thinking of quitting publishing any stuff for the next 10 or 15 years."[34] The reviews, he said, were ruining his writing.

During the first week of November, he and Pauline went to Berlin for the six-day bike races, stayed ten days, bought a painting at Alfred Flechtheim's gallery, and shared a meal with Sinclair Lewis and Ramon Guthrie, who outlived them all to remember it:

> Berlin. Ernest – not Papa for some years to
> come
> – up from Paris to see the six-day bike race.
> Pauline was this time's wife. Dinner with Red
> Lewis.
> A girl – Agatha? – prattled trilingually
> of painters. Cézanne? Van Gogh? Picasso?
> Juan Gris? Mais c'est à rire! Italians, yes.
> But French, Spanish . . . Hemingway stood up
> and crashed his fist down on the table. "El
> Greco is a cockeyed GOOD painter!"
> The gnädige Fraulein squeaked and subsided
> mouselike.[35]

When he and Pauline returned to Paris and the late reviews of *Men Without Women*, he re-read the sixteen chapters of his novel, which seemed "all right part of the time" and at other times seemed like "horse manure."[36] On Thanksgiving Day, while Americans in Paris were eating their turkey, Hemingway wrote Max Perkins that he had about a third of the book – seventeen chapters – done. "I'm putting it in the third person now – got tired of the limitations of the bloody first person – always thinking in one person's head, etc. and the changing is difficult but I think will improve it very much."[37] The shifting voice improved the narrative flow, but it could do nothing for Hemingway's basic dilemma about the story's direction. If Mr. Crane, who was now Mr. House, was the story's center then Ernest needed more information about revolutionists than he had at hand. If the story was about the education of Jimmy House/Crane, then he needed to get on with his schooling.

153

On the streets of New York and in the third person, he had Jimmy's father giving his son dubious advice about how to recognize and deal with homosexuals, a subject about which he seemed to worry a good deal. Testing out his father's wisdom, Jimmy found it of little practical use when approached by the very gay Mr. Elwyn, who had none of the characteristics Jimmy had been warned against: mincing walk, plucked eyebrows, and elongated face. The interlude then took Hemingway further afield to Glenway Wescott and homosexual writers. Jimmy's father, who knew far too much about writers for any soldier of fortune, said that homosexuals made good interior decorators but second-rate writers because they had to fake the love scenes between men and women. Even good American writers did not last long due to cross-breeding. "Sometimes you get one that . . . doesn't go ga-ga at forty five. But lots of American writers are through before they're thirty and most of them are finished by forty five."[38] As Jimmy says about his father,

If he ever got started on writers and books he was liable to go on forever and I could never change him. He was interesting about wars or hunting or fishing or fairies or people or places but he was never interesting about writers or books.[39]

Trying to amuse and please his father, the boy falls back on proven topics: how to talk to whores and how to recognize homosexuals, none of which was getting them any closer to a revolution. Hemingway stopped at Chapter Twenty, boggled, unable to get his characters on the boat to Europe. About that time the letter arrived from Uncle Gus saying how much he enjoyed *Men Without Women* and how much he was looking forward to the novel.

I know the novel will be worth while if it comes up to your expectations. Morally I feel we get most satisfaction if we have self esteem. If when we are alone, we can respect what we think and do. This I feel is also true of our product, the child of our brains and hands. Do these justify our approval, our admiration? Are they what we expected and equal to what we know we can do. If so they are good. . . . Here's hoping your new novel will be just this and no more, no less.[40]

Hemingway could not imagine Gus finding anything to admire about the New York homosexuals. Unable to admit it yet to himself, Hemingway's revolutionist and son were soon to disappear into the writer's scrap heap, not to resurface for another twelve years.[41]

The less than ecstatic reviews of *Men Without Women* did not kill the new novel, but coming as they did when Hemingway's confidence was shaky and his story bogged down, the critics were more influential on his career than they knew. Early and late, Hemingway's professional skin was overly sensitive to critical evaluation. Much later that winter, he let his rancor out on paper:

Valentine
For a Mr. Lee Wilson Dodd and Any of His
Friends who Want it.

Sing a song of critics
pockets full of lye
four and twenty critics
hope that you will die
hope that you will peter out
hope that you will fail
so they can be the first one
be the first to hail
any happy weakening or sign of quick
decay.
(All are very much alike, weariness too
great,
sordid small catastrophes, stack the cards
on fate,
very vulgar people, annals of the callous,
dope fiends, soldiers, prostitutes
men without a gallus)
If you do not like them lads
one thing you can do
stick up your asses lads
My Valentine to you.[42]

But nothing the critics said affected the sale of *Men Without Women.* Published on 14 October, 7,300 copies sold during the following two weeks, wiping out the first printing. A month after its release, 10,000 copies were sold; by December 8, 13,000 copies. When Hemingway returned from Berlin, his first spendable royalty check was waiting for him at the bank: $2615.10 minus the advance of $750.[43] "Did you ever see such eloquent and economical prose," Guy Hickok asked, "as the wording of that check? Not a superfluous word. Not even a superfluous decimal point. That is style. Keep that sentence of prose ever before you. Scan it. Feel the rhythm. Let me scan it. 'Pay to the order of Ernest Hemingway.' It makes its own music."[44]

But with his novel stalled, the money's music was played in a minor key. Putting the manuscript aside, Hemingway turned to his backlog of unanswered mail. A Dominican priest in Chicago wrote to thank him for once saving his friend Don Stewart in the Pamplona bull ring. The priest had heard that Ernest "had become a Catholic within the year. . . . We need writers of your type to help further the cause for which the Dominican order exists in the defense of the Church – the cause of Truth."[45] Ernest's reply was guarded. Don Stewart, he said, was never in danger of his life, and he, Ernest, knew Cameron Rogers only slightly and they had never discussed the Church. "I have been a Catholic for many years," he said,

> although I fell away very badly and did not go to communion for over 8 years. However I have gone regularly to mass for the last two years and absolutely set my house in order within the year. However, I have always had more faith than intelligence or know-ledge and I have never wanted to be known as a Catholic writer because I know the importance of setting an example – and I have never set a good example. . . . Also I am a dumb Catholic and I have so much faith that I hate to examine into it – but I am trying to lead a good life and to write well and truly and it is easier to do the first than the second.[46]

As Ernest was packing the stalled manuscript into his bags for the Christmas trip to Gstaad, two letters arrived from the States. In the first Max enclosed an ad for *Men Without Women* filled with great quotes and headlined: "Not one harsh note in the critical chorus." At the center of the ad was a silhouetted bull whose phallus glowed with incandescent virility. "Only ten thousand bulls got loose in this heated condition," Max said, "and those in the provinces. Heaven protect simple minded cattle there. And it seems to be a fact that the divinity that so strangely shaped *this* end was chance."[47] The second letter was from Hemingway's old war buddy, Bill Horne, whom he had not seen since 1921. Bill said

I wish you would do over again, now, some of those early stories you wrote right after we got to Chicago. . . . The world is reading war stuff now, nine years afterwards, as we decided long ago they would. There's nobody who can write war as you would with that impersonal unaccented style which tells things right along as they happen without prescience or afterthought. Give it a whirl again.[48]

It was good advice but bad timing, what with Christmas shopping, last minute crises, and Ernest's customary sore throat leaving him less than receptive to literary advice. On December 13, with all of Paris frozen in its sleep, Ernest, Pauline, and Bumby boarded the night train to Switzerland where Jinny waited for them at Gstaad. Included in his entourage were Mr. House and his boy from Horton Bay, fathers and sons a long way from home.

GSTAAD: CHRISTMAS 1927

Three months later, when he realized what he should be writing, he could not understand why it had taken him so long to find it, for there were plenty of signs pointing the way: aging vets marching in Paris, *What Price Glory* at the movies, Bill Horne's letter, and Scott's Christmas reading. "I have a new German war book," Fitzgerald said, "*Die Krieg against Krieg*, which shows men who mislaid their faces in Picardy and the Caucuses – you can imagine how I thumb it over, my mouth fairly slithering with fascination."[49] Ernest's own reading of *Before the Bombardment* was another knock at the door which went unanswered until a series of accidents refocused his attention.[50]

As soon as he and his extended family got on the overnight train to Switzerland, nothing went right. Within a week he wrote Fitzgerald that he was suffering from blindness, piles, flu, and a toothache which combined to bring his new novel to a halt. "Had 20 chapters done . . . then got sick . . . just grippy in the head so I couldn't write – then came down here with Bumby and Pauline to get healthy and at Montreux on the way down Bumby when I picked him up in the night to put him on the pot stuck one of his fingers in my right eye and the nail went in and cut the pupil . . . it was my one good eye and I've been in bed and shot to hell one way or another ever since."[51] It was essentially the same letter he wrote to Waldo Pierce, Ezra Pound, and Guy Hickok. Hickok was not impressed with the excuses. "I didn't know Ernest had only one good eye. I know he had only one good leg and I suspected that maybe some of his other organs that are ordinarily found in pairs had been reduced by half, but I never suspected that he had a bum eye."[52]

The eye was a good excuse to put Jimmy and his father on medical hold, but then Gstaad got really boring. The early snow turned to ice under the deep freeze that strangled Europe and froze Paris pipes, but with no fresh powder on top the skiing was terrible, and bridge games grew repetitive, leaving lots of time for letters. Fitzgerald had written from the States, asking for juicy Left Bank news. He joked that he had heard Ernest was "seen running through Portugal in used B.V.D.s, chewing ground glass and collecting material for a story about Boule players," that he was "publicity man for Lindbergh," that he dressed "always in wine-skin with 'zipper' vent" and was "engaged in bootlegging Spanish Fly."[53] Ernest replied that he was "always glad to hear from a brother pederast." The news was that he had given up fiction and "gone into the pimping game." There was no money in Spanish Fly. Fitz had it right about the wine-skin, but it had no zipper, too effete. "I have to watch myself that way," Ernest said, "and deny myself many of the little comforts like toilet paper, semi-colons, and soles to my shoes. Any time I use any of those people begin to shout that old Hem is just a fairy after all." Scott should write him and, in the mean time, try to keep his kid off heroin. "Nobody can convince me that it really does a child of that age any good."[54] It was the season, after all, to be jolly, and even if there was no new snow, Gstaad had plenty of Christmas scenery and good will by the glassfull.

The MacLeishes, fresh from America, were with them at the Rossli, talking, eating, reading, catching up on the gossip. Outside, the winter trade and the winter games went on quite expensively, leaving Ernest uncomfortable in this new routine. Gstaad, pricey enough to be an item in the Paris papers, was not Chamby, was not Schruns. Here the locals worked hard with curling matches and ice carnivals to entertain tweedy English, loud Americans, and displaced Russians. Pauline and Jinny took the edge off Ernest, keeping him appreciated and well tended, while Archie, whose *Hamlet of A. MacLeish* had just been accepted by Houghton Mifflin, gave Hemingway his sounding board. On the back of an envelope, Ernest made a quick note from their conversation:

Imitating everybody, living and dead, relying on the fact that if you imitate someone obscure enough it will be considered original.

Education consists in finding sources obscure enough to imitate so that they will be perfectly safe.[55]

One of their topics was Wyndham Lewis, who had recently struck up a limited acquaintance and correspondence with both of them. This old friend of Ezra's was a prominent London man of letters whose criticism and essays were influential. Earlier in the year, Lewis sent Hemingway an essay based on *Torrents*, which he had liked. Ernest had thanked him for his support and taken his criticism with more grace than usual: "As for my own stuff – I'm sorry there has been so much blood shed. I think it will decrease. The real reason for it (the bloodiness) was, I think, that I have been working for a precision of language and to get it at the start have had to treat things where simple actions occurred – the simplest – and which I had seen the most of – was one form and another of killing."[56] In mid-November, just after the MacLeishes returned to Europe, Lewis visited pleasantly over a Paris lunch with Archie and Ernest, asking them afterward for copies of their recent work.[57] Then, as the Hemingways were packing for Gstaad, Lewis's review of *Men Without Women* arrived courtesy of its author, who found the stories "a blend of Gertrude Stein's manner, Celtic childishness, and the slice of life (the real thing!) redeemed by humour, power over dialogue and an obvious knowledge of the people he describes." The literature of the future, Lewis said,

will be in the hands of a bland and orderly generation about which absolutely nothing is known. Meanwhile, Mr. Hemingway remains easily the ablest of the wild band of Americans in Europe and is obviously capable of a great deal of development before his work reaches maturity.[58]

Over German beer in Gstaad and surrounded by British accents, Ernest and Archie digested the Lewis review and his earlier essay about which Ernest was of two minds. Any publicity helped sell books, but he resented critics who claimed to know more about his writing than he himself did. "Blood Lust," Lewis said, was Ernest's downfall, and Ezra, the old fascist, was its father. Blame it all on Ez.[59] Archie, who appreciated Pound's poetics without caring for his criticism or his attitudes, thought that Lewis was righter than Ernest allowed. To Lewis, MacLeish had earlier written:

As for Ernest – your criticism was just. His stuff has a sensationalist base which I think he would concede and support intellectually. For he is a true stylist (taught, curiously enough, pretty largely by G. Stein (in conversation) if you will believe his assertion!!) whose future is limited only by his willingness to seize it, & his ability to understand the attitude of mind from which proceeds such criticism as yours. The question is what is going to happen inside his head.[60]

That was a good question, one without an immediate answer, for little was happening inside the Hemingway head at present: no stories, no novel, nothing but fragments of a poem:

> yes it is very simple and clear the answer is
>   perfectly obvious
> there is nothing far fetched about it nor any
>   unreasonable difficulty you demand to know
> what was the what was the what was the what
> absolutely I hope that is clear we can now I hope
>   consider
> the matter closed as always there are no difficulties
>   if the
> what was the what was the what was the what was the
>   what was the what
> I think we have finished with that question and the
>   literature of the future I might inform you in
>   passing will be written
> by bland young men of whom at this time absolutely
>   nothing is known.
> Thank you.[61]

At night, when Ernest could not read the Dostoevsky he brought with him from Shakespeare and Co., Pauline read aloud from Henry James's *The Awkward Age*, whose style was in keeping with the rest of the Gstaad winter as far as Ernest was concerned. "He seems to need to bring in a drawing room whenever he is scared he will have to think what the characters do the rest of the time," he wrote Waldo Pierce, "and all the men without exception talk and think like fairies except a couple of caricatures of brutal outsiders. He seems an enormous fake in this."[62] As he wrote those words, he, too, was having trouble thinking of what his characters would do next in a novel in which there had already been far too much talk about "fairies."

Elsewhere there were those who had no trouble at all thinking what to do next with his style. Guy Hickok sent him a parody from the latest *transition* called "The Fixer, A Story of Colonial Life (in the manner of one of the foremost modern American writers)." Myles Standish and John Alden, speaking in clipped Hemingway dialogue, discuss in the manner of "The Killers," "Hills Like White Elephants," and "Now I Lay Me" the advantages of marriage. "If you just get married, everything'll be all right," John tells Myles as they stand at the bar where Jake the bartender serves them whiskey.

"A girl's all right if she's religious enough," said John. All you need's a good girl, Myles."

"I'm lots handier with Indians than with girls. It's simple enough with Indians. All you have to do is let a little air into 'em. After that everything's natural."[63]

It was a little strange to find himself on the receiving end of parody, and stranger still to see how much of his novel was a series of "drawing room scenes" resulting from his not knowing what the characters should do next. In the streets of Gstaad, it was the new year, and the slight snows had turned to ice.

Christmas letters from home did nothing to relieve Hemingway's sagging spirits. His mother, the overly eager painter to whom he had written a long analysis of the Paris art world while hoping to dissuade her from entering it, thanked him from California where she was visiting her brother over Christmas. She appreciated his candid advice, she said, on the difficulty and politics of the art game, but she was still going to send him some of her paintings to enter in "any important show." He could fill out the forms, using his Paris address for her own. "Shall be oh so grateful to you for this looking out for my interests and aiding my climb. It is not what Paris thinks of me but the step forward in the eyes of this country . . . having been acknowledged in Paris – that's what I'm after."[64] She was sending him for Christmas a one-volume complete edition of O. Henry's short stories. At that moment, waiting for Grace in Oak Park, was a letter from an old school mate saying, "I cannot conceive of your son writing of life as he does and being your son."[65] Sometimes Ernest wondered about the same question, but for different reasons.

His sister Madelaine's letter filled in parts of the home life that he liked to keep in mind for those rare moments when he got to missing it.

Christmas, she said, was pretty good because their mother, with whom she did not get along at all, was in California. The family, she assured him, was "damn proud" of him even if it had taken them a while to catch up with his subject matter.[66] All he discovered from his father's letter was that his mother remained in the West and that Sunny's new boyfriend was "clean spoken and pure in thought and does not have to apologize for his parents."[67] His father, who once seemed less heavy-handed with his moral judgements, was more distant than ever, more difficult to recall. *Did you ever have a father?* When he was a boy, he had a father, but that was in another country that he could return to only in his fiction. MacLeish had a father, too, but he died in mid-January, hurrying Archie back to the States to visit the grave. "A necessary expense for a man of letters," Hemingway explained to Pound.[68]

PARIS: JANUARY–MARCH 1928

About the time the frozen pipes burst at rue Férou and Pauline was dealing with plumbers, the *Herald* reported,

> Visiting, departing, arriving and permanently "quartering" writers occupy the Deux Magots. "Where" asks one lean gentleman who lives upon its terrasse, "where is Ernest Hemingway?"[69]

Ernest was in deep snow, skiing with the boys. After six weeks of women and badly crusted slopes at Gstaad, he put Pauline, Jinny, and Bumby on the Paris train while he joined a group skiing cross-country to Lenk and Adelboden.[70] By the time he arrived in Paris the radiator pipes were not fixed and neither was his mind, which continued to struggle with the story of the revolutionist and his son.

Mr. House, as Ernest now called the former Mr. Crane, and son Jimmy remained in the New York hotel looking no different from when he left them there. He fiddled with the manuscript, making minor ink corrections and a few excisions, but nothing of consequence. When the story would not write, he answered more letters. Thomas Hardy was dead, Jack Dempsey retired, and Loie Fuller's whirling scarves now rested close to Isadora Duncan in the grave. The $2,000 *Dial* prize was awarded to Ezra, and Ernest had received second place in the annual O.

Henry short story awards for "The Killers."[71] In California his transient mother was writing of her delight with his award and in the next sentence telling him that his brother Leicester "received the gold medal for the best bird house in the Boy Scout contest last month."[72]

With the January *Dial* (borrowed from Sylvia) in hand, Hemingway wrote Pound, fuming about a T. S. Eliot essay and Modernism. Does "Eliot feel that being sucked in by all that shit as it comes along, Thomism, Steinism, Wyndism, East and Westism etc makes Modern – What is Modern – of our time? Do we have to swallow delicately, always ready to regurgitate and replace with something newer, all the current shit to be of our own time?" Half in desperation, he asked Pound to send the "outline of the good and bad Henry" James as he had offered. If it was already in print somewhere, "just tell me where and I'll get it and copy it."[73] It was a half-hearted question to please Ezra, for Hemingway's reading was just then focused on rather un-Jamesian material: *Lawrence and the Arabs, Recollections of the Irish War,* and *The Riddle of the Irish,* looking desperately for some help on his stalled fiction.[74] A residue from the ski trip was a lovely head cold which in Paris deteriorated into the grippe. "Have been trying to work every morning," Hemingway wrote Perkins, "but all my production seems to be from the nose."[75] The operative word was "trying," for there was nothing to show for his mornings in his study but a new version of Chapter Two, in which he changed the boy's name to Jimmy Breen and the point of view to third person. Nothing helped.[76]

His newly acquired literary fame was another impediment to his writing. The Christmas issue of *The New Yorker* published James Thurber's "A Visit From Saint Nicholas (In the Manner of Ernest Hemingway)," and the January *Bookman* carried a caricature of him.[77] *Vanity Fair* ran a parody with Ernest as matador that began:

I was sitting at a table at the edge of the arena, sipping *Anis del Toro,* and Hemingway was in the center of the ring, under the lights, fighting a bull. As he flung open his dialogue with both hands, the bull charged, tail up. Hemingway swung his plot clear and, as the bull recharged, brought around his dialogue in a half-circle that pulled the bull to his knees. We all applauded.[78]

In February, the *New Republic* carried another flattering parody of his style,[79] and Dorothy Parker wrote a gushing essay in *The New Yorker,* saying,

Ernest Hemingway is, to me, the greatest living American short story writer who lives in Paris most of the time but goes to Switzerland to ski, served with the Italian Army during the war, has been a prize fighter and has fought bulls, is coming to New York in the spring, is in his early thirties, has a black mustache, and is still waiting for that two hundred francs I lost to him at bridge.[80]

Other than having his age, army service, bull- and prizefight records completely wrong, Parker's essay was good publicity, but not what he needed to be reading about himself when Jimmy and his father were stranded in New York, going nowhere.

While Ernest worried over his cold pages, Pauline packed for their trip home to the States. The antique Spanish furniture she had purchased the previous summer would remain in place, for they were keeping the apartment as a hedge against their return. With the baby due in June, they were planning to be back in time for the 1929 San Fermin *feria*. She bothered Ernest as little as possible, not wanting her husband to feel trapped by either their surrounding possessions or their impending baby. On February 29, Gertrude Stein and Alice Toklas came to lunch at Pauline's invitation.[81] Better than Ernest, she understood that it was politically silly to alienate Gertrude, with or without cause. The day, which began with a little sun, turned overcast and drizzling by the time the two ladies left.

Despite the frequently wet Paris weather that irritated Hemingway's throat, he and Pauline were out on the streets more than usual. Sylvia's bookshop was only five blocks from their front door, and less than a block away was the Musée du Luxembourg where Gauguin's Tahitian paintings were on view. Half a block up rue Férou loomed the lovely columns and chunky towers of St. Sulpice church, where they attended Sunday Mass. Two blocks beyond the church was the heart of St. Germain des Prés where potato salad, sausage, and Alsatian beer waited for them at Brasserie Lipp. Across the street were the round tables of Café Flore and Aux Deux Magots. After Ernest quit La Closerie des Lilas during his divorce period, Deux Magots became his café of choice until Glenway Wescott and Louis Bromfield returned to Paris. As the gossip columnist for the *Herald* noted,

There is a rumor to the effect that a terrible split has occurred in the ranks of those who make their headquarters at the Deux Magots. The cause has not yet been ascertained, but it is known that Ludwig Lewisohn, Eliot Paul and Ernest Hemmingway [*sic*] have deserted the Magots for a smaller and quieter cafe not a block away.[82]

With the dollar still going for twenty-five francs, sales of *Men Without Women* approaching 15,000 copies, and Pauline's trust fund producing regular dividends, Ernest and Pauline could afford to indulge themselves with ham and eggs at Café Flore or a painting from one of Flechtheim's galleries.

Their Paris social life was complicated by the proximity of the many residents whom Ernest had alienated through satire, parody, his divorce, or word of mouth. By the time Pauline inherited his unhappy detractors and wounded friends, they were an impressive group, both in size and in membership. The hard core included Robert McAlmon, Harold Loeb, Glenway Wescott, and Kitty Cannell. Hurt but not malicious were Duff Twysden, Lewis Galantière, Gertrude Stein, Alice Toklas, Sherwood Anderson, Louis Bromfield, Ethel Moorhead, George Antheil, and Ford Madox Ford. Added to the list were Hadley's friends who sided with her in the divorce. Pauline, who had her fence-mending work cut out for her, was happy enough to be going home to have the baby. By the time they returned some of the Paris dust might have settled.

Ernest, too, was ready for the trip home, having lived too long in foreign parts. "I should have gone to America two years ago when I planned," he confessed to Perkins. "I was through with Europe and needed to go to America before I could write the book that happened there."[83] Their plans, which they had kept pretty much to themselves, were now settled: sail in March to Havana, Cuba, then by ferry to Key West where Pauline's father would meet them with a new Ford roadster, a gift from Uncle Gus. Two weeks before they left, Art Moss, in what he took to be Hemingway's laconic style, reported:

The Seine Also Rises
"Hello," said Hemmingway [*sic*], "wanna drink?
"Yes," I said. "I wanna drink."
"Give us two drinks, Chips," Hemmy said.
We drank the two drinks.
"So you're goin' away, Hemmy," I said. "Whaddya goin' away for?"
"How should I know why I'm goin' away. I'm goin' to Florida to go fishin' for tarpon."

"Then you ain't gonna do no more bullfightin'," I said.
"No," said Hemmy, "I ain't gonna do no more bullfightin'. Why the devil should I do any more bullfightin'?"
"I don't know," I said, "why should you?"
"God, it'll be swell to be over there with all those big fish," Hemmy said.
"I hope they bite well," I said.[84]

It would also be swell, of course, to be over there with a novel in progress rather than a novel going nowhere. In his explanation to Max Perkins, Hemingway ticked off several good reasons why his new novel would not be finished for the fall season. His various illnesses and wounded eye slowed things down, and he had been "out a good deal." It had taken him five years, he said, to write the stories for *In Our Time*, which was almost true if you allowed that one of them dated from 1922. Those for *Men Without Women* took another five, he claimed, stretching the truth somewhat. *The Sun Also Rises* went quickly in first draft but took another six months to revise. "How much time I wasted in drinking around before I wrote it and how badly I busted up my life in one way or another I can't fit exactly in time," he complained.

I work all the time. But I don't think I can make even an irregular schedule and keep up the quality. I know very well I could turn books out when they should come out (and you have been very damned decent about not even asking me or putting any pressure on me) but we only want good ones – both of us. You see my whole life and head and everything had a hell of a time for a while and you come back slowly (and must never let anyone know even that you were away or let the pack know you were wounded).[85]

He was talking to himself, not to Max, for the only pressure to finish the novel was self-generated.

That is when, quite literally, the roof fell in. The *Herald* reported:

Hemingway Cut In Skylight Crash
Mr. Ernest Hemingway, author who was wounded about the head when a skylight crashed on him at his home Sunday [March 4] morning, yesterday was recovering, according to officials at the American Hospital at Neuilly. Mr. Hemingway's wound, which required three stitches inside and six outside, is healing and he was able to pursue his usual life.

It is understood that Mr. Hemingway's injury will not prevent his intended trip to the United States soon.[86]

What the paper could not report was the odor of his blood as it streamed across his face, or the pricking of the surgeon's needle closing the wound. He had not seen so much of himself exposed since the night in Italy when the mortar blast turned his right knee to jelly, filling his boot with blood. Giddy with shock, he tried to explain to Archie in the night cab streaking to the hospital how the blood tasted and how the smell of it was like being in the ambulance again with the men dripping in the back, but it all came out wrong. The stranger's face in the hospital mirror was too white to be his own, and the bandage swathing his head too large for civilian times.

Pauline met him at the street door, his bandaged head glowing in the dark, took him in hand, and put him to bed, from which he arose early that Sunday afternoon a new man. There was no explanation for it, no logical reason why his blood had set him free. It simply did. When the pain dulled to the opiate's control, he knew exactly what he should be writing. The story had been there all along, ever since the manuscripts disappeared in the Gare de Lyon. The story was the war, the wound, the woman. He knew part of the story by heart, and better yet, he knew exactly where it started, looking out on the dusty road with troops marching past the window and the dust rising and the leaves falling. Two weeks later he told Perkins that he was suddenly getting "a great kick out of the war and all the things and places ... My wife says that she will see that I'm bled just as often as I can't write – judging by the way it's been going this last week."[87] For nine months, he struggled doggedly with Jimmy and his father. Now that was over. Without regret and never looking back, he abandoned them there in New York, waiting for a boat that never came. It was all right. Whatever the process, it had come finally to term, bringing him back through blood to his beginnings. Now he could leave Paris, now turn homeward, for he was, once more, a writer writing.

Chapter Eleven

A PIECE OF THE CONTINENT

Each morning the sun came up like bullfire, turning the island on its spit. If he rose early enough to walk down Simonton to South Beach, he could squint at the red-orange cusp rising out of the dark ocean, and in the late afternoon from the La Concha Hotel, he and his wife could watch it settle down, inch by inch, and then quite suddenly disappear below the blue-black horizon. Between the sun's rise and fall, Key West warmed itself, the tropic humidity rising until sweat ran down the bridge of his nose as he hunched over the pages of his novel begun in Paris. In the eighties by day and seventies by night, the weather was mild by local standards, but to the couple fresh from Paris and without clothes for the climate, it was uncomfortably warm and humid. The wife, edging into her seventh month of pregnancy and turning all night in restless sleep, could not wait to leave for Piggott and home. Each April day was the same, broken only by two thunderstorms, and each morning they woke in their small apartment above the Ford garage swathed in damp sheets. The water, pumped up from the cistern below, tasted like tin, and when the wind died at noon's reach, the odor of departed fish joined them for lunch. Each evening they watched purple martins sweep mosquitoes from the darkening air.

KEY WEST: APRIL AND MAY, 1928

After lunch, as they walked down Simonton Street to the Ford agency, they passed the flowering jacaranda tree, its profusion of blue petals one more sign of burgeoning spring. Elsewhere scarlet bougainvillea, yellow cassia, and reddish-orange flame trees dotted an otherwise salt bleached

168

cityscape. Everywhere, weather-dulled white paint was leeching off of wooden, shot-gun shacks and two-story houses whose rusted screens and sagging porches spoke of better times. The slightly hysterical prosperity of the American Twenties had largely bypassed this southernmost island. With its sponge beds blighted beyond recovery, its cigar factories boarded up, and its Naval base deactivated, Key West was down on its luck. During the previous ten years, half the population left the island; the half that remained had no great expectations. On a side street, a black man was hawking red snappers and yellow grunts from a push cart, calling out in a musical patois.[1]

The Hemingways were back in the USA, but a map was required to prove to both that they were part of the mainland, for Key West was like another foreign country. On the streets there were many voices: local English, harsh Cuban Spanish, and a lilting Caribbean Creole. With the exception of the Havana ferry and the twice-daily trains, the island was in a time-zone of its own device where the only real clock was the rise and fall of tides. It was difficult for Pauline, so close to term, to catch the rhythm of it right or to appreciate the dead center of the day when all but most essential activity stopped. "In the afternoons all the streets were empty," an old man remembered, "and most everybody dozed behind closed doors as if daylight would expose our conditions."[2] Pauline and Ernest had discussed their need for coming home, but they had not talked of this isolation in desert places.

Their crossing on the *Orita* from La Rochelle to Havana was cramped, uncomfortable, and endless. Four days out Pauline complained no one had yet offered her the possibility of a bath. If the barber was open, she was going to buy "the hairnet and the hairpins, and we will fondle far into the night – despite the smallness of the beds, and in the morning the Spanish men will think you are too young even to be married – but I'll have little Pilar kick for them (if they don't mind playing with a girl.)"[3] In his love note reply from "Papa," Ernest told Pauline, "I have often wondered what I should do with the rest of my life and now I know – I shall try and reach Cuba."[4] Later, when they received Uncle Gus's postcard saying, "Hope you had pleasant crossing & the Ford greeted you on arrival," they could only laugh, for no person, no Ford, no greeter met them at the Key West dock.[5] In his largesse, Gus ordered a new Ford Model A Coupé as a gift for the Hemingways, but production problems in Miami delayed delivery.[6] As a result, Ernest and Pauline moved into a shabby, dark apartment above the Trevor & Morris Ford agency to await their automobile.

Soon after arriving, Hemingway sent Max Perkins a telegram: WORKING HARD.[7] In the cool of the morning, he wrote steadily on his war story which, after heavy revisions, now began:

In the late summer of that year we lived in a house in a village that looked across the river and the plain to the mountains. In the bed of the river there were pebbles and boulders, dry and white in the sun, and the water was clear and swiftly moving in the channels.[8]

"That year" was 1915, long before he ever laid eyes on Italy, and the village one he had never seen. The river of his own 1918 wounding was the muddy Piave on the Venetian plain; the river Frederic Henry looked across in 1915 was the blue Isonzo rushing out of the mountains. Based on reading, hearsay, and a few good maps, Hemingway was making a war up in his head more real than any war he had known. It was all there, the country, the people, and the weather always:

I watched the snow falling, looking out of the window of the bawdy house, the house for officers, where I sat with a friend and two glasses drinking a bottle of Asti, and, looking out at the snow falling slowly and heavily, we knew it was all over for that year.[9]

Each day it went like that, the snow falling in his fiction and the sweat running from his brow.

When he wasn't writing, he was fishing in the afternoons off the city docks or along the low, wooden bridges connecting Key West to Boca Chica Key. As with everything else on the island, salt-water fishing was a new experience for Hemingway. As soon as he saw young boys pulling in grunts on hand lines, he realized that all he knew about trout fishing was largely useless, for here the fish, feeding on the tide, would have no use for a Coachman dry fly. He quickly replaced his bamboo fly rod with a casting rod, a salt-water reel, and a bait bucket to carry live shrimp or fresh mullet.[10] By the time the new Ford arrived, Ernest was into the rhythm of the island and in no particular hurry to face Paul and Mary Pfeiffer in Piggott. Pauline, becoming a little anxious about her June delivery, was ready to leave Key West but did not want to break his concentration on the novel.

On April 8, Ernest and Pauline made their Easter duty at St. Mary's Star of the Sea, which was manned by the Jesuits out of New Orleans.

Then Tuesday afternoon, while Ernest was fishing in the ferry bite behind the rail lines, his father and father's brother, Will, appeared quite unexpectedly in Grace Hemingway's ample tow. They had arrived on the 4.30 ferry from Havana and were due to leave that evening by ship for St. Petersburg. Neither father nor son knew the other was anywhere in Florida, for Ernest did not keep his parents informed of his final plans to return to the States, and their letter to him was still recrossing the Atlantic to arrive a week after this chance meeting in the road. There was barely enough time to find Pauline, tour the island, and make promises for the fall. His mother could not stop talking about their Cuban vacation and her painting career, telling "Ernie" she would forward some canvasses to him for Paris consignment. Uncle Willoughby, home visiting from his medical missionary duties in strife-torn China, worked hard to squeeze in family stories, and Clarence, worried about his son driving cross-country on roads yet unpaved, promised to send some good maps with the best routes marked. The Doctor did not tell his son about the unpaid taxes on his wallowing Florida land investments, nor did he say that he was now carefully weighing out each food ration in a effort to control his diabetes.[11]

In front of the now family Ford, father and son, mother and daughter-in-law posed for Uncle Willoughby to take the pictures. Ernest, in an open-collared shirt and a sleeveless sweater vest, is grinning almost shyly, a little embarrassed, with his hands clasped at his groin and his chin slightly tucked. Over his heart there is a noticeable hole in his vest. Already his hairline has receded deeply, leaving his widow's peak prominent and the fresh Paris scar glowing on his forehead. In winged collar, tie, and dark vested suit, his father stands in the heat, head cocked like a sparrow, gazing at the son he has not seen in four years. The positions they assume are almost identical to those in a picture taken when Ernest graduated from high school. The Doctor's now greying hair lies limp on his head, his goatee and mustache have turned completely grey. In his hand he holds an incongruous white captain's cap with a black bill. His black shoes are shined. To their right, slightly separate, stand Grace Hemingway and Pauline. Grace, wearing smoked glasses, is heavy in a black dress down to her ankles, a scarf across her shoulder and a light straw hat from Havana. She is watching Clarence watch Ernest. Close beside her is Pauline, who has dressed for the afternoon in a gaily flowered print dress, loose and long waisted to cover her pregnancy, which is not obvious. Her stylish cloche hat from Paris comes down to her eyes which are focused on the camera, looking away from Ernest.

She is smiling widely and looks quite pretty. It was the first and last time Pauline ever saw Clarence Hemingway.[12]

Soon after his parents' departure, Ernest met Charles Thompson whose family owned, it seemed, half of the island's money-making enterprises: an ice house, ship's chandlery, hardware and tackle shop, and fish company. Georgie Brooks, a local lawyer, suggested to Ernest, who was looking for someone to share a boat, that Thompson might take him out, for he liked to fish as well as any man in Key West.[13] All it took was the first tail-dancing tarpon coming out of the water like some silver dream, gill plates rattling and jaws shaking the hook, to catch Ernest's attention. This was not trout fishing. A thirty-pound tarpon on a twenty-pound test line breaking water close enough to spray the boat was enough to make a man forget about trout fishing.

That first night, Ernest and Pauline joined Charles and Lorine Thompson at their house for drinks and a Key West supper. Before the evening was finished and the Scotch bottle returned to its cabinet, the lives of all four were irrevocably changed. Had Hemingway not connected with Thompson, he might never have returned to Key West; had Pauline not found Lorine, she might never have agreed to the return. It was a good match. Pauline, needing someone educated enough for conversation and companionship, was delighted with Lorine, who was well-read and taught in the local high school. Charles, although he looked younger, was a year older than Ernest, but he was born to be Hemingway's foil, a good listener and always ready to fish or hunt. What the Hemingways gave in return was the world beyond the island, telling Paris stories with good humor and much exaggeration. Ernest, as always, carried so much energy into the room that he forced the rather quiet Charles up to his own charged level.

Through his immediate friendship with Thompson, Hemingway connected with not only the Key West establishment but also the veteran watermen who traded at Thompson's chandlery, worked on their boats, and told stories around the docks at Garrison Bight. It did not take Ernest long to learn the immediate shoal waters or to see by the nautical maps that the fishing stretched out into the Gulf past the Marquesas Keys to the Dry Tortugas. For that expedition he needed something larger than Charles' eighteen-foot outboard and something longer than an afternoon. Letters and telegrams to Mike Strater, John Dos Passos, Waldo Peirce, and Bill Smith urged them to come to Key West for a month of fishing and drinking. It was yet another version of the lost but not forgotten summers at Walloon Lake that Hemingway periodically reconstructed with whatever friends were at hand. By April 21, Hemingway was writing Max Perkins that Dos Passos was on his way down and Waldo was close behind. Bill Smith was coming in by ship on the 24th. The fish, he told Max, were amazing: "tarpon, barracuda, jack, red snappers . . . Caught the biggest tarpon they've had down here so far this season. Sixty three pounds." He asked Max to send copies of his last two books "as soon as possible. Nobody believes me when I say I'm a writer. They think I represent Big Northern Bootleggers or Dope Peddlers – especially with this scar."

Max should not worry about the novel getting finished which Hemingway said "won't be very long and has been going finely." If it was not ready for the fall, he could write some new stories to "keep the stuff going" until the following fall.[14] Hemingway had good reason to be optimistic, for his characters were established: Frederic Henry, a war-weary American ambulance driver with the Italian Second Army; Catherine Barkley, an attractive British V.A.D. a little crazy from having had her fiancé blown to bits in France; Rinaldi, an Italian surgeon, frequenter of whorehouses and Frederic's close friend; and the priest for religious counterpoint. Catherine was an amalgam of his first love, Agnes Von Kurowsky, with one part Hadley, and two parts Pauline. In the background, the war was grinding along as it did, leaving place names – the many battles of the Isonzo – etched on the landscape. With laconic understatement, Frederic was telling the story. "We crossed the river in August," he said, "and lived in a house in Gorizia."[15] It was not Hemingway's war, but one he studied closely and thought he understood – the early and middle parts of the war that led Italy into her debacle at Caporetto.

By early May, Ernest's Key West life was working so smoothly he was loath to leave it. Up early in the morning, he wrote until lunch when he would meet the "Mob," as he jokingly dubbed his gang of cronies, who slept late on Fleming Street at the Over Sea Hotel for a dollar a day and were eating cheap. Afternoons were for fishing and evenings for drink. Prohibition was never taken seriously on the island: there was plenty of cold beer at Raul's, the Cuban Cafe, and Pena's Garden of Roses. Down on Front Street, Joe Russell's hole in the wall served up whatever liquor a man could name, illegal liquor right off the boat from Havana. Russell turned a modest business, sometimes bringing in a load for himself, sometimes wholesaling a little on the side.

Island life, cheap and easy, full of conversation and two-boat afternoons bottom fishing for snapper and jew fish, poling on the flats for bone fish, drifting with the breeze. Before the "Mob" left the island, Ernest hired Bra Saunders and his fishing boat to take them out to the Marquesas and on to the Dry Tortugas where they caught tarpon, drank beer, and told tall tales at night. Crossing the quicksands between Marquesas Keys and Rebecca Shoals, they passed over the dark form of a large, sunken hulk, all that remained of the *Valbanera*, lost in the great hurricane of 1919. Saunders told them the story which began with the worst storm ever recorded at Key West, its winds estimated at over 100 miles an hour but unmeasured after the weather station's anemometer blew away. Caught outside of Havana harbor and unable to enter port, the *Valbanera* ran before the wind until she hit the shoal trying to make it into the Gulf. Thinking he was grounded securely, the captain apparently opened the sea-cocks to hold the ship in place, and the quicksand took her and more than five hundred passengers and crew right on down. When the Greek sponge divers came out, they found her port-side lifeboats still in place, and not a single body washed ashore.[16]

The fishing, the stories, night drinking, the men out together under hot sun and clear stars: all was Ernest's delight, and if he was the biggest spender, he could afford it; his April royalty statement showed that *Men Without Women* had sold 18,839 copies. After subtracting his advance and some minor bills, Scribner's owed him $3718.66. Payment was not officially due until mid-August, but Max assured him that he could collect any or all of it at any time.[17] Debt-free in Key West, where a couple could live well on five dollars a day, the Hemingways had no money problems, only ones of location. Pauline wanted to be in Piggott; Ernest wanted to remain writing and fishing in Key West; his parents expected them to come to Windemere; and the baby needed a regular doctor before late June. To a point, Pauline was tolerant of island life because the book was going well and Ernest happier than he had been in a long time.

By mid-May, however, Paul Pfeiffer, who had waited long enough for his daughter to come home, forced the decision when he arrived by train in Key West. Not about to allow his pregnant daughter to make the arduous cross-country drive in her eighth month, he put Pauline on the train north and remained in Key West to drive with Ernest to Piggott. Ernest was not thrilled to be left alone with his taciturn father-in-law, but he had no choice. A day's tarpon fishing loosened them up considerably, reassuring Paul that his once divorced son-in-law could do something well besides write fiction and make babies. Waldo Peirce, the last "Mob" member to leave the island, fished with them; in comparison with the gargantuan painter and his large gestures, Ernest appeared quite normal.

No matter how well his novel was progressing, Hemingway could not, in good conscience, leave Pauline too long alone in Piggott. During the two months in Key West, he had completed two hundred pages of manuscript, including the night wounding of Frederic Henry. To that point, the novel used little from his own experiences in the Italian war zone, but when the trench mortar shell landed on Frederic at Plava, Ernest relived his own wounding: the white, hot blast of an open furnace door and then roaring wind, his soul singing out of him along a thin wire, dead, knowing he was dead, his soul catching on the wire, and then slowly, very slowly, returning to his broken body.[18] That part of the story he had relived many times, in dreams and not in dreams. Now he revised the details, eliminating much of the sensation, leaving only its essence.

Because the narrative grew each day, unplanned, Hemingway found himself at an awkward hiatus. He knew where the fiction ended, during the disastrous Italian retreat following the Austro-Hungarian break-through at Caporetto in the fall of 1917, but there was no simple way to get Frederic to that juncture without first removing him from the front lines and from Catherine Barkley while his wounds healed. For several reasons, he did not want to use his own hospital experience in Milan. To do so would have been historically inaccurate, for the Red Cross hospital was not opened there until 1918. The greater difficulty, however, was the nurse. Hemingway's recovery in Milan was so intertwined with his romancing of Agnes Von Kurowsky, the attractive nurse who once promised to marry him, that to leave out the love story would be to cheat on the experience. Frederic, older and more experienced with women, was not Ernest at nineteen. Frederic knew Italy well, spoke the language fluently, and had seen the war from its start; in fact, his great advantage was knowing everything Ernest had learned since the war.

In an attempt to return Frederic to the front lines as quickly as possible, Hemingway tried to finesse the problem, beginning his new chapter:

There are only three people of any importance in this story, although my life was full of people, all of whom were important at the time, and I did not see any of the three for over three months. During this time I was at hospitals, first at Dormans, then at Mestre and finally in Milan. I saw them all three before I left the field hospital at the front and all three of them wrote me.[19]

175

But hearing the stilted words, he crossed the paragraph out immediately and let the story of Frederic's recovery go on much as his own had, moving him from the field hospital to a new Red Cross hospital in Milan where he was the first patient. There, waiting for the surgeon to arrive, Frederic got the nurse, Miss Gage, to bring a barber to shave him. Frederic's face was still damp when Ernest had to pack up the loose pages for the trip to Piggott.

Piggott and Kansas City: Summer 1928

On May 20, Pauline left Key West on the evening train; Ernest and her father left by car five days later. It is not easy to say which party had the more difficult trip. Pauline arrived the following morning in Jacksonville, where she walked to her hotel to get out of the day's heat and await the Kansas City train which did not leave until that night. In those days before air conditioning in either hotels or trains, a woman eight months pregnant was not going to be comfortable crossing the South in late May. She spent the night of May 21 and all day May 22 on the train, finally reaching Jonesboro, Arkansas, that evening where she connected to Piggott, arriving late in the night. Ernest and Paul Pfeiffer drove the fourteen hundred miles in six days by car, traveling along two-lane concrete highways that frequently gave way to packed gravel and staying hot nights in tourist cabins. Merely to get off the Keys and on to the mainland took all of the first day because Highway One to Key West was broken by a forty-one-mile ferry ride from No Name Key to Lower Matecumbe, a five-hour voyage of watching gulls and reading the water.

At Memphis, they crossed the Mississippi and turned north on to dirt and gravel roads, coming finally into the small cotton town of Piggott. To the east, rich bottom land stretched twenty miles to the river; to the west the land rolled gently toward the Ozarks. They crossed Sugar Creek, drove up the north side of the village square past the court house and on up the street to where the large Pfeiffer home sat atop Crowley's Ridge. It did not look like the end of the world; the world had simply gone some place else. Long before they reached the front door, Ernest had heard Paul Pfeiffer's unlikely story of the family's remove from St. Louis to Piggott. Unfulfilled by the family business, Paul took his share of Pfeiffer Chemical money and in 1911 went south by train, looking for a place to invest his assets and his time where they would help the most people. On his way back from Texas, he stopped off at the old Palace Hotel to look Piggott over. He saw rich earth, modest farmers, and large possibilities – a town just his size.[20] Leaving Pauline in her Catholic boarding school in St. Louis, in 1913 Paul moved his wife Mary and his two younger children, Virginia and Karl, to Piggott.[21] Now, fifteen years later, Paul owned the bank, the cotton gin, the feed store, and the Piggott Land Company. When the streets needed paving or when the school needed a new building, Paul matched the town, dollar for dollar, to get the job done. With only about two thousand people in Piggott, Paul's feudal estate held little joy for Ernest, a "Christ offal place" he called it.[22] But if one had to be in Piggott, being there as Paul Pfeiffer's son-in-law was by far the best way.

The two-story Pfeiffer home, with its oak-shaded porches and maid's quarters, was a little like Oak Park. Just as Ernest's mother ruled on North Kenilworth, so did Mary Pfeiffer reign on Cherry Street. Paul, a better businessman than Dr. Hemingway, was content to leave the rearing of the family and domestic decisions to his wife. But unlike Grace Hemingway, Mary was content to perfect the house, oversee the kitchen, and gently mold her family. She was the mother Ernest felt he never had, a mother who deferred to her husband's decisions and dedicated her life to her children. She was also dedicated to fine whiskey; not in excess, but an afternoon toddy at poolside and a nightcap after supper was her ritual. Mary also had a private chapel installed off the living room, for Piggott was without a Catholic church. Some Sundays the priest came over from Paragould to say their Mass; some Sundays the family drove to Poplar Bluff, but there was always a Mass.[23]

From Piggott, Ernest wrote his father, thanking him for the road maps and saying that there had been no time to visit with distant relatives along the way. Their doctor in Key West calculated the baby's arrival day as June 27; he and Pauline would be driving to Kansas City for the delivery. However, it was back to Windemere that he wanted to travel, particularly after two days in Piggott, where the main topic of conversation was the cotton crop making in the fields and the possibility of quail hunting in the fall. "I find I'm very homesick for the north," he said, but not a word about his new in-laws.[24]

At first, his writing did not go well in Piggott. Partly it was the setting, where he was a stranger playing strange roles; partly it was the story itself. He assured Max Perkins that the novel's end was in sight,[25] but first he had to get his lieutenant back to the war. No, first he had to get Pauline to Kansas City for the baby to be born. Very first, he had to get out of Piggott and away from cotton farmers and the flat river-bottom land. He and Mother Pfeiffer became close friends, for his grin and his wit remained infectious, but with his father-in-law the Hemingway charm wore thin. Paul Pfeiffer, who moved to Piggott to put the world away, was not much interested in old war stories or the mores of Paris. At night Ernest took Paul Pfeiffer's pregnant daughter to bed in her old room where he woke each morning unsure of who he was: father, husband, lover, writer, son-in-law, intruder? With one eye on the clock and the other on his wife, Ernest measured out two tedious summer weeks in Piggott.

So when Catherine Barkley walked into Frederic's hospital room, it was a great relief to Ernest who thought he knew exactly how this part of the story would unfold. "Something had gone on all the time we had not seen each other," Frederic explained. "It had gone on the same way in both of us. I did not know about it while it was happening. . . . But I knew about it now."[26] It was like being with his nurse back in Milan and being for the first time with Pauline all rolled into one. There in Piggott with Pauline eight months pregnant and with her father's house weighing him down, he tried to explain that first feeling, the one all lovers know but cannot tell. It was like two drops of mercury coming together to make one seamless whole. No, not like that. It was like finding "one day that you are no solider than a postcard that is torn in two and half of it is another person, that nothing makes you happy unless the two halves of the postcard are together."[27] No, it wasn't like a torn postcard either. It wasn't like anything he could find words for in Piggott.

The doctor came to examine Frederic, probe his wounds, and schedule the operation on his ruined knee. Then came the ether-heavy darkness and waking to the pain. "It is not like death's other kingdom," he wrote.[28] Then, crossing out the echo from Eliot's "The Hollow Men," he tried to tell about waking with the cast on his leg and the iron pipe sticking out and then vomiting again and again, helplessly.

Then I lay still and waited for the pain to reach the top and go down but there was no limit to the pain and it had long passed the point where pain had always stopped. I thought our Lord would never send us more [than] we could bear and I had always believed that meant we became unconscious when it was too bad, hence the success of martyrs, but now it was not so but the pain went way beyond what I could bear in the bone and everywhere there was and then inside my chest it started to jerk and jerk and then I cried and cried without any noise, only the diaphragm jerking and jerking.[29]

He crossed it all out, effacing Frederic and his pain, leaving only Catherine and the Milan hospital. Outside his writing room, Pauline, radiant in her pregnancy, waited to be taken to Kansas City; inside there was only Catherine, always ready for Frederic's bed. Finally much of what he wrote those first days in Piggott was merely a way of passing the time, and he crossed out pages ruthlessly.

While Mary Pfeiffer was packing up her daughter for the two-day drive to Kansas City, Ernest received letters from his parents. Typically they both wrote on the same day, neither mentioning the other's letter.[30] His father, advising against having the baby at Petoskey, offered his obstetric services in Oak Park. Not a chance. Ernest was not going to have his sad father birthing his own grandchild while son and mother-cum-grandmother waited apart. That was too many fathers and sons, too many sad stories. On June 7, he wrote Perkins that he was on page 279 and might be finished in July, a half promise he might have kept, but that day the story changed on the page as he wrote. Something was bothering Catherine that she did not want to tell Frederic, but he kept after her until she finally said it: "I'm going to have a baby darling. It's almost three months along. You're not worried are you? Please please don't. You mustn't worry."[31]

They left for Kansas City with Pauline only two weeks away from delivery and uncomfortable no matter which way she twisted in the Ford's front seat. Once they crossed the ferry at Cairo and got on the paved road to St. Louis, the ride smoothed out, leaving only the awkwardness of St. Louis memories better left unspoken. They did not stop, turning west on Highway 40 toward Kansas City. By the time they arrived and moved in at the Lowry house on Indian Lane, the Republican Convention in downtown Kansas City had already nominated the Great Engineer, Herbert Hoover, for the presidency. Ernest stopped by the convention center one morning, but did not stay long.[32]

For a month, the Hemingways lived with Malcolm and Ruth White Lowry on Kansas City's fashionable Indian Lane. Ruth was a cousin, related to Ernest through his Aunt Arabella White Hemingway who married his Uncle Tyler. In 1917, Tyler and the Whites' considerable name got Ernest his first job on the Kansas City *Star*, for Tyler always thought well of this nephew. When Tyler died, Arabella remarried a man named Shepard and moved in quite close to the Lowrys. Between aunt and cousin, the Hemingways were well taken care of in Kansas City, connecting quickly with Carlos Guffey, the doctor who would twice deliver Pauline.[33] Spacious, comfortable, and with a well-stocked liquor cabinet, the Lowry house on Indian Lane was welcome relief for Hemingway, who was sleeping between two pregnant women, one real, the other fictional. With no Piggott and no Oak Park to drag about behind them, his lovers had only the war and their baby for worries. Frederic was asking Catherine:

> "Have you a father?"
> "Yes," said Catherine. "He has gout. You won't ever have to meet him. Haven't you a father?"
> "No," I said. "A step father."
> "Will I like him?"
> "You won't have to meet him."[34]

In the street below their hotel window, "a motor car honked," Eliot's *Waste Land* calling up time's winged chariot, sex and death, the two best stories he knew. "Where will you have the baby?" Frederic wanted to know, for that night he was leaving Catherine to return to the front. He was not to worry, for she would arrange it the best way she could.

When Pauline returned from her doctor's appointment, it was time for lunch; Ernest, leaving the other two in their hotel a little longer, closed the novel down for the day. After sandwiches and a beer, he enjoyed the nearby country club where Malcolm's membership gave him access to afternoon polo games and locker-room drinks followed afterwards by a swim in the Lowry's pool. By June 17, Pauline was a predicted ten days from delivery, and Ernest counted 311 pages of manuscript, telling Waldo Peirce that he now knew how the story ended.[35] All things ended: babies were born and novels finished, but not always as planned.

Hemingway thought he was on the "last leg" of the novel, when he was in fact only half-way through the final manuscript. With Frederic on his way back to the front lines where the retreat from Caporetto awaited him, Hemingway knew the story was a tragedy. What he did not know was how to bring all the pieces together. When he moved Catherine to Milan to give Frederic his summer of love, he ensured that, except in Frederic's thoughts, Catherine and her baby would disappear from the story. It was a dilemma for which he had no immediate answer, letting it work itself out a day at a time. If there were no neat solution, then it was not so different from life itself. *The Sun Also Rises* left a lot of characters without forwarding addresses; maybe this story would end just as ragged.

Every day letters forwarded from Paris, Key West, and Piggott arrived, and every day he worked on the novel, answering only the most pressing mail. Guy Hickok was taking care of the taxes on the rue Férou apartment; Waldo Peirce was trout fishing in Maine; Ernest's sister Marcelline was vacationing in Spain. And Max wanted him to think about serializing the new novel in *Scribner's Magazine*, which would pay a good price, maybe not so high as the more popular magazines, and certainly he could not advise Ernest to give the novel to *Scribner's*, but if it would not sell elsewhere, they would love to have it. The letter was Max personified, hedging his bet, not wanting to offend and unable to say the thing directly.[36] Ernest temporarily ignored the offer, putting all of his energy into his novel.

The day Pauline's labor pains began, Al Smith was nominated by the Democrats for the presidency and Frederic Henry was preparing to go up on the Bainsizza plateau. He had returned to find all his old friends deeply depressed by the war's bloody progress. They were all wounded – Catherine wounded by love; Frederic by the night shell at Plava; Rinaldi carrying the sickness of the brothel into his surgery; the priest so disheartened he could barely function. Everybody gets it sooner or later, Rinaldi insisted. That's where Ernest stopped to take Pauline down town to the Research Hospital; her pains were regular now, and there was nothing he could do but wait. All day he waited, going out alone for lunch and coming back to nothing changed and Pauline getting weaker now. After supper, Dr. Guffey asked Hemingway's permission to remove the baby by caesarean section. When Nick's father opened the pregnant squaw with his sterilized jackknife at "Indian Camp," it had all taken a long time and Nick had not been able to watch him remove the baby or suture the wound. But that was in his fiction, and this operation was now in Kansas City. It was easier in the story where Nick could go back across the lake, sure he would never die, while the woman and her baby were somewhere else. In the story the Indian father, unable to listen to his wife's pain, had cut his throat with a razor. Standing in the hospital hallway with Dr. Guffey and with Pauline white-faced and sweaty inside the delivery room, it was not easy to say, yes, cut open my wife.

A month later Ernest could joke about it, telling Guy Hickok that they opened Pauline up the way a bull gutted a picador's horse, lifting out the heavy baby boy. "It is a different feeling," he said, "seeing tripes of a friend rather than those of a horse to whom you have never been introduced."[37] But in the ninety-degree heat of the Kansas City summer, it was no joke, and with serious stitches lacing up her stomach like a red zipper and gas bloating her belly, Pauline was not laughing. At the telegraph office, Ernest sent out the word to everyone he knew:

PATRICK NINE POUNDS ARRIVED RESEARCH HOSPITAL 7:30 TONIGHT STOP HE AND PAULINE BOTH WELL LOVE ERNEST[38]

At that moment in Bangor, Maine, Waldo Peirce was madly typing a manic letter to Ernest, urging new deep-sea fishing books upon him and advising him to write one of his own, for the competition was minimal. He, Waldo, would help with the Latin names which he was learning for all the salt fishes. "Let's discover a new monster," he suggested, fleshing out the idea somewhat in the manner of James Joyce:

> Taurus Nymphomaniacus Gladeus, Balls like a Bull, wings like a bat, shits like a sawmill, half man and half woman, three hind quarters, self sufficient androginous hermoaphrodizzyacal son of a bitch, a Jacal with seventy three arseholes which he scratches on the sand on the venereal equinox by fair weather only and one hundred and eighty seven cocks with which he buggers himself to death in the rutting season, which is very often, causing few of these comparatively unknown monsters to attain full growth owing to aforesaid pernicious habit.[39]

The day following Pauline's caesarean, *The Oak Parker* published "Ernest Hemingway, One of Ours," saying that Ernest "apparently hasn't an ideal to his name and 'respectability' is not one of his literary traits. Still, Oak Park must accept him . . . because he is one of the acknowledged leaders in contemporary literature." The author was unhappy that a writer who could not plot, who stole his characters from life, a writer who had nothing to write about, should be the Pied Piper for the young who wanted so desperately to become part of the Lost Generation. "The Killers," she said, was now required reading in certain University of Chicago writing courses, and Robert Frost had declared it the "world's greatest short story." So no matter how low his characters, how boring his anti-plots, how disgusting his scenes, Hemingway was "the village genius" whether Oak Park liked it or not.[40]

After reading the article, Ernest composed a note for the woman who wrote it:

YOU ARE CERTAINLY AN UNATTRACTIVE LITTLE NEST EGG OF OTHER PEOPLE'S IDEAS AND PHRASES.

He signed but did not send the telegram, telling his father who sent him the clipping that he had "never read a collection of such drool."[41]

While Pauline suffered through three weeks' confinement and Ernest tried to keep to his writing schedule, letters and telegrams from all quarters – Paris, Oak Park, New York, and Piggott – flowed into Kansas City filled with good wishes. Mary Pfeiffer wanted Pauline and her baby home as soon as possible where Jinny was waiting to take care of the boy. Ernest, she said, could then hide out with her blessing in what ever wild part of the country he wished to finish his novel.[42] Among the predictable messages came the studied zaniness of Scott Fitzgerald, who had not yet heard of Patrick's birth but who was back in Paris and friends once more with the Murphys. Without knowing much about Ernest's novel in progress, Fitzgerald kidded Hemingway: "While you're in America don't cast any doubt on my statement that you held a bridgehead (or was it a hophead) at Caporetto for three days & utterly baffled the 2nd Austrian Army Corps."[43]

At that moment on Bainsizza plateau, it was the night before Caporetto and Frederic was talking with Gino about the bloody war. Gino said that their summer loses could not have been in vain. Frederic did not answer, but thought to himself:

I was always embarrassed by the words sacred,

glorious, and sacrifice and the expression in vain. We

sometimes standing in the rain almost out of earshot so
that only the shouted word came through
            now
had heard them/ and read them /~~now in~~ for a long time

and I had seen nothing sacred

,on proclamations that were slapped up by bill posters
over other proclamations,

and the ~~only things glorious were the cavalry riding with
lances, the clean oiled mechanism~~

that were called
the things /glorious had no glory and the sacrifices ~~were~~

were like the stockyards of Chicago if nothing was done
with the meat except to bury it
~~or were vain.~~/ There were many words that you could not

stand to   ~~and certain num~~
/hear and finally only the names of places /had dignity.

Certain numbers were the same way and certain dates and
                                        have them
these with the names of places were all you could say and

have them
/mean anything ~~and they meant everything~~. Abstract words

~~{~~such as glory, honour, courage, or hallow~~}~~ were ~~a little~~
obscene

                              villages
obscene beside the concrete names of /~~places~~, the numbers

the names of rivers
of roads,/the numbers of regiments and the dates.[44]

It took him half the morning to get it right. Outside the house on Indian
Lane, the sun was roasting the city, melting the asphalt in the street; on
the Bainsizza, fog pooled in the swales of the rolling plateau while rain
fell intermittently, blurring the grey landscape.

When the bombardment began up the line, Frederic was not yet
concerned. But then, at three in the morning, with wind rising and rain
falling in sheets, "Croatians came over across the mountain meadows and
into the front line."[45] He got those Croatians exactly where he wanted
them, the only place they should have been that rainy morning on a
plateau he had never seen.[46] The Kansas City June grew into sweltering
July while Frederic, in the cold Italian rain, tried desperately to reach the
safety of the Tagliamento River. In the hospital room Pauline's bright
wound was slowly healing when Catherine Barkley abandoned her Milan
duty, betrayed by her pregnancy. On July 4, Hemingway wrote his
parents that conditions had not been "ideal" for finishing his novel, but
he saw no way they could bring the baby to Windemere. "Where ever
we go," he said, "we must stay for a while. I wrote Dad asking about
getting a cottage at Walloon but was discouraged." As he wrote it, he

knew that Jinny Pfeiffer was waiting in Piggott to care for Patrick, and he was making plans for a trip west with his friend Bill Horne. He signed the letter "Ernie," but failed to mail it until July 15 when he added an additional explanation: "I'd love to come to Windemere but can't work and see anyone and would be as pleasant to have around as a bear with carbuncles until this book is finished."[47]

Dependent upon strangers and the privacy of unfamiliar places, he wrote hard on the road, a man possessed and without a home. By mid-July, he was able to joke about it with MacLeish.

> I am now on page 455 (one of the shittiest yet and I hoped it would be one of the best) – as near as I can figure out I will go on writing this book forever. I am next going to try writing in Wyoming. I have had some success writing in Key West – writing in Piggott was equally difficult – writing in Kansas City has charms of its own but have we given the great west a chance? No. Therefore I will hope to conclude the volume in Wyoming. If it doesn't go well I will move on to Idaho. Will probably finish neck deep in the Pacific ocean.

That Sunday morning in Kansas City he could not know that his ending would not be right until he was back in Paris, having finally traveled full circle. He told Archie, "Once I get this fooking book done (it rides me and poops me all day and all night) I will write you out of house and home with letters."[48]

In that Kansas City month, Hemingway had written Frederic from Milan to the Bainsizza in time for the Second Army's confused, muddy retreat toward the Tagliamento. Every detail, every turn of the road, was map accurate without ever intruding or calling attention to itself. Through it all Frederic tried to carry out his orders, but the rain-drenched roads were jammed with peasants in horse-drawn wagons, trudging troops, and stalled vehicles. For hours they sat listening to the rain on the ambulance roof, dozing in the lull. And Frederic thought,

> If there was no war we would all be in bed. In bed I lay me down my head. Bed and board. Stiff as a board in bed. Catherine was in bed now between two sheets over and under her which side did she sleep on? Maybe she wasn't asleep. Maybe she was lying thinking about me. Blow blow ye western wind well it blew and it wasn't the small rain but the big rain down that rained. It rained all night.

You knew it rained down that rained. Look at it. Christ that my
love were in my arms and I in my bed again. That my love
Catherine. That my sweet love Catherine down might rain. Blow
her again to me. ~~That was another one about the western wind.
Not so good because there was music instead of the small rain
down might rain to quiet the western ocean~~. Well we were ~~caught~~
in it. Everyone was caught in it and the small rain would not quiet
it. Good night Catherine, I said out loud, I hope you sleep well.[49]

He bracketed the entire section, marking it: "Cut out maybe."

But he never did because it was right, the whole section was right,
words leading to other words across the page and the pages filling right.
It went on like that, day after day, pages with few if any changes, and he
could smell the hay in the Italian barn where they stopped and taste the
pasta and hear bombs falling on the further road when Austrian planes
harried the main retreat. He was there with Frederic trying to get three
ambulances across the river and losing them to the mud of side roads.
He was there pulling the trigger when Frederic coolly "dropped" the
deserting sergeant as if he were a game bird. That morning when
he wrote MacLeish, Frederic was climbing out of the river into which he
had jumped to avoid being shot as a German spy. The next day on foot
he crossed the Venetian plain, making his way carefully toward the rail
bridge near Latisana where he hopped on to the slow freight carrying
heavy artillery toward Milan.

PIGGOTT AND WYOMING: LATE SUMMER 1928

Ernest, Pauline, and Patrick returned to Piggott by train, arriving the
day before Hemingway's birthday and two days before Pauline's. After
sharing their birthday party around the Pfeiffer pool, Ernest could not
wait to get out of town. He complained to Waldo Peirce, "I'm no nearer
finished on my fucking book than ever . . . six more weeks to work. The
bloody heat ruins my head. . . . There are no fucking alibis in life – the
stuff is good or not – your reasons for it not being are not worth a
turd."[50] He did not tell Peirce that despite Kansas City heat, a strange
house, and his wife's caesarean, he had written one hundred and seventy
pages of manuscript in thirty days, creating Frederic's remarkable retreat
from Caporetto, start to finish. That same day he wrote Perkins that he

was leaving for Wyoming to finish the book, which would still need cutting and revising, but he would do that in Paris when he returned there in November. "Am damned sick of the heat," he wrote. "Been over 90 almost every day for nearly a month."[51]

Five days in Piggott and Ernest was gone, riding the train back to Kansas City where he joined with his old friend from Chicago, Bill Horne. He stopped long enough to do some shopping and write two letters to Pauline. Then he and Bill started west in Hemingway's Ford, bound for a dude ranch in Wyoming. With western roads largely unpaved, cross-country driving in 1928 was a serious test of endurance. America was out on the road, but a road replete with multiple hazards and few conveniences. Ernest and Bill made their way north and west from Kansas City, picking up Highway 30 west of Omaha, and then Highway 71 which was paved only as far as St. Joseph, where it turned to rolled gravel and then to dirt and back to gravel all the way to Cheyenne. From there due north it was mostly dirt roads across the high plains to Sheridan. The posted speed limit was thirty-five miles an hour, but they seldom made it.[52] They carried a spare tire, a hand pump, plenty of extra inner tubes, and a couple of patching kits for frequent flats. They also carried spare spark plugs, water for the radiator, and a can of gasoline. Between Kansas City and Cheyenne, a few of the new service stations were open, but in the smaller towns they had to search for the gasoline pump in front of general stores and old livery stables. Where they could find them, they slept in the new tourist courts with tiny cabins and what passed for a hot bath. By the second night they had crossed Nebraska and arrived in Casper, Wyoming, where Ernest telegraphed Pauline his love. Driving twelve-hour stints and longer, they made the 1,040-mile journey in three days.[53]

Outside of Sheridan at the Folly Ranch, where Bill Horne's fiance joined the two men, there were a few dudes and too many dudeens to suit Ernest. In three days he wrote only eight pages of manuscript and caught forty-four fish. On the fourth day he returned to the many-gabled Sheridan Inn where he ripped off thirty-five pages in four undisturbed days. On 8 August, he moved out to Eleanor Donnelly's Lower Ranch where, without dudes like himself to bother him, he wrote seventeen and a half pages the first day.[54] In one exhausting day, he rowed with Frederic and Catherine (reunited at Stresa) all through the rainy night on Lago Maggiore, hiding from the border patrols and finally making it safely into Switzerland by morning light. With a good map, he could see the towns coming up in the dark and see the promontories looming above him; he could feel the blisters forming on Frederic's hands. Those smooth pages needed almost no revisions, going straight into print as they were first written. The novel was driving itself toward the finish he had realized for it when Pauline was cut open in Kansas City. As he went to sleep that night, Frederic and Catherine, posing as cousins and under nominal arrest, were following the Swiss soldier into Locarno. The next day he moved the lovers toward Montreux where he knew the rails, the roads, and the inns in detail, and where he could draw on all the warmth he remembered from two winters there with Hadley. Frederic was wounded in the Plava offensive the April before; now Catherine would come to term in April.

While the manuscript pages piled up, so did the unanswered letters on top of his dresser. Dos Passos wrote from some obscure Russian village where he was living on "pears and old bread and a Dutch cheese." Waldo was slaying fish in Maine, and Hadley was hiking in France. She said, "Try & ease up the tired mind & heart in that grand sun dried west and forget all the women & children & the various woes they have bro't you. I have tho't about you a great deal & I am sure you need a great rest & and as usual have had the good sense to look in the right place for it."[55] By the time he got that letter, he was giving their cottage above Montreux and all their memories to Frederic and Catherine. From Paris, Guy Hickok reported, "Jews going to Zion, Irish going to Lourdes, Socialists going to Brussels, Third party women going to Geneva, Kikes going to the Follies and old Eagle readers coming all the way to Paris to 'pay their respects' to me. Sheik hunting girls going to Algiers, [and] Flyers splashing all the water out of the Atlantic."[56] He enclosed a photograph of Hadley and a note from Ezra: "Wots the Pig got? Wott gott has the Pig gott? Piggott mit uns!"

Stranded in Piggott until she recovered her strength, Pauline was less than amused by Ezra's joke. Patrick, she told Ernest, was putting on weight and looking distinctly Chinese, while she was losing weight and missing her husband. From Kansas City, Ernest sent her a pair of fishing waders so that she would be properly equipped in Wyoming. Over the phone he tried to explain about the "wading pants," which sounded to Pauline like "wedding pants." On August 3, she wired him: WEDDING PANTS GREAT SUCCESS BUT LONESOME LOVE PAULINE. By letter she said that they "fit very practically, especially in the feet. I look like somebody in a duffel bag."[57]

Each day her letters came just as they had during their now historic "Hundred Days," chatty letters that did not complain or cause problems.

She kidded him about his habit of saving every piece of paper that passed through his hands, and made sure he remembered why he was missed. "When I get with you again," she promised, "I'm going to be a model of wifely arts and crafts. It's going to be *lovely, lovely, lovely* to be with you again, and Wyoming will be perfect." Having seen her renowned husband, the young men of Piggott, she said, were all growing mustaches. Maybe, when they got back to snow country, he would grow a beard again and she would "wash it in snow water once a week and that will keep it maybe from turning green." As for the "18 beautiful blonds" who drove him away from the Folly Ranch, she would be with him in about three weeks, her teeth fixed, her "figger" flattened out. "So sweetheart, try your best to sleep and I'll be there every night, and fish and write well, and maybe finish the book or almost, and then we'll have a glorious, glorious month dressed in wedding pants night and day."[58]

Day and night in Switzerland, Catherine and Frederic lived as well as they could through the winter while the baby grew and Catherine slowed down. When the spring rains began, they moved down the lake to Lausanne to be close to the hospital. There in their hotel room, Catherine said:

"I know I'm no fun for you darling. I'm like a big flour barrel."

"No you're not. You're beautiful and you're sweet."

"I'm just something ungainly that you've married."

"No you're not. You're more beautiful all the time."

"But I will be thin again Darling."[59]

Catherine and Pauline, each with narrow hips, would both be thin again and sometimes in the night he was not sure who was in bed with him or where the bed was or if he cared. Each day, writing a letter to Pauline and writing about Catherine, he lived with both women in his head.

On August 7, Pauline wired: ARCHIE WIRES HAS SEVEN POUND BOY GLAD YOURE BETTER LOVE PAULINE. A day later she sent by registered mail and insured for $4,000 the 486 pages of manuscript Hemingway had left for safe keeping in Piggott. It was the most insurance the post office would issue, and as she handed it across the counter, the memory of Ernest's stolen manuscripts had to cross her mind. In the letter that followed, she said she was packing for her trip west. "I weigh 111 lbs and feel fine but am careful for you," she said.[60] On August 14, the priest came over from Paragould to baptize Patrick in the Pfeiffer chapel; that afternoon Pauline left for her dental appointment in St. Louis.[61] Three days later, as Pauline was boarding the train for

Sheridan, Catherine's labor pains began before dawn in Lausanne. Once Frederic got her into the hospital room, she sent him out for breakfast, and when he returned they had moved her to the delivery room. The doctor assured him that everything was going well. Beside Catherine was a tank of nitrous oxide gas for her pain.[62]

"I want it now," Catherine said. The doctor placed the rubber mask over her face and turned a dial and I watched Catherine breathing deeply and rapidly. Then she pushed the mask away. The doctor shut off the petcock.[63]

As Hemingway's writing day ended, Frederic remained beside Catherine as her pains grew more intense, and he was still there in the delivery room when Ernest went into Sheridan the next day to meet Pauline's train.

From the station, he wrote a note to Guy Hickok, complaining that the train was two hours late and claiming to be only two days from the end of his novel. Despite Prohibition, there was good beer from the local brewery and "good wine from a wop – a nice French family (bootlegger) where we sit on the vine shaded porch and drink as at the Double Maggots – youth will be served." When the book was finished, he and Pauline planned, he said, to vacation around Yellowstone and the Tetons, fishing and hunting, but they would be back in Paris by November.[64] For two days after Pauline arrived, he did not write a word; then, returning to Catherine and Frederic, he finished their story in thirty-six pages written in a three-day burst.[65]

All that morning the pains came and went, sometimes bigger ones, sometimes not, and all the while Catherine being as brave as possible. Early in the book when Frederic gave her the cliche about the brave dying but once to the coward's thousand deaths, she had said: "The brave dies perhaps two thousand deaths if he's intelligent. He simply doesn't mention them." "She said she wanted to be brave, and now, with the pains breaking her down and her face turning ashen, she was getting her chance. Everybody got his chance. Frederic had his twice at the rivers: once at Plava when he was blown up while eating cold pasta, and then again on the Tagliamento where he watched the firing squad doing their duty. The first time was an industrial accident, and the second time he deserted. That was his choice, but Catherine had no choice, and finally, when the gas would no longer work, the pain broke her completely:

"Oh please darling please make it stop. *There it comes. Oh oh oh.*"
She breathed sobbingly in the mask. "It doesn't work. It doesn't
work. Don't mind me darling. Please don't cry. Don't mind me.
I'm just gone all to pieces. You poor sweet. I love you so and I'll
be good again. I'll be good this time. *Can't they give me something?* If
they could only give me something."[67]

When the pains produced no baby, the doctor finally performed the
caesarean section, lifting out the bloody boy who looked like a skinned
rabbit.

Frederic watched the doctor "sewing up the great long forceps-spread
thick edged wound." The doctor assured him the scar will flatten. Only
after Catherine is recovering in her room does Frederic learn that his son
was born dead, strangled by his umbilical cord. Frederic thinks he should
have the boy baptized, but cannot move. He thinks, *that's what you did.
You died. You did not know what it was about. You never had time to learn. They
threw you in and told you the rules and the first time they caught you off base they
killed you.*[68] He returned from supper to find that Catherine had begun to
haemorrhage and they could not stop the blood and she was dead.

That was the end of the story, not the one he started to tell, but the
one that told itself. Outside the ranch cabin, the evening air carried the
first chill of fall. The cook was ringing the iron triangle, calling the
hands in for supper.

Chapter Twelve

THE DEAD

With sun bright behind him and his pistol steadied on the car door, he watched the burrow where nothing moved. The prairie dogs had disappeared at the sound of the motor, and now he waited for them to come back. The dust the car raised settled back on to the dirt road, empty for miles ahead and miles behind. Only the dry rasping of grasshoppers broke the silence, that and the metal ticking of the engine as it cooled. Ahead, out of range, a red-tailed hawk hunted on afternoon thermals, circling effortlessly westward. They looked away at the hawk and then back to the burrow where an almond-shaped head peered out, his black eyes and nose making a triangle on the grey, pointed face. They had not seen him come back. He was simply there. The man with the pistol waited, not moving, not taking aim, not yet. The dog stared straight at them, listening to the ticking sound of the cooling engine, unable to sort them out from the mass of the Ford. Then, quite slowly, he edged out of his hole until his entire body was visible, perched on the edge of the burrow, muscles tensed. Still the man waited. The dog sat back on its haunches, scanning the horizon, his belly white in the sun and his paws held limp against his chest. Slowly now the hunter raised his pistol, bracing his arm against the door and sighting through the open sight along the blue-black barrel. When the dog stood up on its hind legs, absolutely still, the man squeezed off the shot. The hollow-point bullet hit the dog squarely, tumbling it backwards away from its burrow. When he got to it, the animal was no longer moving. It was a clean head shot.

PIGGOTT: EARLY FALL 1928

For a month they disappeared into Wyoming's empty spaces, glad to have the novel's first draft finished, glad to be free again. The country was open, filled with distance and wide vistas of yellow grain, prairie grass, cattle, and sheep, all reminding Hemingway of Spain. On the horizon were blue-black mountains, miles away but looking quite close, their peaks still white with last winter's snow. There was sun and little shade, empty spaces without people, and where one found people, they came at face value, for the land did not allow much pretension. There were men alive who remembered the Missouri Breaks where rustlers were once hunted down to be hung without juries or to be shot like wolves by bounty hunters. Eastern dudes and dudeens, hairy chaps flapping, might now be found on homesteaded ranches too small to make a living in a land water poor, but it was still a dangerous land where men went armed out of habit. There was plenty of game for the hunter, prong-horned antelope on the plains, deer, elk, and black bear in the mountains. On the wing were prairie chickens and grouse, and in the fall, ducks came through heading south. There were good streams and rivers for fishing trout, rainbows and browns. It was a country Ernest read about as a child.

Down dirt roads and across mountain passes, he and Pauline drove their dusty Ford through the Big Horn Mountains and down to Trapper Lodge at Shell to visit Owen Wister, the writer who invented the Western. "Not since I talked with Henry James at Rye in 1914 have I opened up at such a rate," Wister said later.[1] Their conversation included stories of Teddy Roosevelt, Wister's old friend and Ernest's boyhood hero. Wister told Ernest what kind of country he might expect to see in the Yellowstone area and shared with Hemingway his recently published collection of short stories, *When West Was West*.[2] Ernest told him about Scribner's forcing him to remove certain words from *The Sun Also Rises*, and his fears of more drastic censorship for his new novel. It was one of those rare encounters for Hemingway, an older writer with whom he connected instantly and without competitive feelings. It was also a laying on of hands, a passing of the torch. Through Wister, Hemingway connected with those gentlemen writers of the 1890s; a "sweet old guy," Ernest called Wister, who "writes damn well too."[3] Before parting, the two men made plans to meet again that winter in Paris.

Out of Shell, the couple drove west to Cody, stopping sometimes to shoot at prairie dogs who watched from the edge of their burrows with cautious curiosity. "They are like getting planes in war time," Ernest said, "for every one that is confirmed you lose a bunch down the holes – only unlike the war you go home at night."[4] On the open Wyoming prairie, where one could occasionally find a bleached buffalo bone, Hemingway drove with his .22 pistol and his new 12 gauge Winchester within arm's reach. Earlier in August, Hemingway wrote Waldo Peirce, "So far have shot three marmots (rock dogs) almost as big as badgers with the pistol and the head off a water snake."[5] This response to nature was in the American vein, a response that Hemingway learned from most of his childhood reading, from the Sears catalog, and from his hunting father: any moving animal or bird was fair game. In this respect, Hemingway was no different from most boys of his generation, but as with all of his interests, he was more ardent than most, fishing and hunting to the limit.

He and Pauline crossed the Sylvan Pass, entering Yellowstone, largely empty of summer tourists and beginning to color up for fall. Elk and moose fed in the wide valleys that opened on to incredible scenery, a West beyond the imagination. At the north-east corner of the park, they took the little-used exit that dead-ended at Cooke City across the Montana line. A dirt road led into an almost abandoned mining town of log cabins, sagging roofs, rusting iron, grey weathered siding, a general store, and the Cosmopolitan Hotel. When the surrounding mines shut down, the money stopped, and the hard rock miners drifted on to the next strike. Behind, they left mine tailings to leach heavy metals into the creeks and faded towns like Cooke City. At the end of the road, the Hemingways put into Shaw's Camp, where their cabin was warm and the lodge food better than expected.[6] From here they fished trout from Clark's Fork of the Yellowstone, promising to return one summer soon. It was here, also, that they decided not to return to Paris in November, but instead to go back to Key West for the winter. Their decision was based partly on the memory of the miserable Paris winter with its attendant sore throats, partly on the need to revise the novel undisturbed. With *Scribner's Magazine* offering $10,000 for the serial rights, providing there were no objectionable passages, Ernest was looking at too large a payday to risk the uncertainties of a Paris or Gstaad winter.[7]

As summer played itself out, Ernest turned the Ford east toward Kansas City, where they stopped long enough for Pauline to be examined by Dr. Guffey and for Ernest to write a few letters. By 25 September, a month after the still untitled novel was finished, they drove back into

Piggott where the fields were white with late cotton. The baby Patrick, now twice his birth weight, they found content in Jinny's care and the nurse's arms. In jest, Ernest wrote to Fitzgerald that he was thinking of advertising his fathering services in the magazines:

> Are your children Rickety, deformed, in any way unsatisfactory. See E. Hemingway (then pictures of the product – all by different Mothers). Perhaps He can help You. Mr. Hemingway understands your problem. He is the author of Mr. and Mrs. Elliott [*sic*]. He knows what you are up against. His own problem is different. Mr. Hemingway has to avoid children. Since the age of fourteen he has been embarrassed by a succession of perfect Little Ones. Now he has decided to make this great gift available to All. Tear off the enclosed coupon and mail it in a plain stamped envelope and you will receive his booklet Perfect Children for You All.[8]

Beneath the joke was the irony that Hemingway, age twenty-nine, father of two with wife and ex-wife, was never quite easy in domesticated circumstances. He wanted to be "Papa," his adopted nickname, but without entailments. From Oak Park his father wrote, still longing to take his son hunting in the Smoky Mountains of Carolina but giving up the trip to be the responsible Doctor. For the first time, he signed the letter "Dad", putting the word in quotes and initialling them CEH as if his son might not know who was writing.[9]

There were other letters to be answered, letters from Evan Shipman, Peirce, MacLeish, Owen Wister, Perkins, and Guy Hickok. Mornings, after an early exercise run along Crowley's Ridge, he sat with his portable typewriter on the shaded Pfeiffer porch, two-fingering the keys in his newsman's manner. To Wister, with whom he had hoped to talk again that fall in Paris, he wrote that he was going to Key West instead. "It was there that I had the best time and worked best," he said, "so I thought it would be better to re-write the book there and by staying that long I would know something about the place and could write some stories." In Piggott, a dull, shut-in country, he said he was homesick already for Wyoming, but in his letters he was always homesick for somewhere else.[10]

To MacLeish, Ernest wrote to confirm his interest in visiting with Archie and Ada, maybe even seeing a football game, but "Patrick complicates things." "By all the laws of civilization we ought to look after Pat for a while otherwise you'd see us this week end." The Piggott cotton he said was "as white as a Mammy song," and Pauline, after a month in Wyoming, was stronger than ever, "but she has a scar that makes my forehead look like nose picking (a terrible simile)."[11] To everyone, he wrote how anxious he was to begin the revisions to his novel in the seclusion of Key West. He told Max Perkins that he felt good about the book and was never healthier. His main concern was putting together enough cash to invest in bonds that would provide seventy-five to a hundred extra dollars each month. He had seen too many friends, like Fitzgerald, dribble away their income with nothing to show for it. For this reason, he had not yet cashed the $3,700 royalty check and would appreciate the $5,000 advance against the serialization of the novel. He worried about his promise of first refusal to Ray Long with the Hearst people. Maybe he could talk his way out of that dilemma. Maybe Long wouldn't want the book.[12]

Perkins sent the $5,000 check, saying it was either a down payment on the serial or an advance against the novel.[13] He included copies of Edward Adam's *Nigger to Nigger* and Conrad Aiken's *Costumes by Eros* to relieve Hemingway's boredom in Piggott. Max also kept Hemingway informed about the life and times of Scott Fitzgerald, his wanderings and his still unfinished novel four years in the making. Ernest replied that Zelda was the source of 90 percent of Scott's problems; if only he had married a supportive wife, Scott might have been "the best writer we've ever had."[14] This simplification was becoming a frequent Hemingway response: whatever troubles a male friend might have, they were caused by his wife. He did not care for the wives of Lincoln Steffens, John Hermann, or Lewis Galantière. His own break-up with Gertrude Stein he would blame largely on Alice B. Toklas. His father's deteriorating mental and physical condition he attributed to his mother's selfishness. Hadley, had she not mentioned his affair with Pauline, might have saved their marriage.

Supportive wives, on the other hand, were a creative man's best asset. Dorothy Pound, for example, never complained in public about Ezra's long-standing relationship with Olga Rudge. Pauline, who knew Ernest to the bone, was quick to read his needs and understand his penchants. If she seemed a less than enthusiastic new mother, leaving Patrick to her sister's care, it was because she was determined to be the supportive wife and slim lover. Pauline knew that Ernest did not fare well alone, a trait proved beyond question during their hundred-day separation with its talk of suicide. Nor did he remain alone for long; his sexual magnetism drew women to him almost without his effort, as she well knew from her own first meeting with him and from observing his effect on other women. Thus when he planned a month-long trip to Chicago and the east coast, Pauline was ready to start packing, but her sister's tonsillitis interfered. They had been in Piggott and with Patrick only three weeks before Ernest left for Oak Park. While the nursemaid tended to Patrick, Pauline remained behind to care for Jinny, but not for long.[15]

In the Piggott bank for safe keeping Hemingway left behind his 652-page novel and a short story begun on the Pfeiffer porch and still unfinished. The story, which would eventually be called "Wine of Wyoming," was a curious experiment in structure (four parts), and in point of view (effaced narrator becoming the final focus). It was also his homage to Owen Wister, whose Wyoming cowboys had thrilled him as a boy and whose "The Right Honorable the Strawberries" was a rough model. Both stories seem to center on foreigners in the American west: Wister wrote of the titled Englishman whose values could not sustain him on American frontier; Hemingway wrote of the Fontans whose French Catholicism is tested in Prohibition America. Both stories were indebted to Conrad and Henry James: put a character down in a foreign country to test his values, where they must be self-sustaining.[16]

In the first three sections of his story, which Hemingway composed in Piggott, the narrator listens to the Fontans' conversation, heavily French, as they discuss the inexplicable behavior of Americans who come to their house to buy Père Fontan's home-brewed wine and beer. They arrive drunk; they leave drunk. Those that stay pour whiskey into the good wine and then vomit on the table. The Fontans, while trying to maintain their French heritage, cannot understand these Americans who do not savour wine. Nor does the wife truly believe that Al Schmidt, as she calls the presidential candidate, is actually a Catholic. Sitting in the morning sun on the porch in Piggott, Ernest typed steadily on the story, which was going on in his head and around the Pfeiffer living room as well. Here too were Catholics isolated in Protestant country, and, like the Fontans, the Pfeiffers drank moderately and favored Al Smith in the November election 'as did Ernest'. Uncle Gus wrote from New York that he was voting for Hoover because of Smith's stand on alcohol, but did not expect by mail to convince Ernest to change his position. Hemingway supported Smith, but, unregistered, he could not vote that November.[17]

The heart of the story, however, was not the Smith election or Prohibition; the real issues were moral values and the problem of being a Catholic in America, where there were too many different churches and no substantive religious life. It was not any good to be a Catholic in America, Madame Fontan allowed. "But I think it's better to be catholique if you are." When the narrator, who says he is a Catholic, asks her if she goes to Mass in America, she replies, "No. I don't go in America, only sometimes in a long while. Mais je reste catholique. It's no good to change the religion."[18]

It was a problem in the story and in the house: how to be a Catholic in America; how to love your Catholic wife when the Kansas City doctor said no more babies for at least three years. The fact was that neither of them, Ernest or Pauline, was any longer merely an American; they had lived too long in Europe and the experience had changed them irrevocably. If Hemingway's fictional Fontans were having difficulties maintaining a home in a foreign country, so was their creator unsettled. For over six months now, he had been living in rented or Pfeiffer rooms where nothing belonged to him but his socks on the dresser. Had anyone asked them where their home was, their answers would have come slowly and with qualifications: not Piggott, nor Key West, and never Oak Park. The only address they could have given was their apartment on rue Férou, but they could not live forever in France. The fictional Fontans, displaced French, beleaguered by the law and worked hard by life, had made their home in this strange country. As Hemingway put the unfinished story away, Fontan was promising the narrator three bottles of the new wine that evening.

"I'll be back," I said.

"We count on you," Fontan said.[19]

The next morning, Hemingway put his suitcase back into the Ford and drove north alone in the rain toward Chicago.[20] He passed through St. Louis two days behind Al Smith; neither man stopped. Both men were traveling a little anxious. Polls showed Smith trailing Herbert Hoover by wide margins through most of the country. Hemingway was returning to Oak Park where he had not lived in nine years.[21]

OAK PARK: OCTOBER 17–22, 1928

It was all changed and the distances different; the vacant lots all but disappeared. Flat-roofed apartments, once found only on the south side of the tracks, were now everywhere. Oak Park streets were crowded with new automobiles, and flashy radios were advertised in several store windows. As he drove through his old neighborhood, he saw bare stript trees and wet leaves down in all the yards. He felt almost invisible until he stopped in front of 600 North Kenilworth where the house looked the same as he remembered it. But when he walked into the living room, where walls were now covered with his mother's oil paintings, he realized that home too was different from when he left. Marcelline, married and with a daughter in Detroit, could not make the reunion. Ursula had come down from Minnesota, leaving her husband at home.[22] Sunny, his younger sister, was approaching her twenty-fourth birthday. Little Carol, eight when he left, was now a high-school junior at seventeen, and Leicester, the brat, was almost fourteen. His father, with his Florida tan now faded, appeared gaunt, nervous, and a little too talkative. In his old room Ernest unpacked his bag, hanging clothes in the closet that still smelled faintly as it had when he was young. The Doctor followed him up the stairs: together again, father and son.

During the previous twelve months Hemingway had received more letters from his mother and father than at any time since his Italian wounding. Grace's letters, full of her painting career, said nothing about his father's progressive angina nor his now diagnosed diabetes. In the kitchen Ernest saw the scale where his father's meal portions were weighed; "a touch of the sugar" his father called it. Insulin injection was available for diabetics, but the Doctor did not use it. Clarence Hemingway, who resented deeply his growing physical impairments as signs of personal weakness, refused to discuss his health. Grace put the best face she could find on her husband's erratic behavior, hiding her fears beneath her habitual smile.[23] Ernest may have seen symptoms in his father's letters, where the handwriting varied widely as if composed by different men. Through them ran the desire to return to his youthful and unmarried hunting days in the North Carolina mountains. In Oak Park, Ernest, who saw how much the trip meant to his father, may have wished he had taken the time to accompany him. He also saw the surface defenses his mother and siblings devised to shield themselves from his father's unpredictable behavior, now too happy, now too silent. Often irritable and suspicious, Clarence Hemingway was locking his drawers and questioning the motives of his family. During the week Ernest was home, his father tried hard to be enthusiastic about retiring soon to Florida where they would be almost neighbors.

A small medical practice would supplement the income Clarence hoped to realize soon from their Florida land. Some time around 1925, the Doctor, whose income was never large, had mortgaged his debt-free house for $15,000 to which he added their small savings and part of a paid-up insurance policy. With the money he bought several lots in Clearwater, Gulfport, and St. Petersburg, intending to live largely off the income derived from sales and rents.[24] In doing so, Clarence Hemingway, like almost every other American in the era, was trying to catch the economic wave that was creating wealth out of thin air. Across the country, men of no fortune were piling up paper wealth in Wall Street's bull market; at least once a week one read of some poor boy who retired wealthy having invested his meager savings in hot stocks. Take a ride on the Reading, take a flier on steel. Dr. Hemingway, whose father's real estate sales once helped create Oak Park and whose brother George continued to develop the Village, was naturally drawn to property investments rather than stock certificates. The Doctor's inclination was encouraged by Grace's cousin, Fred Hall, who had made quick money in the Florida market.[25]

In 1925, Florida, where old Anson Hemingway had vacationed for some years, appeared to be the golden opportunity; for over two years, land prices had doubled and redoubled, making fortunes for sharp speculators who were aided by the national media's hyping of Florida as America's future vacation and retirement center. With his characteristic poor timing, Clarence Hemingway invested in the Florida boom as it reached its peak. By early 1926, national magazines predicted that the inflated values would diminish sharply and that it was a "virtual certainty that many thousands of persons who have invested their whole savings will be wiped out."[26] By summer of that year, *The Nation* announced that "the Florida boom has collapsed . . . uncountable numbers of Americans, who believe cards and gambling sinful, have staked their all in Florida's feverish game and lost."[27] As if to let the remaining hot air out of the land boom's balloon, a hurricane that September swept through Miami, killing 1,200 and leaving the town a shambles.[28] By October of 1926, Anson Hemingway was dead and the Florida land boom moribund.

Through it all, Clarence Hemingway let his bet ride. Unlike many speculators who bought on the margin, he bought his lots outright, allowing him to wait while the market recovered. His only mortgage payment was on his Oak Park property, which was worth more than he had borrowed. By the summer of 1928, there were cautious predictions that the Florida land market was on the edge of recovery.[29] If Clarence Hemingway kept up his tax payments in Florida and his mortgage payments in Oak Park until he sold the Oak Park house, he could pay off the mortgage and move to Florida with money in the bank. On paper, the plan was reasonable. Even the second Florida hurricane in September of 1928, which cut a hundred-mile-wide swath across Palm Beach, killing at least 1,250 people, did not really affect the Hemingway lots which were still valued at more than their purchase price.[30] Dr. Hemingway assured his son that he would soon be squeezing oranges right off his own tree.

What Clarence did not tell Ernest was that he now feared the Oak Park streets where no one could be trusted, that he had difficulty remembering his patient's names, that he had more heart pains than any one knew. In a locked drawer his bank book had not been balanced for several months; in his files a backlog of uncollected bills accumulated. Some days he was unable to see patients; other days he was unnaturally euphoric. Earlier, Sunny had written her brother that "Dad has given up the N.C. trip in favor of working here. He's rather hard pressed with real estate investments in Florida and thinks he can't get away. No one can argue with him."[31] Reality was gradually slipping from Clarence Hemingway's grasp, leaving him isolated and trapped by imagined fears and his financial muddle. Grace did not understand what was happening to her husband. For over twenty years she had watched his periods of depression grow progressively worse and steadily longer. Hoping that Ernest's visit would help her husband, she was on her best behavior not to irritate her son, which irritated him no end. The Doctor was not the only male in the family she did not understand.

Five days at home was about all Ernest could take of his mother's constant rapture over her new career in painting, although he had to admit that her canvasses – landscapes, rural scenes, and still lifes – were well executed. There was nothing wrong with his mother's technique, except that it was post-impressionist, not post-cubist.[32] With a forced show of enthusiasm, he agreed to try to place her canvasses with a gallery or a salon exhibit when he returned to Paris. She was, love her or not, seemingly unchanged all these years, still mystic, still running in high gear, still full of herself. She did not tell her son that her hair was beginning to fall out, which she concealed under the great mass of it. Dr. Ormsky wrote Clarence that it might be due to some disturbance in her basic metabolism; had he better information, he might have said it was worry over her husband. "Mrs. Hemingway," Ormsky said, somewhat understatedly, "is certainly an astonishing woman."[33] Her elder son might have added a few more adjectives, but would not have disagreed with "astonishing."

On Monday morning, Ernest repacked his bags, said his goodbyes, and left North Kenilworth for the last time but one. There were embarrassing tears in his father's eyes as they shook hands, and his mother gave him a hug. He watched them waving in the rear view mirror as he turned the corner. By noon he was relaxing with a drink in Bill Horne's hotel room at the Whitehall where Pauline's daily letter was waiting for him: "I'm so happy with you, so happy, happy, happy & you are so lovely and complete and satisfying and perfect. And how lovely it is to be in bed with you at night and read."[34] Because she could not join him for another seven days, he sent her Paul Rosenfeld's latest book and a Thomas Mann novel.[35] Wednesday morning, his father's letter arrived at the hotel, only a note, hoping to see him some more before Ernest headed east. It was signed "Love 'Dad'", but without qualifying initials, just "Dad" in quotes. Enclosed in the envelope was his father's only remembered attempt at verse:

I can't seem to think of a way
To say what I'd like most to say
To my very dear son
Whose book is just done,
Except give him my love and "HOORAY."[36]

Ernest put the letter away, uneasy with his father's emotion and unable to tell the Doctor that he was spending another week in Chicago before Pauline arrived. He had not even told them about her coming, for he did not want to go through that awkward family meeting or to explain why they were leaving the new baby in Piggott. Later he would feel guilty about his omission, but now it was merely relief he felt, glad to have done his duty without any real arguments.

On Tuesday, October 30, he and Pauline were kissing shamelessly on the platform at the Chicago station. They had barely enough time to finish shopping before going out to supper that evening with Bill Horne and his fiancee. On Thursday morning, before their train left for New York, Ernest and Pauline attended All Saints' Day mass at the Cathedral of the Holy Name. After the service, Father Fitzsimmons enlisted Ernest into the Arch-Confraternity for the Relief of the Souls in Purgatory. Signed and sealed, the document, which included the promise of a requiem High Mass, was a kind of spiritual insurance policy, bestowing plenary and partial indulgences on its members or on souls in purgatory of their choosing.[37]

About the time Ernest and Pauline walked out of the church in Chicago, Hadley was in London sitting at a writing desk in the Hotel Metropole where she was staying with Paul Mowrer. She was alone, she wrote, for Paul was at an official dinner where her presence would have been awkward. Bumby was in Paris with Marie where he enjoyed the moccasins Ernest had sent. She appreciated Ernest's $500 check, and, relenting, agreed to send Bumby to America in January if she could find someone to take him. The Mowrers now owned an "adorable place at Crecy-en-Brie" where she was to have her own room. She did not say that Winifred Mowrer also had a new room of her own in Paris that had nothing to do with Paul.[38] "I got thin and agile at Annecy," Hadley said, "and no longer wear a corset. Olga says my face is much more interesting with the bones showing."[39]

En Route Chicago: November 18, 1928

It was dark outside the train, dark and cold in the Pennsylvania hills and darker still in the far reaches of the Republic. Lights went quickly past their window as *The Spirit of St. Louis* rattled westward, carrying Ernest and Pauline, both exhausted and he hungover, back to Chicago where they would pick up their Ford for the long drive to Piggott and Key West. Their fortnight trip east was finally over: the MacLeishes in Conway, Perkins in New York, Mike Strater and Fitzgerald at Princeton. It had ended the night before in a drunken evening at the Fitzgerald home they called Ellerslie Mansion. As they waited for the porter's first call to dinner, Ernest wrote Scott a thank-you note:

We had a wonderful time – you were both grand – I am sorry I made a shall we say nuisance of myself about getting to the train on time – We were there far too early – when you were in the hands of the Cop I called on the phone from our platform and explained you were a great writer – the Cop was very nice – He said you said I was a great writer too but he had never heard of either of us. I told him rapidly the plots of some of your better known stories – He said – this is absolutely literal – "He seems like a Dandy Fellow."[40]

Ernest said nothing about Scott's four-years-and-still-unfinished novel, or Zelda's obsessive ballet practice to "The March of the Toy Soldiers."

In fact, there was a good deal better forgotten about the entire weekend. Three days afterwards, Mike Strater said that his head was only beginning to recover. "A bullfight is sedative in comparison. Next time we had better try Lower California instead of Delaware. And he [Scott] is such a nice guy when he is sober."[41]

After a week on the MacLeish farm in Conway, Massachusetts, which ended with Hoover's landslide victory over Al Smith for the presidency, the Hemingways had moved into the Brevoort Hotel in New York City. There were lunches with Max, dinners with Mike Strater, and business at Scribner's where Ernest discussed the magazine's offer to serialize his new novel. On 16 November, they picked up Mike Strater on their taxi ride to Madison Square Garden for the Friday night fights where they planned to meet Evan Shipman, but among the 19,000 boxing fans they never caught sight of each other. In the semis, Al Singer took out a local featherweight in the fifth round with a clean head shot, and Gorilla Jones from Akron got a tough decision over a kid named Silver. Later Shipman wrote that "the coon from Akron was the one I liked the best of the evening."[42]

The next afternoon, Strater and the Hemingways joined Scott Fitzgerald and 50,000 other chilled spectators to watch Princeton defeat Yale 12–2 in a football game that included six intercepted passes.[43] Scott, with his still romantic notion of Princeton football, was delighted, as was Strater, who graduated from Princeton and who was Scott's model for Burne Holliday in *This Side of Paradise*.[44] The four friends boarded the football special for Philadelphia sober and arrived with Scott drunk. The evening that followed at Ellerslie became more raucous as Scott tried to be the witty host while Zelda, in her tutu, stared a lot as the men got drunker. "It was great to have you both here," Fitzgerald wrote later, "even when I was intermittently unconscious."[45] Traveling westward in the dark, Hemingway may not have yet realized that the best days of his friendship with Scott were already behind him. They would see each other off and on for another few years, but never share the same camaraderie.

CROSS COUNTRY: EARLY DECEMBER 1928

Back in Key West, Hadley's letter arrived saying that Bumby's continuing coughs and grippe had become alarming. "Paul and I feel he must have a change of air." *Paul and I.* He read on. *Paul and I* had decided that Bumby needed the Key West sunshine, not the filthy weather of a Paris winter. Unless she heard otherwise from him, they were leaving November 28 on the *Ile de France*, arriving in New York on 4 December. With Hadley and his son already four days at sea, there was no way to delay the visit and barely time to make the two-day train trip back to New York. Much as he enjoyed traveling, the last eight months by ship, train, and car had left him sated: Paris to Key West to Piggott to Kansas City to Sheridan to Piggott to Chicago to New York to Chicago to Piggott to Key West. Now he had to face four more days on the train with Hadley in the middle of it. Having seen little of her since their divorce, he must have wondered how she would be now that she was *Paul and I.* He repacked his bags, enclosing the manuscript of his new novel, which he had not looked at for three months. Four boring days on the train would give him time to begin his revisions. Before leaving, Hemingway scribbled a quick note to his father saying that he would be in New York until 6 December.

He spent all day Sunday with Pauline putting their rented quarters in order. Lorine Thompson, in constant communication with Pauline, found them a two-story, furnished frame house at 1110 South Street, close to the beach and the Casa Marina Hotel.[46] With four bedrooms upstairs, there was room for Patrick and for Hemingway's sister, Sunny, who arrived at Ernest's expense to help type his manuscript. With Bumby's arrival, the bedrooms would be full and the spacious house suddenly crowded: a wife, two sons, a sister, a maid, and expenses to match: $30 a month plus taxes on the apartment in Paris, $125 a month for the Key West house, plus maid, food for six, car insurance, utilities, liquor, fishing, and visiting friends. The bills added up. It seemed impossible that only six years earlier he and Hadley, for $18 a month, moved into three rooms above the *bal musette* in Paris, where they knew no one and lived quite simply.

On Monday evening, December 3, Pauline kissed her husband goodbye at the Key West station where he boarded the Havana Special for its return trip to New York. Forty hours later, unsteady from the rocking of the rails, dislocated and hungry, Ernest arrived in the impersonal morning bustle of cold New York. For someone else's perfectly sound reasons, the dining car had disappeared from the train in Washington before dawn. He took a cab straight to the Brevoort Hotel and breakfast. At that same moment, Hadley and Bumby were debarking from the *Ile de France* at the West 15th Street dock while government agents boarded the ship, searching for and seizing 700 bottles of illegal liquor.[47] She and her son checked into the Earle Hotel just off Washington Square on Waverly Place. Unlike the Brevoort, which was French in manner and rather expensive, the inexpensive Earle was not to be found in the guidebooks. Hadley's budget was already devastated by the passage, for the *Ile de France* was the newest, most luxurious, and most expensive ship of the French Line. But on short notice and with so many Americans returning to the States for Christmas, Hadley was lucky to have booked the only space available.

With each having established a separate base camp, one on the edge of the Village and the other in fashionable midtown, Hadley and Ernest met that afternoon in a public place to make the exchange of Bumby. With seeming confidence, Hadley, sleeker and better dressed than Ernest remembered her, relayed Paris gossip and café news. He told her of his travels and the new book, but did not pry about Paul Mowrer. It was all too painful for words, smiling at each other while the small boy rattled on in his private Creole. Before their marriage, Hadley had asked, "Ernest, you don't have lots and lots of 'infatuations' do you? What could I do if you did? Course if you do I guess you can't help it."[48] Sitting there across the table from her now famous and former husband, she had learned the answer but forgotten the question.

Late Thursday morning, Ernest and his son were in Abercrombie and Fitch, Christmas shopping. Among other gifts, Ernest bought a harpoon gun which fascinated Bumby, a five-year-old whose precocious questions amused the clerks. Having been admired all his young life by famous and forgotten literati, godmothered by Gertrude Stein, raised by his Breton cook and nanny, and educated in the Paris cafés, Bumby was accustomed to being the center of someone's attention. As Ernest quickly rediscovered, the surveillance of his son, whom he had not seen for nine months, was a full-time job. But Ernest was a good companion on the New York streets, where the father and son reunion became a private adventure.

The morning was cold in New York but colder in Oak Park, where for two days now the temperature had not risen above freezing. On North Kenilworth, the Doctor woke early as usual, checked the furnace, ate a measured breakfast while complaining to Grace about pains in his foot, and then left for the hospital where he had patients to visit. In his coat pocket he carried the emergency medicine for his now more frequent attacks of angina, but he carried nothing to fend off the depression that once again enveloped him. The black mood often came like this in winter with the leaves down and the trees gaunt, and almost always it came after his brother Willoughby visited from China. Clarence forever regretted not going to China with Will as a medical missionary.

When the Doctor returned home for lunch, it was one o'clock in New York where the speculators were watching six billion dollars vanish as the bears caused a small crash in the market.[49] Ernest and his son, untouched by Wall Street's humors, were lunching in the French restaurant at the Brevoort where they had already checked out. They still had a little over two hours before the Havana Special was scheduled to leave Penn Station. By the time they finished lunch, the police had arrived at North Kenilworth, and by train time, the Oak Park neighborhood knew what had happened. At the station, Evan Shipman met them on the platform, helping load presents and baggage into Pullman car E-72 for the two-day return to Key West. "Were there any casualties?" he asked later. "And what did the people in the lowers [berths] say? I can see Bumby practicing with that Springfield harpoon on the porter."[50] As father and son boarded the train, a frantic telegram from Hemingway's mother was arriving at the Scribner offices, too late to catch Ernest before the train pulled out.[51]

Across the river and through the Jersey fens, the Special made quick stops at Newark and Trenton, picking up cold passengers to warm them on Florida beaches or in Havana bars. As the train left Trenton, the Pullman porter brought Ernest a ten-word telegram from his sister Carol which had been relayed up the line from Penn Station:

FATHER DIED THIS MORNING ARRANGE TO STOP HERE IF POSSIBLE [52]

His throat knotted up and he could not speak. At the window, Bumby chattered on about the grey and passing urban scene; strangers across from him were reading their papers. Others were settling into new found seats. *FATHER DIED*. Along the road bed, broken bottles, rusted iron, and stray paper flickered past. Into a far field, dark birds were descending out of a dull sky. *"Is dying hard, daddy?" "No, I think it's pretty easy, Nick. It all depends."* His fictional doctor said that to his son, and now the Doctor was dead. This was how he would remember it, the train's broken rhythm, his son looking out into December light and his father dead. He held back tears in that public place, trying to loosen his constricted throat. It all seemed to take a long time. When he looked up, the porter was still standing beside him in the aisle. To kill his hurt, he forced himself to think quite clearly, assessing possibilities, measuring distance against time. His train was only thirty minutes outside of Philadelphia, where he could connect to Chicago overnight. But Bumby? He could take Bumby with him, but he wanted to be there alone, unencumbered, free to cry if the tears came.

The porter, McIntyre, returned with train schedules and telegram forms, all Hemingway needed to work things out. When he finished the first set of telegrams, he explained it carefully to McIntyre. He was leaving Bumby to the black man's care, leaving money for the diner, leaving money for McIntyre to send these telegrams. He warned the porter about his son's strange language and how McIntyre must be sure that the boy did not get off the train before Key West where his mother awaited him. Then he tried to explain the situation to Bumby, who listened without fully understanding but without fear. He was accustomed to going places with those paid to care for him. Marie was always taking him somewhere when his parents disappeared, and now it was McIntyre, who wore a uniform and ran the train. Bumby was delighted.

Within fifteen minutes of having received Carol's telegram, Hemingway had absorbed its impact, brought his emotions under control, digested schedules, and arrived at a workable solution. Outside of Philadelphia, he sent his first wire to Max Perkins:

PLEASE WIRE $100 IMMEDIATELY WESTERN UNION NORTH PHILADELPHIA STATION. MY FATHER IS DEAD. MUST GET FIRST TRAIN TO CHICAGO.[53]

When the Havana Special stopped at the North Philadelphia station, Ernest hugged Bumby goodbye and waited on the platform until the train pulled out, his son waving at the window. It was 5.15 p.m. and the light was failing outside. It was like the war, a cold station with unknown people going in different directions, the clock running, a destination to be reached. He had less than three hours to exchange his ticket and find cash to supplement the $40 in his pocket.[54] The first thing was to persuade the Penn Railroad to refund his ticket for a berth on the 8.00 p.m. overnight to Chicago, the same train he and Pauline had taken to Chicago less than three weeks earlier; then he wired Oak Park his arrival time the following evening and called Pauline collect, explaining the situation, and asking her to contact Hadley in New York.

Still needing money and knowing that his telegram had probably missed Perkins, Hemingway phoned Strater in New York, but Mike was out. He left a message, hung up, and dialed Fitzgerald's number in Delaware.[55] Scott responded immediately, and the money arrived at the station's Western Union office in time for Ernest, minutes before boarding his train, to send Max another telegram:

DISREGARD WIRE GOT MONEY FROM SCOTT[56]

All that remained now was the long and lonely journey into the heart of the country where his father's body waited for him. As the night train pulled out of the Philadelphia station, morticians in Oak Park were making final repairs to Clarence Hemingway.

OAK PARK: DECEMBER 7–16, 1928

When they met him at the Chicago station, his first question was how did his father die, but the answer was lost in hissing steam and platform clatter, hard to hear and hard to understand. They had to say it twice: *he killed himself.* Ernest had thought so often about his own suicide, threatened it at dark moments, imagined it fully, but never his father's. Nick asked his father why the Indian killed himself? *I don't know, Nick. He couldn't stand things, I guess.* Clarence Hemingway, despondent, sat down on his marriage bed, fitted grandfather's Civil War pistol to his right temple and pulled the trigger.[57] In the night traffic, the drive to Oak Park took place in time suspended. They stopped on Lake Street at Drechsler's funeral home where his father's body lay in its coffin; pancake make-up obscured the dark bruising left by the gunshot. Ernest had to look closely to find the patched wound, for the small bullet from his grandfather's pistol had entered with surgical neatness. *Couldn't stand things, I guess.* Clarence Hemingway did not look peaceful, or sad, or sleeping. With lightly powdered cheeks somewhat sunken, hair well brushed to cover the balding frontal lobe, the body in the coffin was almost a stranger. His father was somewhere else.

Uncle George Hemingway explained again what it was that Clarence could not stand. Earlier that Saturday afternoon, he first told the coroner's jury that it was the Doctor's worry over his diabetes and angina that pulled the trigger. Knowing that he was a "hopeless case," Clarence had taken the quick way out. His mental condition, George

Hemingway said, had been sound and his financial affairs were "in good condition." Neither statement was true, as George well knew, but he was not going to have his brother going down as a mental case, nor did he want Clarence's financial problems discussed in public. It would be bad if Oak Park thought there was insanity in the family, and worse for George's real estate business if anyone knew he had denied Clarence financial help when he most needed it. So George said nothing about his brother's periodic depressions or about his shaky investments in the Florida land market.[58]

When they arrived at North Kenilworth, Grace was in bed, sedated, and all the children but Madelaine were gathered in the front room awaiting Ernest's homecoming. His mother began to cry as soon as he walked into her room; unable to speak of Clarence, she was worried about Sunny in Key West getting the letter Grace had written in near hysteria. Passing the closed door to his father's bedroom, Ernest went downstairs to send the telegram to his sister:

DISREGARD FIRST LETTER. MOTHER SAYS CHEERFUL ONE SENT TONIGHT. EVERYONE FINE REALLY. ALL SEND LOVE. DUKE ALSO. FUNERAL TOMORROW. PLAN-NING LEAVE SATURDAY NIGHT. LOVE ERNIE.[59]

He sent a second telegram to McIntyre, instructing him to wire collect if Bumby was safe, and a third telegram to Pauline. Then the five children, sitting around the fireplace, tried to understand their loss: young Les, who opened the door on his bleeding father; the girls, who, never understanding the Doctor's "nervousness," long resented his dark moods; and Ernest, who could have made the hunting trip to the Smokies but did not, and now never would.

Adding to the tension was the conflict between Ernest and his older sister Marcelline, who had taken charge of the crisis before her brother's arrival. Ernest made it quite clear that he was now head of the family and would make all necessary decisions. Deeply shaken by their father's suicide, neither Ernest nor Marcelline was completely rational, and both, without fully understanding it, harbored many of the Doctor's problems. Marcelline's own "nervous condition" had prostrated her the summer of 1921, while Ernest's cycle of black moods and ecstatic highs was becoming more apparent to him. Afterwards Marcelline tried to put the best public face possible on the situation, calling Ernest a "great comfort to Mother and all of us."[60] Leicester remembered Ernest telling him they should be praying for their father's soul in purgatory and saying, "I'm going to give Marcelline a piece of my mind, first chance I get."[61] Years later, Marcelline complained to her mother bitterly about Ernest's treatment of her at the funeral, particularly when he said that their father's soul, as a suicide, was condemned to everlasting hellfire.

The next morning, the hearse from Drechsler's delivered the body to Grace's music room where friends and neighbors stopped by to pay respects. Ernest announced that he was having a Mass said for the repose of Clarence's soul, using the benefit of the Arch-Confraternity he joined a month earlier. At that time, he knew no souls in purgatory to remember, and now his father was dead. After Ernest led the family in the Lord's Prayer, they removed the casket for the two o'clock funeral service to the First Congregational Church where Clarence was a deacon. Afterwards, in bitter cold, they buried him in Forest Home Cemetery where his mother and father, Anson and Adelaide, lay close by.[62]

After the funeral, Ernest opened the Doctor's locked drawers to find an unbalanced check-book, uncollected bills due him and his own bills past due, unpaid back taxes on the Florida property, and one insurance policy depleted to buy land. Ernest, who once resented his father's insistence on keeping accurate financial accounts, could not believe that Clarence had left his affairs in such disorder. Gone were his meager savings, including the small inheritance from Anson Hemingway. Now his father's problems were his own. Soon after the funeral, he sent Marcelline home, put Leicester on a raw meat diet to improve his frail health, and generally took charge as he wished his father had done.[63]

Nothing removed Ernest's own sense of having failed his father. To his younger brother, Hemingway said that when their father wrote him asking for financial help, he had sent a check which Clarence received the morning of his death. Ernest found the letter, unopened, where the Doctor placed it on his bedside table. If the Doctor had only opened the letter, he might not have pulled the trigger.[64] But there was little truth in the story. If Clarence wrote such a request, it is the only letter from his father Ernest did not save. On the Doctor's table there was, in fact, a letter from Ernest, the one giving his schedule in New York. After Grace sent the first telegram to Scribner's, Carol found and opened her brother's letter, realizing that Ernest was already on the train bound for Key West. The information it contained allowed her to send the second telegram which reached him outside of Trenton. Carol said nothing, then or later, about any check enclosed in the letter which has also disappeared. If his father had only asked, Ernest would have given him the money. *"Is dying hard, Daddy?" "No, I think it's pretty easy, Nick. It all depends."*

But what killed Clarence Hemingway was not unpaid bills or lack of money; they were only pieces of paper, numbers on a bank statement, the visible residue. None of the children, least of all Ernest, was ready to admit that long-standing and deadly genetic problems were the invisible cause of their father's death. Moody depression and creeping paranoia killed the Doctor, along with insomnia, hypertension, and diabetes. At fifty-seven his life slipped through his fingers like beads of mercury, a thing which he no longer had the will to control. He left no explanatory note except the one that would appear and reappear in his children's medical records. However, no explanation Clarence could have left his son would have eased the pain and anger Ernest felt at losing his father to what seemed a coward's death. It was a loss for all time, never far beneath the surface of his mind. Three years later he would say in a note, "To commit suicide except as a means of ending unbearable pain may be compared to cheating at solitaire, but a man making such a comparison is a confident fool."[65]

After the funeral Grace stayed on her feet, determined to face down the local stigma of her husband's suicide, while Ernest worked out the economics of her widowhood. Her only assets were two cottages on Walloon Lake, several Florida lots, the mortgaged Oak Park house, and a $25,000 insurance policy.[66] Grace's once sizable inheritance from her father had been gradually depleted over the years, leaving her now sorely dependent upon the kindness of her children, and Ernest, taking on the authority of his fallen father, was not about to suffer what he always saw as her domineering attitude. He insisted she sell the North Kenilworth house, which had been on the market for some time, and move into smaller quarters. Uncle George and Marcelline's husband, Sterling Sanford, would invest the insurance policy, the income on which would be supplemented by boarders and music students. Ernest also set up reasonable tasks for his mother to complete, principally collecting unpaid bills. For the first time in his life, his mother deferred to his judgement, and in his father's house Ernest was now the "Papa."

Every day, in the room used by his father for an office, Ernest worked on his war novel, going over the penciled pages eliminating dross. There were transitions to improve, sentences to clarify, and names to make regular. He inserted new chapter breaks and began to number the chapters for the first time. By Wednesday, December 12, he had revised as far as the night battle at Plava, stopping just before Frederic Henry was blown up.[67] The next day, having finished with his father's business, Hemingway spent all morning and part of the afternoon deep in his fiction, worrying over the wounding and rebirth of his ambulance driver. In the first draft the blast was like a furnace door opening, white hot and wind rushing, and Frederic, unable to breathe, felt his soul leave his body, going out and out before sliding slowly back as if riding a thin wire.[68] That was all Ernest knew about near-death experience, the soul sliding out and then returning. Eliminating the thin wire and other excesses, Hemingway made a fair copy of the heavily revised passage. By the end of his working day, he had moved Frederic from the field hospital near Gorizia back to Milan, where he stopped just as Catherine Barkley was entering the room. In the margin, he reassured himself, "going better so far." In his dead father's house that was once home, he kept a piece of himself detached and living in his fiction.

Friday morning, December 14, as Hadley was boarding the *Berengaria* to return to Europe, Ernest reunited Frederic and Catherine, revising that radiant moment of their first sexual encounter so heavily that it required recopying to be legible. In the garden at Gorizia, where Catherine was a little crazy from losing her fiance at the Somme, Frederic was playing a game, taking whatever she would give him.

"You did say you loved me, didn't you?"
"Yes," I lied.

Now the first time she saw him wounded, she was in bed with him, withholding nothing, and he was in love with her. Frederic tried lamely to explain what he could not understand, and the more he talked the worse it got. Ernest cut all the explanations to have Frederic say: "When I saw her I was in love with her. Everything turned over inside of me." By day's end he had revised one hundred and forty pages, eliminating nine and adding six, telling himself on MS-344, "can almost type it as it stands."

Saturday morning he prowled the familiar rooms, looking for something he could not name – not his old books or his father's stuffed loon, not his old camping gear – something hard and imperishable that he could not find. Finally he told his mother that all he wanted was his grandfather's pistol still at the Coroner's office. She promised to retrieve

213

it for him.[69] That afternoon he carefully repacked his manuscript in the suitcase, ate an early supper, and waited for Uncle George to drive him to the Chicago station. Having come home for the last time, Ernest Hemingway was finally leaving Oak Park. *Couldn't stand things, I guess.*

KEY WEST: DECEMBER 1928

Having lost his own father the previous year, Archie told Ernest:

I know how the death of your father changes him in your mind and he becomes what he was when you were very young and your heart is destroyed with tenderness for him. No one can talk to you then. You are walking in your own boyhood and everyone is very far away. But there is one thing I am going to say to you ... You must not let your mind work over and over the way it happened. I know how your mind works round and round your pain like a dog going over and over the same track and what a torment it is to you. But now you must not. It is too serious. The consequences to you too grave.[70]

It was sensible advice but hard for Hemingway to follow. To Dos Passos he wrote that "every other day we shoot snipe for the day after. My old man shot himself on the other hand (not in the other hand, in the head) as you may have read in the paper."[71] Count on it: fathers fail their sons. Depend on it: sons forgive neither their dead fathers nor themselves.

When Hemingway returned to the manuscript passage where Frederic's driver is shot by the Italian rear-guard, he made a fair copy of the revised page, including Aymo's death.

We pulled him down on the other side and turned him over. "His head ought to be up hill," I said. Piani moved him around. He lay in the mud on the side of the embankment, his feet pointing down hill, breathing blood irregularly. The three of us squatted over him in the rain. He was hit low in the back of the neck and the bullet had ranged upward and come out under the right eye. He died while I was stopping up the two holes. Piani laid his head down, wiped his face with a piece of the emergency dressing, then let it alone.

"The cocksuckers," he said.[72]

There were only two added sentences and a few changed words on the page; it did not need recopying, but he did it anyway, for it was not only the driver's head wound he was trying to staunch.

By 8 January, Pauline and Sunny had typed out the first twenty chapters; two days later the count was twenty-nine. With the conclusion in sight, Ernest began inviting the "Mob" down for winter fishing. MacLeish, hard pressed for cash, begged off, but Waldo Peirce, Dos Passos, Mike Strater, and Katy Smith were all due to appear. Hemingway told Perkins to pack his old clothes and tennis shoes and come down to fish, for it was the only way he was going to get the manuscript.[73] On 14 January, he wrote Guy Hickok that he was "on chapter 34 and working like a bastard to get it (the book) done by the end of January."[74] Eight days later the typescript was complete.[75]

The next day, a telegram from Perkins arrived:

FOX FILM CONSIDERING KILLERS FOR TWO REEL MOVIE TONE STOP MIGHT GET $2,500 MORE LIKELY $2,000 STOP WIRE DECISION STOP EXPECT TO SEE YOU BY MIDDLE OF NEXT WEEK STOP[76]

Ernest's reply was immediate:

TAKE WHATEVER CAN GET STOP FINISHED BOOK YESTERDAY SPLENDID TO SEE YOU HEMINGWAY[77]

As it turned out, he needed the money to cover his mother's expenses. Unable to find the Doctor's account books to collect from patients, she now faced back taxes on the sixteen Florida lots and two quarterly installments on the house mortgage. Ernest told her that it was a bad time to sell the land. He would pay the outstanding taxes and also supplement her income with one hundred dollars of his own money each month.[78]

Grace was relieved and deeply touched by her son's offer. Eight years earlier, when she evicted him from the family's summer cottage, she had compared their relationship to a bank account on which he was overdrawn. In some detail she pointed out how he might repair his credit rating with deposits such as other sons regularly made, like showing some "interest in Mother's ideas and affairs . . . praise her cooking, back up her little schemes . . . a surreptitious paying of bills, just to get them off Mother's mind."[79] Between mother and son, that long-saved letter remained always an unspoken and unforgiven act. Ernest never referred to it; neither did Grace. References were unnecessary. "Surely God will bless," his mother now told him, "when you have such a generous heart. You will never know what a relief it was to my poor worried head . . . to receive your letter yesterday. Why Ernest! it's like being reprieved when you expected to hang." Now she could afford to restore Carol's allowance, renew some magazine subscriptions, attend a church dinner, and treat herself to "a shoe shine and a soda" once in a while.

His gift had lifted her out of poverty, than which there was no deeper disgrace in Oak Park. The Doctor's insurance policy had paid off $21,000 and "there was one thousand all together in his 2 checking accounts and mine," she reported. "I have bought with Sterling's and the bank's advice 12 one thousand dollar bonds . . . the other 10 thousand I invested in 2–5 thousand [dollar] real estate mortgages @ 6 percent." The investments would provide $110 a month, supplemented erratically by fees from music and painting lessons as well as an occasional sale of a painting. Her son's beneficence had doubled her monthly income. With Marcelline's husband, Sterling Sanford, committed to paying the mortgage for the year, Grace could once more hold her head high at the meetings of the Nineteenth Century Club. Meanwhile she had twice been to the Coroner's office before finally securing the release of the suicide pistol, which she now held awaiting Ernest's instructions. "Do you want me to send it down to you," she asked. "Les wants you to leave it to him when you are through with it, but you have first choice. . . . We're thrilled about your success with the new book. Has it a name – or had we best not know till others do?"[80]

After considering a long list of titles, Ernest had, in fact, finally named the book which was begun in Paris, finished in Wyoming, revised in Oak Park, and typed in Key West, a book obliquely encompassing much of his life. In it, he gave his war wounding, his nurse, and all of Italy to Frederic Henry; to Catherine he gave Pauline's hard labor and her operation. From his life with Hadley, he took their good times at Chamby when the roads were iron hard and they deeply in love. Catherine sounded a lot like Pauline, who had made Ernest her religion, risking her soul on the promise of his love. From maps and books and hard listening, he made up the war he never saw, described terrain he never walked, and had written an historic retreat so accurately that his Italian readers would later say he was present at Caporetto. He was there, not as anyone supposed, but there saying goodbye to a part of his life about which he could never write quite like this again. He called the book *A Farewell to Arms.*

ENVOI

APRIL 5, 1929

In the late afternoon off Havana harbor, the *Yorck* noses into the Gulf Stream's purple-blue water as she heads east toward Europe. Noisy gulls hover in her wake while passengers hang on the railings, watching the island gradually diminish. Ernest, in his double-breasted grey suit with matching fedora, is standing awkwardly with one foot on the wooden deck, his other cocked against the forward hatch to balance Patrick on his knee. Small and fat, Patrick stares intently at his parents, who are both smiling. Pauline's black pumps balance her black cloche hat; her left hand holds her light coat closed. A bright sun casts dark shadows.[1] Behind the camera with Madelaine, Bumby is looking somewhere else.

The Hemingways are returning Bumby to Hadley and themselves to Paris, their plans amorphous. His father buried and his novel finished, Ernest is in two minds about their future. In Key West, they have stored a few belongings against possible return; in Paris, where 25,000 Americans are now permanent residents, Guy Hickok has paid up the taxes on their rue Férou apartment.[2] In the *Yorck's* cargo another new car, a gift from Uncle Gus, crosses with them.[3] In New York, the first installment of *A Farewell to Arms* is ready to appear in the May issue of *Scribner's Magazine*, which finally put up $16,000 for the serial rights. "AWFULLY PLEASED PRICE OK," Ernest wired,[4] but when he saw in the first galleys how the editor was rewriting his fiction, he was furious. "I'd rather return the money and call it all off," he told Max, "than have arbitrary eliminations made without any mention of the fact that they are being made. If that's to be done let someone else sign it."[5]

On Broadway, the Marx Brothers are closing in *Animal Crackers*, and Eddy Cantor is opening with *Whoopee!* Hoover has replaced "Silent" Cal Coolidge in the White House, where the business of the government remains Business. If prosperity continues at its present level, Hoover is cautiously suggesting tax cuts in 1930. The stock market, after a rocky few days, has righted itself. US Steel is down ten points, Eastman Kodak down fifteen, selling out some of the little players and giving the manipulators room to operate. Most brokers concede that stocks were overvalued, but as the analyst for the *New York Times* said, "It is to nobody's interest that the speculative bubble burst in such a manner as to spread disaster all around." That afternoon, Babe Ruth hit his first home run of the spring preseason, and the impeachment trial of Huey Long began in Louisiana. (Yes, he bought legislators' votes, but he never lied about doing so.) Elsewhere, revolutionists are dying in China and Mexico; textile workers are striking in North Carolina and Tennessee. At the news stands, readers of *Liberty* magazine await a new serial, *The Red Napoleon*, whose communist villain, believing "the supremacy of the white race must be ended, . . . invades America to kill the white men and capture the white women."[6] It is the last year of the Twenties, and its signs are mixed.

In the Illinois cemetery where spring grass is rising green, his father lies beneath a simple stone:

Clarence Edmonds Hemingway M.D.

1871   1928

John 15, 13

The Doctor's $300 funeral bill was paid by Sterling and Uncle George, as Ernest thought only fitting. Marcelline and Sterling were rich, he told his mother, "and have always been great friends of the family while I live by my pen and have been more or less an outcast." It was Uncle George's problem to see the house sold, or cancel the mortgage himself, for he had "done more than anyone to kill Dad and he had better do something in reparation . . . or I will have his hide." Ernest had never written about the family, but "with the death of the ones I love a period has been put to a great part of it and I may have to undertake it," he threatened.[7]

In five years he had written five books, three of them to become American classics. His short story, "The Killers," was being taught in college classrooms as a modern masterpiece, and Hemingway imitations were appearing in slick magazines. He had come home to renew himself, having lived too long, he thought, in Europe. Within the space of a year, he had traveled twelve thousand miles, finished his novel, met his in-laws, had his wife's womb cut open to bear his son, and finally stood over his father's grave. On the road again, he now traveled much heavier than ever before, more baggage and more responsibilities: a wife and an ex-wife, two sons, and a dependent mother. The heaviest piece of his newly acquired baggage was his dead father whom he loved and lost as a boy, and who now was with him forever. Turning back toward Europe, he was a native son in transit, unsure if he was merely visiting or returning for another decade. Oak Park was behind him, never again to see his face; the family cottage at Walloon was a haunted house. Had any one asked, he, who once knew the answer by heart, could not have said for certain which way led toward home.

NOTES

LIBRARIES

JFK   = Hemingway Collection, John F. Kennedy Library, Boston, Mass.

Lilly   = Lilly Library, University of Indiana

PUL   = Firestone Library, Princeton University

UTex   = Humanities Research Center, University of Texas

UVa   = Alderman Library, University of Virginia

YUL   = Beinecke Library, Yale University

HEMINGWAY TEXTS

TOS   = *The Torrents of Spring* (New York: Scribner's, 1926).

SAR   = *The Sun Also Rises* (New York: Scribner's, 1926).

AFTA   = *A Farewell to Arms* (New York: Scribner's, 1929).

AMF   = *A Moveable Feast* (New York: Scribner's, 1964).

88P   = *88 Poems*, ed. Nicholas Gerogiannis (New York: Harcourt/Bruccoli Clark, 1979).

SL   = Carlos Baker (ed.), *Ernest Hemingway Selected Letters* (New York: Scribner's, 1981).

CSS   = *The Complete Short Stories of Ernest Hemingway* (New York: Scribner's 1987).

221

OTHER FREQUENTLY CITED TEXTS

Baker = Carlos Baker, *Ernest Hemingway, A Life Story* (New York: Scribner's, 1969).

Brian = Denis Brian, *The True Gen* (New York: Grove Press, 1988).

Bruccoli (1) = Matthew J. Bruccoli, *Scott and Ernest* (New York: Random House, 1978).

Bruccoli (2) = Matthew J. Bruccoli, *Some Sort of Epic Grandeur* (New York: Harcourt Brace, 1981).

Bruccoli and Duggan = Matthew J. Bruccoli and Margaret Duggan (eds), *Correspondence of F. Scott Fitzgerald* (New York: Random House, 1980).

Donnelly = Honoraria Murphy Donnelly, *Sara & Gerald* (New York: Times Books, 1982).

Drabeck and Ellis = Bernard Drabeck and Helen Ellis (eds), *Archibald MacLeish, Reflections* (Amherst: University of Massachusetts Press, 1986).

Hannemann = Audre Hannemann, *Ernest Hemingway, A Comprehensive Bibliography* (Princeton: Princeton University Press, 1967).

Kert = Bernice Kert, *The Hemingway Women* (New York: Norton, 1983).

Lynn = Kenneth S. Lynn, *Hemingway* (New York: Simon & Schuster, 1987).

Mellow = James Mellow, *Invented Lives* (Boston: Houghton Mifflin, 1984).

Meyers = Jeffrey Meyers, *Hemingway* (New York: Harper & Row, 1985).

Miller = Linda P. Miller, *Letters From the Lost Generation* (Rutgers University Press, 1991).

Smith = Paul Smith, *A Reader's Guide to the Short Stories of Ernest Hemingway* (Boston: G. K. Hall, 1989).

Turnbull = Andrew Turnbull (ed.), *The Letters of F. Scott Fitzgerald* (New York: Scribner's, 1963).

Winnick = R. H. Winnick (ed.), *Letters of Archibald MacLeish* (Boston: Houghton Mifflin, 1983).

Young Hemingway = Michael Reynolds, *The Young Hemingway* (Oxford: Blackwell, 1986).

Paris Years = Michael Reynolds, *Hemingway: The Paris Years* (Oxford: Blackwell, 1989).

NOW AND THEN

1. Brian, p. 52.
2. Ibid., pp. 52–3.
3. Kathleen Cannell–Bernard Saranson, private collection.
4. Brian, p. 49.
5. Donnelly, p. 165.
6. Gerald Murphy–Sara Murphy, Sept. 4–9, 1937, Miller, pp. 199–200.
7. Brian, p. 54.

Chapter One: THEN

1. Hemingway notebook, JFK, dated 6 March 1926. Entry goes on to say that it was reading about the death of Litri (a bullfighter) and the suicide of P. L. Storm that made him think about death.
2. "Preludes to a Mood," *New York Times Book Review*, Oct. 18, 1925, p. 8.
3. "Good Prose," *The Nation*, 122 (Feb. 10, 1926), p. 162.
4. Turnbull, pp. 195–6. Turnbull dates the letter ca. Dec. 30, 1925. However, Hemingway did not write Fitzgerald about the Liveright refusal until Jan. 1, 1926, which probably dates the Fitzgerald letter contemporary with his wire of Jan. 8, 1926 to Perkins. See Bruccoli and Duggan, p. 187.
5. *SL*, p. 195.
6. Item 200, JFK. Although this typescript is by a professional typist, it has no Hemingway changes on the opening paragraph, and it is the same text that appeared in galleys from Scribner's and which Hemingway later cut. The original Hemingway typescript for the opening chapters is probably the typescript now at UVa.
7. Item 195, JFK. A fairly late draft that has the names correct as they appear in the final typescript.
8. Pauline Pfeiffer's lending library card at Shakespeare and Co., Firestone Library, Sylvia Beach Collection, PUL.
9. *Mrs. Dalloway* (New York: Harcourt, Brace (Harvest Book), 1925, 1953), p. 140.

10. Ibid., p. 39.
11. Kert, pp. 171–2. Fishing licenses at Pamplona in 1927 list Pauline at five feet and four inches, Hemingway at six feet: JFK.
12. Brian, p. 71.
13. Paris edition of the Chicago *Tribune* (hereafter *Tribune*), Mar. 4–11, 1926. Their Paris rent, no more than 700 francs a month, was about $300 for the year. After their divorce Hadley and their child, Bumby, were able to live the next seven years on Hadley's trust fund and the income from *The Sun Also Rises*.
14. Undated letter from A. G. Pfeiffer to Pauline Pfeiffer, JFK. On Jan. 16, 1926, Gus wrote the Farmer's Loan and Trust Company a letter referring to the establishment of this trust on Jan. 2, 1926. This letter is also at the JFK. Pauline refers to her "new trust fund" in a letter to Hadley (Feb. 4, 1926) written immediately after Hemingway's departure for New York. By Feb. 1, 1926, Hemingway was registered at the Hôtel Vénétia on Montparnasse.
15. Harold Loeb last said this in Brian, p. 71.
16. Kert, p. 172.
17. EH–Bill Smith, 2 Jan. 1926, private collection.
18. Dos Passos–HH, undated but written in late Feb., JFK.
19. Gerald Murphy–HH, Mar. 3, 1926, Miller, p. 15.
20. EH–Max Perkins, Mar. 10, 1926, *SL*, p. 197.
21. The register at Hotel Rössle, Gaschurn, shows that the Hemingways, the Murphys, and John Dos Passos stayed at the inn between March 12 and 17. The register and the family ownership of the Rössle is continuous from 1801.
22. Pauline Pfeiffer–EH [8 March 1926], JFK.
23. See Rössle bill for rooms 9, 12, and 15, JFK.
24. Donnelly, pp. 21–2; Hemingway's later famous phrase, "grace under pressure," may well have originated at Gaschurn. A month later, trying to explain the difference between "guts" and courage, he used the phrase in a letter to Scott Fitzgerald: EH–F. Scott Fitzgerald, ca. April 20, 1926, *SL*, p. 200. Murphy remembers that Sara and Hadley went to Bludenz while the men were at Madlener Haus; the Rössle room bill, however, shows that there were two people eating at the Rössle while the men were away.
25. See Feb. 1926 postcards from Dos Passos to Hemingway, JFK; and see Townsend Ludington, *John Dos Passos* (New York: E. P. Dutton, 1980), pp. 242–3.
26. *AMF*, p. 209.

27. *SAR*, p. 114.
28. Pauline Pfeiffer's lending library card, Sylvia Beach Collection, PUL.
29. Pauline Pfeiffer–EH and HH, Mar. 16, 1926, JFK. Dos Passos was Portugese, not Spanish.
30. *Mrs. Dalloway*, p. 237.

Chapter Two: SUN AND SHADOWS

1. "Latin Quarter Notes," *Tribune*, Mar. 31, 1926. The Hôtel Vénétia is a supposition, but it is where Hemingway stayed in February on his way to New York.
2. Max Perkins–EH, Mar. 15, 1926, Scribner author files, PUL.
3. *TOS*, p. 20.
4. EH–Max Perkins, 1 April 1926, *SL*, p. 198.
5. *SAR* MS, Item 194, Notebook I, p. 8, JFK.
6. *SAR*, p. 115, now says only Henry, but it was Henry James in the typescript Hemingway sent to Scribner's.
7. Item 194, Notebook III, p. 51, JFK.
8. *SAR*, p. 20.
9. *Tribune*, Apr. 12, 1926; EH–F. Scott Fitzgerald, ca. Apr. 20, 1926, *SL*, p. 199; EH–Herbert Gorman, Easter 1926, JFK.
10. *Tribune*, Apr. 7, 1926; see Meyers, Lynn, and *The Paris Years* on the feud with Mencken. Later reprints of the book did not carry the dedication.
11. *SAR*, p. 236.
12. See incoming letters from Jean Watson of Curtis Brown to EH, Apr. 7, 13, 17, 1926, JFK. On Jul. 31, according to EH note on envelope, he made Edgar Mowrer his German agent. Mowrer was a well-known foreign correspondent and the brother of Paul Mowrer, whom Hadley later married.
13. Basil Woon, *The Paris That's Not in the Guide Books* (New York: Brentano's, 1926), pp. 263–9; see also *Tribune*, April 1926, for information on tourist arrivals. During the week of the bike races, eleven ocean liners full of tourists arrived from New York; on Apr. 24, eight liners left New York within a twenty-four-hour period.
14. EH–F. Scott Fitzgerald, ca. Apr. 20, 1926, *SL*, p. 199.
15. Ibid.; *Tribune*, Apr. 20, 1926; guest book, Sylvia Beach Collection, PUL.

16. Fitzgerald was making more money than Hemingway would see for another three years. In 1925 his income was $18,333; in 1926, it was $25,686. See Fitzgerald ledger reprinted in Matthew J. Bruccoli (2), appendix 2, pp. 532–3. EH–Max Perkins, Apr. 24, 1926, *SL*, p. 202. What Hemingway did not tell Max was that Fitzgerald had also enclosed a $100 check in that letter. See Baker files, PUL.
17. EH–F. Scott Fitzgerald, Apr. 20, 1926, *SL*, pp. 200–1. Sophie Irene Loeb was an internationally known social worker famous for her ideas on child welfare and child care.
18. EH–Max Perkins, Apr. 24, 1926, *SL*, pp. 201–2.
19. EH–Max Perkins, Apr. 24, 1926, *SL*, p. 202.
20. See Hanneman, p. 12.
21. Perkins was right to hedge his bet; the first edition of *TOS* did not sell out until July of 1928. Hemingway's contract called for 15 percent royalties; given that at least 90 copies of *SAR* were sent out to reviewers, the remaining 5,000 copies at their market price of $2.00 a copy would have earned Hemingway exactly $1,500.
22. Item 200, JFK, is the composite typescript for the novel, the first 122 pages of which are by the hired typist.
23. See A. Scott Berg, *Max Perkins, Editor of Genius* (New York: E. P. Dutton, 1978), pp. 94–6.
24. Max Perkins–EH, May 18, 1926, JFK.

Chapter Three: SUMMER'S LEASE

1. *The Common Reader* (New York: Harcourt Brace, 1925, 1953), pp. 92–3. Pauline Pfeiffer's checkout card, Sylvia Beach Collection, PUL; on March 16, Pauline checked out *The Common Reader*, returning it on April 20; on April 26 she checked out *Moll Flanders*, returning it on July 26.
2. See EH–F. Scott Fitzgerald, 4 May 1926, *SL*, p. 203: "In Spain of course I can't talk at all – am in for 3 mos. of listening and reading the papers." By 1926, Hemingway had spent a little over three months in Spain since the summer of 1923. His command of Spanish was good enough to do what he wanted to do in the country, but it was not good enough to hold meaningful conversations with native speakers. In his May 15, 1926 letter to Fitzgerald (*SL*, p. 204) he said, "I don't want to look up my Spanish friends because then I'll have to be talking Spanish, if I can talk Spanish."

Letter is misdated as ca. May 20, but internal evidence indicates May 15.

3. EH kept bullfight programs for May 17 and May 23, 1926. See *El Sol* (Madrid newspaper) May 14–28, 1926, and letter to Fitzgerald, May 15, 1926. See also his own somewhat fictionalized version of these two weeks in "The Art of the Short Story," *Paris Review*, 79 (1981), pp. 85–102.

4. *CSS*, p. 273. Later he said that he wrote this story/play in the afternoon, but the manuscript of "The Killers" is dated as having been written between "2:15 and 8 p.m." on the same day. See Smith, for the most cogent discussion of this issue.

5. See Items 535 and 536, JFK.

6. In first draft the name is Dominick Nerone; it became Ole Andreson in holograph revision. The Nerone name came from an early Chicago friend of Hemingway's from 1921: see *Young Hemingway*. Item 536 is typed through the first ten pages and then goes to holograph for another nine pages which are numbered 1–9. This holograph ending is tagged "add the Killers." The typed draft is called "The Matadors" with that title crossed out and "The Killers" added in holograph.

7. George Plimpton (ed.), *Writers at Work: The Paris Review Interviews*, 2nd series (New York: Penguin Books, 1977), p. 232. Here and elsewhere Hemingway claims he began and finished the story on May 16, 1926. The early version of the story, however, differs from the final version only in the last three typed pages.

8. Item 202-C, JFK, dated Sept. 25, 1925, Chartres.

9. Item 728, JFK.

10. Other titles for this story were "A Broken Heart" and "After the Fourth." With any of the short stories, the reader should always refer to Smith as the most reliable source on manuscripts and other matters. See also Smith's "The Tenth Indian and the Thing Left Out," in James Nagel (ed.), *Ernest Hemingway: The Writer in Context* (Madison: University of Wisconsin Press, 1984), pp. 53–74, and Robert E. Fleming, "Hemingway's Dr. Adams – Saint or Sinner!" *Arizona Quarterly*, 39 (Summer 1983), 101–10.

11. Hadley Mowrer interview with Carlos Baker, 1962, Baker files, PUL. Thanks to Bernice Kert for loaning her copy. This trip, given the terrible April–May weather, could have taken place only during the first week of April or the first week of May. May is the more likely of the two.

12. Sylvia Beach Collection, PUL. Books checked out on May 5 and 14, returned Sept. 13.
13. Hadley Mowrer interview, Baker files, PUL.
14. See *Young Hemingway* and *Paris Years* on this point. Hemingway's fears were not peculiar or exaggerated. The 1917–18 epidemic of Spanish flu killed more Americans than World War I.
15. Assuming that Hadley would arrive on May 14, Murphy bought her a swimming ticket for the Antibes beach. Hadley arrived on May 16.
16. EH–F. Scott Fitzgerald, May 15, 1926, *SL*, pp. 204–5. This letter is misdated as ca. May 20, but internal evidence indicates May 15.
17. Miller, pp. 16–17.
18. HH–EH, May 18, 1926, JFK. None of Hemingway's letters to Hadley from this period have apparently survived.
19. HH–EH, May 21, 1926, JFK.
20. EH–Sherwood Anderson, May 21, 1926, *SL*, 205–6.
21. HH–EH, May 22, 1926, JFK.
22. EH– Clarence Hemingway, May 23, 1926, *SL*, p. 207.
23. Pauline Pfeiffer–EH, May 20, 1926, JFK; marked as arriving in Madrid on May 24, 1926.
24. HH–EH, May 24, 1926, JFK.
25. Hemingway telegraph bills, JFK; HH–EH, telegram, May 27, 1926, JFK.

Chapter Four: A PURSUIT RACE

1. Zelda Fitzgerald–F. Scott Fitzgerald, late summer 1930, Bruccoli and Duggan, p. 247.
2. Nancy Milford, *Zelda* (New York: Harper and Row, 1970), pp. 120–1.
3. Miller, pp. 17–8; Bruccoli (2), pp. 253–5; Bruccoli and Duggan, pp. 196–7.
4. Letters in JFK. On June 15, Hadley renewed two subscriptions to the Book Lounge (Miscellany Box, JFK). Pierre Devoluy, *The French Riviera* (London: The Medici Society, 1924), pp. 52–63; Kert, pp. 180–1.
5. The original is undated in JFK. From EH's letter to Perkins on June 5, it is obvious that Fitzgerald's critique came before that date. For a smoother copy of this letter see Bruccoli and Duggan, pp.

193–6. See also Bruccoli (2), pp. 248–53, and Bruccoli (1), pp. 35–55, for a fuller discussion of this relationship.

6. Bruccoli (2), p. 253.
7. EH–Max Perkins, June 5, 1926, *SL*, p. 208.
8. Cut galleys are at UVa; see Hershel Parker's interesting overview on such Hemingway cuts in his essay "Textual Criticism and Hemingway," in Frank Scafella (ed.), *Hemingway: Essays of Reassessment* (Oxford: Oxford University Press, 1991), pp. 17–31.
9. Sherwood Anderson–EH [nd], JFK; EH answered this letter on July 1, 1926.
10. *New York Evening Post Literary Review*, June 12, 1926, p. 9; *New York Times Book Review*, June 13, 1926, p. 8; *New York World*, May 30, 1926, p. 4M.
11. Donnelly, pp. 18–20, 34.
12. Drabeck and Ellis, p. 46. See also "Introduction," in Miller.
13. See Linda Miller's essays, "Gerald Murphy and Ernest Hemingway," Parts I & II, *Studies in American Fiction*, Autumn 1984, pp. 129–44 and Spring 1985, pp. 1–13; and "Ernest Hemingway and the 'Understanding Rich'," *North Dakota Quarterly*, Winter 1987, pp. 125–36.
14. John Dos Passos, *The Best of Times* (New York: New American Library, 1966), p. 149.
15. See photo section of Miller.
16. Milford, *Zelda*, pp. 120–3.
17. *Death in the Afternoon* (New York: Scribner's, 1932), p. 273.
18. Hemingway's passport indicates that they entered Spain on July 1, 1926. See Calvin Tompkins, *Living Well is the Best Revenge* (New York: Viking Press, 1971), p. 98.
19. See *Paris Years*.
20. Donnelly, p. 24.
21. See plate section.
22. *Death in the Afternoon*, p. 275.
23. Gerald Murphy–"Hadern" (i.e. Hadley and Ernest) [14 July 1926], Miller, pp. 19–20.
24. Ibid.
25. Donnelly, p. 24; Tomkins, *Living Well is the Best Revenge*, pp. 99–100.
26. Baker, p. 152.
27. Sara Murphy–EH, July 14, 1926, Miller, pp. 20–21.
28. Gerald Murphy–EH/HH, July 14, 1926, JFK.

29. See Kert, p. 182; Alice Sokoloff, *Hadley* (New York: Dodd, Mead & Co., 1973), pp. 87–91.
30. Pauline Pfeiffer–EH/HH, July 15, 1926, JFK, sent to Hotel Aguilar in Madrid.
31. Brian, p. 76.

Chapter Five: ROOM WITH NO VIEW

1. "Suburban Passenger Train Derailed Outside Gare de Lyon," *Tribune*, Aug. 16, 1926.
2. Item 307, JFK. See Scott Donaldson's definitive discussion of Hemingway's construction and revision of Items 307, 308, and 309 in "Preparing for the End: Hemingway's Revisions of 'A Canary For One'," *Studies in American Fiction*, 6 (Autumn 1978), pp. 203–11.
3. "A Canary For One," *CSS*, pp. 258–61.
4. See Item 348, "Cross Roads," JFK. Hank Erforth, a farmer, remains angry at kids who did not stop to help while his house was burning down. Seeing all his furniture out in the yard, they thought he was merely moving.
5. HH–EH [16 September 1926], JFK: "I want you to take the Massons and Miró when you move the big things out."
6. The Hadley letters to Hemingway during the period of separation are badly dated or undated, many of them written on the same day, several sent by Paris pneumatic. These two letters appear to have been written ca. Sept. 16–18, 1926, JFK.
7. Item 648a, p. 14, JFK; see Donald Junkins' editing of this manuscript and its companion piece, Item 648b, in The *Hemingway Review*, 9 (Spring 1990), pp. 2–49. Many scholars have placed the Murphy studio on the fifth floor at 69 rue Froidevaux; however, Linda P. Miller, Murphy scholar and editor of his letters, says it was a ground floor studio on the basis of Murphy's letters.
8. HH–EH, Aug. 20, 1926, 8.30 a.m., JFK.
9. July 24, 1926, *SL*, pp. 211–12; the echo of Winterbourne's condition in *Daisy Miller* is probably a conscious allusion.
10. Max Perkins–EH, July 20, 1926, JFK, original in Scribner author file, PUL. Whether Perkins' use of "been too long abroad" is also a Henry James allusion is problematic; however, in the same letter he again brings up the issue of using Henry James's name in the text.

If letters seem out of sequence, remember that ten days was the minimum time between the States and Europe for mail delivery. Hemingway did not have this Perkins letter at hand when he wrote on July 24.

11. EH–Max Perkins, Aug. 21, 1926, *SL*, p. 213.
12. EH–Max Perkins, Aug. 26, 1926, *SL*, pp. 214–15.
13. Holograph addendum to Item 536, pp. 8–9, JFK.
14. "The Killers," *CSS*, p. 221.
15. Robert E. Fleming, "Hemingway's 'The Killers': The Map and the Territory," *Hemingway Review*, 4 (Fall 1984), pp. 40–3. See also EH–Max Perkins, Aug. 21, 1926, *SL*, pp. 213–14.
16. EH–Max Perkins, Aug. 26, 1926, *SL*, p. 215.
17. James Rorty–EH, Sept. 8, 1926, JFK; Jonathan Cape–EH, Aug. 31, 1926, JFK.
18. Max Perkins–EH, Aug. 23, 1926, JFK; EH–Max Perkins, Sept. 7, 1926, *SL*, p. 216.
19. Edith Finch–EH, Aug. 14, 1926, JFK; EH–Edith Finch, Aug. 18, 1926, JFK. See Smith, pp. 154–5. The story/play was published by The As Stable Pamphlets in November 1926. Hanneman is incorrect on publication date.
20. EH–F. Scott Fitzgerald, ca. Sept. 7, 1926, *SL*, p. 216.
21. Fitzgerald's *Ledger*, reproduced in Bruccoli (2), p. 532.
22. Sara and Gerald Murphy–EH, [n.d., ca. Sept. 2, 1926], Miller, pp. 23–4.
23. Donnelly, p. 25; Linda P. Miller, "Gerald Murphy and Ernest Hemingway, Part I," *Studies in American Fiction*, Autumn 1984, pp. 137–40.
24. Sara and Gerald Murphy–EH [n.d., ca. Sept. 2, 1926], Miller, pp. 23–4.
25. Gerald Murphy–EH, Saturday [Sept. 4, 1926], Miller, pp. 21–3. Whether Murphy's analysis of the Hemingway marriage is based solely on his first-hand observations or partially on Hemingway's description of it we will never know. However, Murphy's analysis sounds suspiciously close to Hemingway's developing version of what went wrong with both his marriage and his father's.
26. EH–F. Scott Fitzgerald, ca. Sept. 7, 1926, *SL*, p. 217.
27. HH–EH, Aug. 20, 1926, JFK.
28. Kert, p. 183.
29. HH–EH, Sept. 13, 1926, JFK.
30. "With Latin Quarter Folk," New York *Herald*, Sept. 15, 1926.

31. "With Latin Quarter Folk," New York *Herald*, Sept. 21, 1926.
32. HH–EH [16 September 1926], JFK.
33. Program with results recorded in JFK.
34. HH–EH, Sept. 17, 1926, JFK.
35. Herbert Gibbons, *The Ports of France* (New York: The Century Co., 1926), pp. 31–41. Pauline Pfeiffer–EH, *Pennland* stationary, Sept. 24, 1926, JFK. *Muirhead's North-Eastern France* (London: Macmillan, 1922), pp. 18–20.
36. Pauline Pfeiffer–EH, Sept. 24, 1926, JFK.
37. Hemingway's borrower's card, Sylvia Beach Collection, PUL; Lawrence S. Morris, "Frolicking on Olympus," *The New Republic* Sept. 15, 1926, p. 101.

Chapter Six: The Hundred Days

1. HH–EH, [n.d., early Oct. 1926, from internal evidence], JFK.
2. PP–EH, Oct. 11, 1926, JFK.
3. Item 597b, JFK.
4. *88P*, p. 84.
5. These include "A Canary For One," "In Another Country," "Now I Lay Me," "A Simple Enquiry," "A Pursuit Race," and "My Own Life." See Smith for more details of composition.
6. Item 597c, Notebook (69 rue Froidevaux address), JFK.
7. EH–Archibald MacLeish, Dec. 20, 1925, *SL*, p. 178.
8. See Turnbull, pp. 296–7; EH–Fitzgerald, ca. Dec. 24, 1925, *SL*, p. 182.
9. EH–Max Perkins, Apr. 24, 1926, *SL*, p. 202.
10. Hemingway's borrower's card, Beach Collection, PUL. The three-month subscription cost 150 francs ($5).
11. E. Allison Peers, *Spain* (New York: Farrar & Rinehart, 1930), pp. 236–40; E. M. Newman, *Seeing Spain and Morocco* (New York: Funk & Wagnalls, 1930), pp. 171–7; *Baedeker's Spain and Portugal* (Leipzig: Karl Baedeker, 1908), pp. 200–9. The pillar is reported variously as marble or jasper.
12. Barrera de Sol tickets for Oct. 14 and 17, JFK.
13. See Drabeck and Ellis; Beach Collection, PUL; MacLeish Collection, Library of Congress; Winnick, p. 196. It is interesting to note how many of Hemingway's Paris friends were Ivy League graduates: Pound, Stein, Dos Passos, Murphy, MacLeish, Harold

Loeb, Harold Stearns, Mike Strater, and (almost) Fitzgerald to name the most obvious.

14. Drabeck and Ellis, p. 232; at the base chapel of Naval Air Station, Pensacola, Kenneth MacLeish's wings (#74) are pinned on the wall.

15. Hemingway inscription for Gerald Murphy of *Today is Friday*, private collection; MacLeish–C. E. Frazer Clark, Mar. 1, 1973, private collection; *Herald*, Oct. 17, 1926.

16. *El Sol*, Oct. 11–18, 1926.

17. "Cinema of a Man," in *New Found Land* (Paris: Black Sun Press, 1930), reprinted in *Collected Poems* (Boston: Houghton Mifflin, 1952), p. 46.

18. MacLeish–John Peale Bishop, June 26, 1925, Winnick, pp. 165–6; Drabeck and Ellis, pp. 29, 61.

19. Pauline docked in New York on October 4. Her first batch of letters reached Paris about October 14 while Hemingway was in Spain. The confusion and anxiety of their separation were heightened by the 20–30-day turnaround on their correspondence.

20. Pauline Pfeiffer–EH, Oct. 1, 1926, JFK.

21. Pauline Pfeiffer–EH, Oct. 5, 8, 1926, JFK.

22. HH–EH, Oct. 18, 1926, JFK.

23. Dos Passos–EH, n.d. [ca. Oct. 10, 1926], JFK.

24. Clarence Hemingway–EH, Oct. 7, 1926, JFK; *Herald*, Sept. 20–1, 1926. Clarence's inheritance was $3,116.07, statement on estate settlement, UTex.

25. EH–Clarence Hemingway, Oct. 22, 1926, JFK.

26. For example, Jed Kiley, in a book which Hemingway refused to allow printed while he was alive because of its errors, speaks quite knowingly of his good friend Ernest Hemingway and about Gerald Murphy's fifth-floor walk-up studio where he visited Hemingway during the Hundred Days. The studio was on the ground floor, and Kiley was never an old friend.

27. *Tribune*, Nov. 7, 1926.

28. Typical of the genre was Sisley Huddleston's book, *Mr. Pavane: A Paris Fantasy* (London: T. Butterworth, 1926), with a character named Ezra Ounce.

29. "Around the Town," *Herald*, Nov. 17, 1926. The "literary pal" is Harold Loeb.

30. "Latin Quarter Notes," *Tribune*, Dec. 9, 1926. "Fifty Grand," having been rejected by several New York periodicals, first appeared in this French translation.

31. "Latin Quarter Notes," *Tribune*, Dec. 28, 1926.
32. The Avenue du Bois de Boulgone became Avenue Foch in 1929. The apartment belonged to Pierpont Morgan Hamilton. Archibald MacLeish–Martha Hillard MacLeish, Oct. 7, 1926, Winnick, pp. 184–5; Brian, p. 72; Arlen J. Hansen, *Expatriate Paris* (New York: Arcade Publishing, 1990), p. 234.
33. Pauline Pfeiffer–EH, Oct. 11, 1926, JFK.
34. Pauline Pfeiffer–EH, Oct. 25, 29, 1926, JFK.
35. EH–Pauline Pfeiffer, Nov. 12, 1926, *SL*, pp. 220–2. This letter was originally dated October 12, but internal evidence, as Carlos Baker points out, indicates the later date.
36. Item 492A, JFK, an early draft of "In Another Country."
37. Item 492, JFK, a second type draft of "In Another Country."
38. HH–EH, Nov. 8, 1926, JFK.
39. HH–EH, Nov. 9, 10, 1926, JFK.
40. HH–EH, Nov. 14, 1926, JFK. These cards are misdated as November 15, but are written on "Sunday," which was November 14.
41. HH–EH, Nov. 16, 1926, JFK.
42. Virginia Pfeiffer–Pauline Pfeiffer, date uncertain but probably Nov. 17, 1926, JFK. When the rains began to deluge Chartres, Hadley cut the week short and returned to Paris on 18 November.
43. EH–HH, Nov. 18, 1926, *SL*, pp. 226–8. Hemingway's offer of *The Sun Also Rises* royalties included those from his British publisher, Jonathan Cape, who had offered a contract for the book on Nov. 9, 1926 (letter, JFK).
44. HH–EH, Nov. 19, 1926, JFK.
45. "Marital Tragedy," *New York Times Book Review*, Oct. 31, 1926, p. 27.
46. Conrad Aiken, "Expatriates," *New York Herald Tribune Books*, Oct. 31, 1926, pp. VII-4.
47. Dorothy Parker–EH, Nov. 3, 1926, JFK.
48. "To a Tragic Poetess," *88P*, pp. 87–8.
49. Pauline Pfeiffer–EH, Nov. 27, Dec. 4, 1926, JFK. The first letter may be the first written reference to Hemingway's "iceberg theory."
50. Ezra Pound–EH, Nov. 3, 1926, JFK. The idiosyncratic spellings are all Pound's. "Calidge Colvin" is Pound's mockery of then President Calvin Coolidge. The "Peace Conference" refers to Hemingway's poem "They All Made Peace – What Is Peace," *Little Review*, Spring 1923. Later Hemingway said that "Neo-Thomist" referred

to the "temporary embracing of the church by literary gents." See, *88P*, pp. 147–8.

51. *88P*, p. 83. First appeared in *Exile*, Spring 1927.
52. Hemingway's borrower's card, Beach Collection, PUL. He returned the book Feb. 28, 1927.
53. "News of New Books," *Tribune*, Nov. 8, 1926.
54. Item 524, JFK. The Gertrude Stein word portrait of Hemingway is called "He and They Hemingway."
55. For details of the Hemingway–Stein relationship see *Young Hemingway* and James Mellow, *Charmed Circle* (New York: Avon, 1975).
56. Item 524, JFK.
57. Beach records, day books, and inventories, Beach Collection, PUL.
58. See "A Strange Enough Ending," *AMF*, pp. 117–19, which begins: "The way it ended with Gertrude Stein was strange enough."
59. Item 594a, JFK. On 19 November 1926, Hemingway mailed the satire to Perkins, asking him to place it for him; it was subsequently published in the *New Yorker*, Feb. 12, 1927, pp. 23–4, as "My Own Life." The bicycle pump may be the rusted one Joyce's young lad found in *Dubliners*, a book Hemingway greatly admired.

Chapter Seven: FORTUNE AND MEN'S EYES

1. *Herald* and *Tribune*, Nov. 26, 1926.
2. EH–Pauline Pfeiffer [2 December 1926], JFK.
3. EH–F. Scott Fitzgerald, ca. Nov. 24, 1926, *SL*, pp. 231–3. On Nov. 22, 1926, Hemingway sent Perkins "In Another Country" for *Scribner's Magazine*.
4. Item 618, JFK. See Paul Smith, "The Bloody Typewriter and the Burning Snakes," in Frank Scafella (ed.), *Hemingway: Essays of Reassessment* (Oxford: Oxford University Press, 1991), pp. 80–90.
5. Item 619, JFK. This typed fragment may be an insert rather than a second draft, but it was written after Item 618.
6. Item 620, JFK.
7. The close reader will note several differences between each of these drafts and the final published version of this story which was called "Now I Lay Me." See Smith for more detailed information.
8. This insight belongs to Nina Fournier.
9. Item 620, JFK.

10. Hemingway met with the lawyer on December 3 (EH–Pauline Pfeiffer, *SL*, p. 234). The divorce papers, signed and dated December 8, are in JFK. Burkhardt signed for Hadley.
11. EH–Grace and Clarence Hemingway, Dec. 1, 1926, *SL*, p. 233.
12. Grace Hemingway–EH, Dec. 4, 1926, JFK.
13. Clarence Hemingway–EH, Dec. 13, 1926, JFK.
14. EH notes written on front of Perkins' envelope (mailed Dec. 4, 1926) at JFK: "Friday [Dec. 24] night Bumby's tree; 3–4 pm Sherwood; Thursday [Dec. 23] noon 12 Evan [Shipman] to go out to Vincennes [trotting horse race]; Friday am get winter coat, Hadley's pants – dinner shoes and sweat shirt from 113 [Notre-Dame-des-Champs] with Evan." A second meeting took place in January after Pauline returned.
15. "Sherwood Anderson's Arrival Here Sets Literary World Agog," *Tribune*, Dec. 17, 1926; "Sherwood Anderson Sees No Danger Of American Ever Becoming Cultured," *Tribune*, Dec. 18, 1926; "Who's Who Abroad," *Tribune*, Dec. 19, 1926.
16. The review, "Hemingway Seems Out of Focus" first appeared in the *Chicago Daily Tribune* (Nov. 27, 1926) and was reprinted in the Paris edition (Dec. 19, 1926).
17. Grace Hemingway–EH, Dec. 4, 1926, JFK; Clarence Hemingway–EH, Dec. 13, 1926, JFK.
18. "Molina Wins Easy Decision," *Herald*, Dec. 23, 1926. On his program (JFK) Hemingway scored the fight: Molina 45 – Brown 40.
19. Archibald MacLeish, "Family Group", *New and Collected Poems* (Boston: Houghton Mifflin, 1976), p. 22.
20. Ralph D. Paine, *The First Yale Unit*, vol. 2 (Cambridge, Mass: Riverside Press, 1925), pp. 350–73.
21. Item 228, JFK. MacLeish's degree was in law; the doctoral degree in philosophy probably came from Ralph Church, who was seeing Hemingway in Paris at this time and pursuing such a degree.
22. Pauline Pfeiffer–EH, Dec. 15, 1926, JFK. The second story to which Pauline refers is "Now I Lay Me," which at one point EH was calling "In Another Country – Two."
23. At one time or another he did this in fiction, poetry, or letters to Ezra Pound, T. S. Eliot, Ford Madox Ford, Gertrude Stein, Harold Loeb, Louis Bromfield, Glenway Wescott, Ernest Walsh, Dorothy Parker, Scott Fitzgerald, Sherwood Anderson, Archibald MacLeish, and John Dos Passos. Not all of these pieces were finished or published.

24. Ezra Pound–EH, Dec. 21, 1926, JFK.
25. As always with Hemingway's short fiction, the reader should consult Smith and ignore misinformation such as my own gaffe in *Hemingway's Reading* (Princeton: Princeton University Press, 1981), p. 22, where I said the story was published in *Exile*.
26. EH–F. Scott Fitzgerald, ca. Nov. 24, 1926, *SL*, p. 232.
27. EH–Pauline Pfeiffer, undated, two versions, JFK. The last sentence could refer to the fall salons in Paris in which there was almost no Cubist art present. The *Tribune* called attention to this absence as a fad passing. But "Cubist" was one of the code words used by the two lovers.
28. Others have said that Pauline arrived on the *New Amsterdam*, but only the *Cleveland* arrived on January 8 at Cherbourg. See "Shipping News" in either the *Tribune* or the *Herald* for January 1927.
29. "Notes of a Rapid Reader," *Saturday Review of Literature*, 3, 21 (Dec. 18, 1926), p. 1; not in Hanneman.
30. "Bodies of 3 Alpine Skiers Recovered; Five Others Missing," *Herald*, Jan. 4, 1927; "Austrian Skier was Killed near Bludenz today," *Herald*, Jan. 5, 1927; see also *Herald*, Mar. 4, 5, 1927. Hemingway transposed the avalanches of 1927 to the winter of 1926 in *A Moveable Feast* where they were metaphorically more appropriate.
31. See Kert, pp. 199–200. Virginia Pfeiffer was born in 1902, according to Laura Huxley, who should know.
32. HH–EH [early January 1927], JFK. The uncashed check is also in this collection. Bumby was with Marie Rohrbach, as he often was when Ernest and Hadley traveled.
33. Sylvia Beach–EH, Jan. 3, 1927, JFK, speaks of Joyce's suggestion. Eugène Jolas–EH, Jan. 3, Feb. 27, 1927, JFK; Ezra Pound–EH, Jan. 18, 1927, JFK.
34. Max Perkins–EH, Jan. 14, 1927, JFK. They paid $75 for the piece.
35. Donald Freeman–EH, Jan. 6, 1927, JFK. EH noted on envelope, "answered 28 Jan." The stories were "A Pursuit Race," "A Simple Enquiry," and "Hills Like White Elephants."
36. Ezra Pound–EH, Jan. 30, 1927, JFK. Perkins' letters to Hemingway, starting in November 1926, begin talking about the collection of stories.
37. EH–Max Perkins, Jan. 20, 1927, *SL*, p. 241. The story was published in *The American Caravan: A Yearbook of American Literature* (New York: Macaulay, 1927). A measure of Hemingway's

growing stature can be found in the number of times he was asked to appear in the first issues of new periodicals: *This Quarter, Exile, Transition, Caravan, New Masses, Commerce, S4N*.

38. Ezra Pound–EH, Jan. 29, 1927, JFK.
39. Max Perkins–EH, Jan. 28, 1927, JFK. Selling at $2, the 11,000 copies at Hemingway's 15 percent royalty rate would have generated $3,300 minus his $1,000 advance. See EH–Max Perkins, Dec. 21, 1926, *SL*, p. 240. Divorce judgement: Hadley interview with Carlos Baker.
40. HH–EH, Feb. 1, 1927, JFK.
41. HH–EH, undated but clearly written after January 15, and before January 27, 1927, JFK. Only 5,000 francs of the 5,100 franc check cleared due to lack of funds. Hadley took the 5,000 francs leaving a balance of 44 francs, not quite $2.
42. Francis Coats–EH, Jan. 7, 1927, JFK.
43. Ella Winter Steffens–EH, Jan. 11, 1927, JFK.
44. John Dos Passos–EH, Jan. 16, 1927, JFK.
45. Sinclair Lewis–EH, Jan. 31, 1927, JFK. Lewis's echo of Emerson's greeting to Whitman on the publication of *Leaves of Grass* probably went unrecognized by Hemingway.
46. Guy Hickok–EH, Jan. 21, Feb. 8, 1927, JFK.
47. See *Paris Years*, pp. 192–4 for more information on the composition of this story. See also Paul Smith, "From the Waste Land to the Garden with the Elliots," in Susan Beegel (ed.), *Hemingway's Neglected Short Fiction* (University Microfilms Inc. Press, 1989), pp. 123–30.
48. Chard Powers Smith–Carlos Baker, May 27, 1969, Baker Collection, PUP. Olive Smith died in childbirth in Naples on March 11, 1924, but Hemingway apparently had no knowledge of her death when he wrote the story.
49. Chard Powers Smith–EH, Jan. 2, 1927, JFK.
50. "With Latin Quarter Folk," *Herald*, Jan. 16, 1927. The quote came from Christopher Morley's column, "The Bowling Green," *Saturday Review of Literature* (Dec. 18, 1926), p. 451.
51. EH–Chard Powers Smith, ca. Jan. 21, 1927, *SL*, p. 242.
52. February 18–28, Hemingway is in Paris to pick up Bumby for vacation in Switzerland. On February 24 Hadley and his son were taken off his passport; on March 1, Bumby was put back on. On February 28, Hemingway returned two books at Shakespeare and Co.

53. Paul Mowrer–EH, Jan. 9, 1927, JFK.
54. In the Baker Collection, PUL, there are several letters from Chard Powers Smith to Carlos Baker that arrived too late to incorporate into his 1969 biography. There the question is raised but unanswered as to whether Hemingway actually mailed the letter or not. Smith died in 1977 at age 83, the author of several volumes of poetry, and history and of one biography of his mentor, Edwin Arlington Robinson.
55. Caresse Crosby, *The Passionate Years* (New York: Dial Press, 1953; repr. Ecco Press, 1979), pp. 169–71.
56. *Shadows of the Sun*, ed. Edward Germain (Santa Barbara: Black Swallow Press, 1977), pp. 131–2.
57. Grace Hall Hemingway–EH, Jan. 21, 1927, JFK.
58. EH–Grace and Clarence Hemingway, Feb. 5, 1927, *SL*, pp. 243–4.
59. Marcelline Hemingway Sanford–EH, Feb. 7, 1927, JFK.
60. Clarence Hemingway–EH, Jan. 27, 1927, JFK.
61. Dorothy Parker, "The Paris that Keeps Out of the Papers," *Vanity Fair*, Jan. 1927, p. 71.
62. EH–Max Perkins, Feb. 19, 1927, *SL*, pp. 246–7. Even in this retraction, Hemingway does not say that he drove ambulances for the American Red Cross. Until very recently Scribner's continued to say on the backs of Hemingway books that in World War I he "served as an ambulance driver and infantryman with the Italian army." In fact, he was stationed in Italy as a Red Cross ambulance driver, one who never served as an infantryman with any army anywhere. See Reynolds *Hemingway's First War* (Princeton: Princeton University Press, 1976; paperback Oxford: Blackwell, 1989) and *Young Hemingway*.
63. For a detailed accounting of the public life, see John Raeburn, *Fame Became of Him* (Indianapolis: Indiana University Press, 1984), where he frequently anticipates and often becomes the source for my understanding of Hemingway as media event.
64. *Time*, (Oct. 14, 1927), p. 38.
65. EH–Max Perkins, Feb. 14, 1927, *SL*, pp. 245–6. For unstated reasons, "Up in Michigan" was never part of the final set of stories and was not republished until 1938.
66. Archibald MacLeish–EH, Feb. 14, 1927, JFK.
67. Archibald MacLeish–EH, Feb. 20, 1927, JFK.
68. *Herald*, Feb. 14, 1927. Plays closed included *Sex* and *The Virgin Man*.

69. "A Simple Enquiry," *CSS*, pp. 250–2.
70. Guy Hickok–EH [late January 1927], JFK. Refers to the Palace of Justice divorce judgment in Hadley's favor which took place 27 January.
71. Guy Hickok–EH, Feb. 8, 1927, JFK.
72. Ezra Pound–EH, Feb. 15, 1927; Guy Hickok–EH [late February 1927], JFK.

Chapter Eight: RITUAL ACTS

1. In mid-February Hadley sent Ernest a telegram asking for their joint passport so that she could arrange for her own passport (undated telegram to Gstaad, JKF). On February 24, 1927, Hadley and John Hadley Nicanor Hemingway were removed from the passport (JFK). On March 1, 1927, John was put back on the EH passport with a new picture so that EH could take him to Wengen where Pauline and Virginia moved in search of better snow.
2. HH–EH, Feb. 17, 1927, JFK.
3. Pauline Pfeiffer–EH, Mar. 17, 1927, JFK.
4. EH passport, JFK, shows March 10 entry into France. Hadley's new wardrobe was the result of checks totaling $550 cashed between February 17 and March 4, 1927. On March 11 she cashed another $200 check before leaving for Chartres. These canceled checks were at the Taube Inn in Schruns, Austria, the summer of 1988.
5. "Four Divorces to Americans Here," *Herald*, Mar. 11, 1927; on the same day the *New York Times* ran a similar story which spoke of their three year-old child being in the custody of the mother.
6. "Mrs. Ernest Hemingway, Author's Wife, Gets Divorce in Paris," *Tribune*, Mar. 11, 1927.
7. Hemingway's borrower's card, Beach Collection, PUL. The Garnett book was *Go She Must!*, which EH apparently returned the same day.
8. Telegram received Mar. 9, 1927, JFK.
9. Ezra Pound–EH, Mar. 11, 1927, JFK. Card and copy of *Exile* were sent to Gstaad and forwarded to Paris. The flyer is attached to the postcard at the JFK. Pound also sent on March 14, 1927, the printer's explanation to Hemingway.
10. O. C. Valentine–EH, Mar. 4, 1927, and C. H. Towne–EH, Feb. 5, 1927, JFK.

11. The will is in JFK. It has two dates. The first, November 1927, is typed in the heading by Pauline's lawyer. The second, March 14, 1927, Pauline entered in ink in the appropriate blank space.
12. EH passport, JFK, shows him entering Italy on March 18 and exiting on March 24. During the seven Italian days they drove roughly 1,100 kilometers. They apparently came back early, for Pauline did not expect them until April 2.
13. These details and others come from Hemingway's "Italy, 1927" which was reprinted as "Che Ti Dice La Patria?" (What Do You Hear From The Fatherland?) in *Men Without Women* (New York: Scribner's, 1927) and in *CSS*, pp. 223–30.
14. Pauline Pfeiffer–EH, Mar. 15, 1927, JFK.
15. Pauline Pfeiffer–EH, Mar. 17, 18, 1927, JFK; Hansen, *Expatriate Paris*, pp. 94–5. The "clipping books" were collections of reviews on his books.
16. Pauline Pfeiffer–EH, Mar. 17, 1927, JFK. Others have said that on the Italian trip, Hemingway found the priest who baptized him, but no hard evidence has been cited to support the claim. As H. R. Stoneback has pointed out, at the Italian field station where he was brought wounded, most priests would have assumed his Catholicity and administered Extreme Unction, the last rites, rather than the sacrament of baptism.
17. Pauline Pfeiffer–EH, Mar. 20, 1927, JFK. Hemingway was a compulsive saver of his own papers, leaving full trunks behind at way-stations throughout his life.
18. Pauline Pfeiffer–EH, Mar. 21, 1927, JFK.
19. "Che Ti Dice La Patria," *CSS*, p. 230. See also Hemingway's passport, JFK.
20. Guy Hickok–EH, Mar. 27, 1927, JFK.
21. See Pauline Pfeiffer–EH, Mar. 18, 20, 1927, JFK.
22. Virgil Thompson–EH, Mar. 22, 1927, JFK.
23. Clarence Hemingway–EH, Mar. 6, 22, 1927, JFK.
24. Grace Hemingway–EH, Feb. 20, 1927, JKF.
25. Jess Archer Davidson–Grace Hemingway, Mar. 20, 1927, Hemingway Collection, UTex.
26. The proof of the review was enclosed in the Max Perkins–EH letter, Mar. 9, 1927, JFK. It ran in *Atlantic*, 139 (April 1927), pp. 12, 14.
27. EH–Max Perkins, Apr. 1, 1927, originally read in Scribner author file in Scribner's offices in New York and now at the Princeton

University Library. The "stuff" he could not get is also referred to in "Italy – 1927." It is probably the baptismal certificate, but that was never mentioned as a reason for making the trip.

28. "People Here and There," *Herald*, Apr. 2, 1927. The store opened May 20, 1927.

29. When Augustus G. Pfeiffer died in 1953 he owned 44 percent of the Warner–Hudnut stock and left $8.3 million to his research foundation. His rare collection of chess sets was left to Metropolitan Museum of Art (*New York Times*).

30. F. Scott Fitzgerald–EH, Mar. 14, 1927, JFK.

31. "Check List of New Books," *American Mercury*, 5 (August 1925), p. xxxviii.

32. F. Scott Fitzgerald–EH, [March, 1927], Turnbull, p. 299. See Bruccoli (1), pp. 56–60. Mencken's *American Mercury* turned down at least three of Hemingway's stories in 1924, and Hemingway neither forgave Mencken nor ever submitted anything to him again. See *Paris Years*, pp. 199, 235.

33. F. Scott Fitzgerald–EH, Mar. 27, 1927, JFK.

34. EH–F. Scott Fitzgerald, Mar. 31, 1927, *SL*, p. 248.

35. Item 758, JFK.

36. Items 328A, 329, 330, 517, and 727, JFK. See Smith, pp. 193–6.

37. Guy Hickok, "On Those Synthetic States," *The Exile*, Spring 1927, p. 21.

38. "Italy – 1927," *New Republic*, May 18, 1927, pp. 350–3. The essay/story was finished and professionally typed by April 21. On May 4, Edmund Wilson received and read the piece. Wilson–EH, May 4, 1927, JFK.

39. "With Latin Quarter Folk," *Herald*, Apr. 30, 1927.

40. Guy Fangel–EH, Apr. 12, 1927, JFK.

41. Hemingway's borrower's card, Apr. 23: Alan L. Maycock, *The Inquisition from its Establishment to the Great Schism*, Beach Collection, PUL.

42. Gerald Murphy–EH, Mar. 19, 1927, JFK. All evidence indicates that Murphy did not show up and that Hemingway remained in the studio until his May wedding.

43. Robert D. Crozier, SJ, " 'The Paris Church at Passy': A Note on Hemingway's Second Marriage," *Papers on Language and Literature*, Winter 1979, pp. 84–6. Crozier, misreading the handwritten document, lists St. Pierre de *Monteripe* as the second church for the reading of the banns. It was, in fact, St. Pierre de *Montrouge*, a large and

important church in the fourteenth arrondissement in which the Murphy studio was located and where Hemingway had lived for the three previous months as required by the Church.

44. Hemingway Notebook, Wedding Notes, JFK. See also H. R. Stoneback's crucial essay, "In the Nominal Country of the Bogus: Hemingway's Catholicism and and the Biographies," in Scafella, *Hemingway: Essays of Reassessment*, pp. 105–40.

45. Hemingway apartment papers, JFK.

46. Why Hadley and Ernest both moved out of the Notre-Dame-des-Champs apartment but continued to pay rent is unclear. No necessities, other than psychological ones, forced both to leave. It would have obviously been less expensive for one to have remained in residence. Hemingway continued to use it as a convenient storage facility.

47. F. Scott Fitzgerald–EH [18 April 1927], Turnbull, p. 300.

48. Hemingway–Pfeiffer wedding materials, Patrick Hemingway Collection, PUL. While Pfeiffer money rolled in from all sides, the Hemingway contingent was notable only for its absence on the gift list, for Ernest had not yet told his parents of his second marriage.

49. EH–Max Perkins, May 27, 1927, *SL*, p. 252.

50. Madelaine Hemingway–EH, Apr. 23, 1927, JFK. Madelaine also said she would not have suggested the trip if she had known he was getting married. Hemingway's wired reply is written out on the back of the envelope.

51. Hadley sailed April 16. Ernest's part of the divorce was final on April 21.

52. EH–Max Perkins, May 4, 1927, *SL*, pp. 250–1. "After the Fourth" became "Ten Indians." "A Lack of Passion" remained unpublished. "Now I Lay Me" is not mentioned but does appear in the collection.

53. EH Wedding Notebook, JFK.

54. Identity card, dated May 10, 1927, JFK. "Extrait des actes de mariage du quatorzième arrondissement de Paris, Année 1927" made "le quatorze mars mil neuf cent vingt-huit," JFK.

55. *Baedeker's Handbook for Paris* (Leipzig: Karl Baedeker, 1924), p. 331. This area is now somewhat changed and no longer called Place de Montrouge.

56. "Extrait des actes de mariage du quatorzième arrondissement de Paris, Année 1927" made "le quatorze mars mil neuf cent vingt-huit," JFK.

57. "Extrait du registre des actes de mariage de la paroisse de St. Honoré d'Eylau," made on May 26, 1976 and reproduced in Crozier, "'The Parish Church at Passy'". Hemingway's year of birth is listed as 1897, which some have interpreted as his effort to make himself closer to Pauline's age. However, his age is given correctly on the civil certificate, which may mean that the recorder simply made a mistake on the church records.

58. Ada MacLeish note appended to Archibald MacLeish letter to Carlos Baker, Jan. 31, 1965, Baker Collection, PUL.

59. "Mme. M'Leish to Make Debut in Paris on Monday," *Herald*, May 7, 1927. While Archie was in Paris to write, Ada was there to train her soprano voice with intentions of performing in Boston.

60. Clara E. Laughlin, *So You're Going to France* (Boston: Houghton Mifflin, 1927); Baker, pp. 185–6; Kert, pp. 203–4.

61. Laughlin, *So You're Going to France*; period (1924) postcards describing the area, personal collection.

62. Patrick Hemingway in a letter to Bernice Kert, August 1978.

63. Andrée Viollis, "Celebrating the Great Festival of Provence," *Travel*, 52 (April 1929), pp. 22–4, 46, 48.

64. *CSS*, p. 257; earlier titles were "After the Fourth" and "A Broken Heart."

65. Item 472, JFK. The manuscript tells of incidents following the San Fermin *feria* of 1925 and was probably written just before Hemingway began *The Sun Also Rises*, ca. July 21, 1925.

66. T. S. Eliot, "The Waste Land," *The Complete Poems and Plays* (New York: Harcourt, Brace, 1952), p. 42.

67. Item 473, "Hills Like White Elephants" MS, JFK. Quotations are from the MS, which has so few revisions that it is almost the same as the published story. At the bottom of the MS is the following note in Hemingway's hand: "Mss for Pauline – well, well, well." There is no indication when this note was appended, and there is no evidence that either Pauline or Hadley ever had an abortion.

68. EH–Max Perkins, May 27, 1927, *SL*, pp. 251–3.

Chapter Nine: PILGRIM'S PROGRESS

1. Borrower's card, May 31, 1927, Beach Collection, PUL. The book was *Parnell* by St. John Ervin.

2. Gerald Murphy–EH, 22 May 1927, Miller, pp. 26–7.

3. Madelaine Hemingway–EH, May 12, 1927, JFK.
4. Guy Hickok–EH, 7 June 1927, JFK. "Italy – 1927" appeared in *New Republic* (May 18, 1927), pp. 350–3.
5. HH–EH, Apr. 30, 1927, JFK.
6. HH–EH, May 9, 1927, JFK.
7. HH–EH, May 21, 1927, JFK.
8. "With Latin Quarter Folk," *Herald*, June 26, 1927.
9. "Around the Town," *Herald*, May 19, 1927.
10. See Sara Murphy–Pauline Hemingway, June 17, 1927, PUL; Gerald Murphy–EH, June 18, 1927, Miller, pp. 27–8. Both refer to EH's letter about the ballet.
11. Bruce Reynolds, *Paris With the Lid Lifted* (New York: George Sully & Co, 1927), pp. 205–7.
12. Gerald Murphy–EH, June 15, 1927, postcard, JFK.
13. "The rail ends do not meet," *88P*, p. 92.
14. EH–Paul Chautard, June 7, 1927, JFK.
15. EH–Barklie Henry, ca. Aug. 15, 1927, *SL*, p. 255.
16. EH–Mother Pfeiffer [Mrs. Mary Pfeiffer], n.d. [ca. June 1927], and EH–Mr. and Mrs. Paul Pfeiffer, n.d. [ca. late June 1927], Patrick Hemingway Collection, PUL.
17. Brian and Marcus Tate, *The Pilgrim Route to Santiago* (Oxford: Phaidon Press, 1987); *Baedeker's Spain and Portugal* (Leipzig: Karl Baedeker, 1908); Edwin Mullins, *The Pilgrimage to Santiago* (New York: Taplinger, 1974); Walter Starkie, *The Road to Santiago* (Berkeley: University of California Press, 1965); Georgiana King, *The Way of Saint James*, 3 vols (New York: G. P. Putnam's, 1920).
18. EH–Archibald MacLeish, Aug. 29, 1927, MS Division, Library of Congress.
19. EH–Max Perkins, June 24, 1927, Scribner author file, PUL.
20. Max Perkins–EH, July 14, 1927, Scribner author file, PUL.
21. Mildred Temple–EH, June 15, 1927, JFK.
22. Mildred Temple–EH, June 22, 1927, JFK.
23. EH–Mildred Temple, June 24, 1927, Scribner author file, PUL.
24. EH–Max Perkins, June 24, 1927, Scribner author file, PUL.
25. Barklie Henry–EH, July 25, 1927, JFK.
26. "The Main Death," *Black Mask*, June 1927.
27. Tyley Hancock–EH, Aug. 23, 1927, JFK.
28. Archibald MacLeish–EH, Aug. 13, 1927, JFK.
29. EH–Archibald MacLeish, Aug. 29 1927, MS Division, Library of Congress. EH's parody of *The Jew of Malta* quotation comes after he

has used part of it for his title, "In Another Country." William Bullit became American Ambassador to France.

30. Clarence Hemingway–EH, Aug. 8, 1927, JFK. Letter was addressed to EH's bank and forwarded, arriving at the same time as the MacLeish letter which EH answered from Santiago.
31. *Boulevardier*, 7 (Sept. 1927), pp. 6, 50–2. Thanks to Matt Bruccoli for sharing his microfilm.
32. EH–Horace Liveright, Dec. 7, 1925, *SL*, p. 173; EH–F. Scott Fitzgerald, Dec. 31, 1925, *SL*, p. 184.
33. EH–F. Scott Fitzgerald, Mar. 31, 1927, *SL*, p. 249.
34. "From A Littérateur's Notebook," *Tribune*, Jan. 2, 1927.
35. EH–F. Scott Fitzgerald, ca. Sept. 15, 1927, *SL*, p. 261. Butcher was the same *Tribune* reviewer who disliked *The Sun Also Rises* and who lectured on her dislike at Oak Park's Nineteenth Century Club, to which Grace Hemingway belonged.
36. Ernest Hemingway, "The Real Spaniard," *Boulevardier*, Oct. 1927, p. 6.
37. EH–Max Perkins, Sept. 15, 1927, Scribner author file, PUL. *For Whom the Bell Tolls* should have won in 1941, but no prize for fiction was awarded that year. See Baker, pp. 363, 510.
38. EH–Max Perkins, Sept. 15, 1927; the reference to writers who talk about the work and don't write was to Fitzgerald, who was now three years into *Tender is the Night*, which would not appear for another seven years. EH–F. Scott Fitzgerald, ca. Sept. 15, 1927, *SL*, p. 261.
39. EH–Clarence Hemingway, Sept. 14, 1927, *SL*, pp. 257–9.

Chapter Ten: THE NEW LIFE

1. EH–Mrs. Mary Pfeiffer, Oct. 1, 1927, Patrick Hemingway Collection, PUL. He eventually dedicated the book to his friend and poet, Evan Shipman.
2. Mary Pfeiffer–EH, Sept. 7, 1927, JFK.
3. "On To Paris," Official Plans and Information Issued by the American Legion France Convention Committee, brochure, n.d. See also *Tribune* and *Herald* for last two weeks of Sept. 1927.
4. *Herald*, Sept. 1927.
5. *Herald*, Sept. 15, 20, 1927; Judi Culbertson and Tom Randall, *Permanent Parisians* (Chelsea, Vermont: Chelsea Green Pub. Co., 1986).
6. "American Banker Discovers Little Tension In Italy," *Herald*, Sept. 18, 1927.

7. *Collegiate Tours to Europe, Summer of 1927* (Chicago: The Art Crafts Guild, Inc. Travel Bureau, 1927), 32 pp.
8. EH–Mrs. Paul Pfeiffer, Oct. 1, 1927, Patrick Hemingway Collection, PUL.
9. Hemingway notebook dated March 1926 owned by Toby Bruce and copied in the Baker files, PUL.
10. The "New Slain Knight" working title is crossed out on the pencil MS, Item 529b, JFK. The MS runs twenty chapters with minor revisions in ink. There are two alternate chapters, one from a shifted point of view, both done apparently as revisions. This MS, previously closed to scholars, was opened to me by the Hemingway Estate under special permission.
11. See *Young Hemingway* for more detailed information on Dr. Hemingway's gradually deteriorating condition.
12. Clarence Hemingway–EH, Sept. 28, 1927, JFK.
13. MS-14; there are two pages numbered 14. At page 142, EH renumbered all previous pages sequentially. At some later point in revision, he added this page, which he also numbered 14. For fictional needs, Hemingway moved his parents' summer cottage from Walloon Lake to Lake Charlevoix.
14. "The Twa Corbies," in Arthur Quiller-Couch (ed.), *The Oxford Book of English Verse* (Oxford: Oxford University Press, 1939), p. 450. Hemingway first came to know and love this poem in high school. In his March 1926 notebook, he transcribed the second verse while making notes for a novel about an escaped convict.
15. "To the Editor of the Tribune," *Tribune*, ca. mid-Oct. 1927, clipping, JFK.
16. Grace Hemingway–EH, Oct. 14, 1927, JFK; *SAR*, p. 39.
17. Hadley's sixth-floor apartment at 98 Boulevard Auguste Blanqui lay well below Montparnasse but the Glacière Metro stop almost at her front door put her within easy reach of the Quarter and took Bumby to within a few blocks of his father's apartment on rue Férou.
18. EH–Clarence Hemingway, Oct. 20, 1927, JFK. Although many have called this the "Jimmy Breen" novel, the name, Breen, appears only in the late revision to one chapter. Hadley was booked to arrive on the *Lancastria* (see my *Hemingway: An Annotated Chronology*, Detroit, Mich.: Omnigraphics, Inc., 1991), but she arrived three weeks before the *Lancastria* docked.
19. Item 529b, JFK, Chapter Six, p. 6/89.

20. This portion of the unfinished novel was published in the Finca Vigia edition of the short stories as "A Train Trip," p. 565. A typo on p. 565 should read Ad Wolgast, not Moegast.
21. Item 529b, JFK, Chapter Six, p. 6/89.
22. Item 529b, JFK, Chapter Seven, pp. 17–18/110–11.
23. Item 529b, JFK, Chapter Nine, p. 1/127.
24. EH–Archibald MacLeish, Oct. 8, 1927, *SL*, p. 262.
25. Item 529b, JFK, Chapter Ten, pp. 1–12.
26. "Latin Quarter Notes," *Tribune*, Oct. 12, 1927. This story has been variously reported with generally the same conclusion. It apparently became a momentary *bon mot* in the Quarter, for Wescott never forgot the insult.
27. Item 529b, JFK, Chapter Thirteen, p. 14.
28. Item 529b, JFK, Chapter Thirteen, p. 10.
29. Telegram repeated in Gus Pfeiffer–EH, Oct. 18, 1927, JFK.
30. Dorothy Parker, "A Book of Great Short Stories," *New Yorker*, 3 (Oct. 29, 1927), pp. 92–4; "Men Without Women," *Time*, 10 (Oct. 14, 1927), p. 38.
31. Joseph Wood Krutch, "The End of Art," *The Nation*, 125 (Nov. 16, 1927), p. 548.
32. Lee Wilson Dodd, *Saturday Review of Literature*, 4 (Nov. 19, 1927), pp. 322–3.
33. "An Essay in Criticism," *New York Herald Tribune Books*, 4 (Oct. 9, 1927), 1, 8. As John Hollander points out ("Hemingway's Extraordinary Reality," in Harold Bloom (ed.), *Modern Critical Views: Ernest Hemingway* (New York: Chelsea, 1985), p. 126), Woolf seems to think "that the operation in question is a tonsillectomy."
34. EH–F. Scott Fitzgerald, ca. Nov. 3, 1927, JFK.
35. Sportplatz bike races were November 3–9. Alfred Flecthheim–EH, Nov. 14, 1927, JFK, refers to 500 marks for the "Sintenis." Ramon Guthrie, "For Approximately the Same Reason That a Man Can't Marry His Widow's Sister," *Maximum Security Ward* (Farrar, Straus & Giroux, 1970), p. 98; thanks to Bud Rovit for pointing this poem out to me, one of his many gifts.
36. EH–I. S. Godolphin, 5, Dec. 1927, PUL.
37. EH–Max Perkins, Nov. 24, 1927, Scribner author file, PUL. Chapter Seventeen is less than two pages, breaking off for the shift in point of view. He tried the same shift to no advantage when revising *The Sun Also Rises*.
38. Item 529b, JFK, Chapter Nineteen, p. 5.

39. Item 529b, JFK, Chapter Twenty, p. 1.
40. G. A. Pfeiffer–EH, Nov. 20, 1927, JFK.
41. Robert Jordan in *For Whom the Bell Tolls* and Thomas Hudson in *Islands in the Stream* are both related to Jimmy Crane's revolutionist father, and both novels are deeply concerned with fathers and sons.
42. "Valentine," *88P*, p. 93; first published in the "Final Number" of the *Little Review* (May 1929), p. 42.
43. Scribner royalty payments, Scribner author file, PUL; Max Perkins–EH, Nov. 18, 1927, PUL; Max Perkins–EH, Dec. 8, 1927, PUL. Royalties were paid on sales to the end of October. The first printing of the book sold out within two weeks.
44. Guy Hickok–EH, Nov. 19, 1927, JFK.
45. Fr. Vincent Donovan–EH, Thanksgiving Day 1927, JFK.
46. A corrected and revised draft of the letter written ca. Dec. 9, 1927, JFK. Fr. Donovan answered the letter on Dec. 26, 1927, JFK.
47. Max Perkins–EH, Nov. 30, 1927, JFK. The ad in the *New York Times Book Review* for Nov. 27, 1927 announced the book was in its "Third Large Printing."
48. William Horne–EH, Nov. 29, 1927, Baker files, PUL.
49. F. Scott Fitzgerald–EH [ca. Dec. 10, 1927], Turnbull, p. 302, mentions receiving EH's check from Max Perkins who enclosed it in his letter of Dec. 8.
50. Hemingway's borrower's card, Beach Collection, PUL: Osbert Sitwell's book was checked out Nov. 26 and returned Dec. 7 when EH was checking out books for the Schruns trip.
51. EH–F. Scott Fitzgerald [ca. Dec. 18, 1927], JFK. Letter was torn up and then pieced back together with a brief cover to explain it.
52. Guy Hickok–EH, Dec. 22, 1927, JFK. Hemingway did, in fact, have congenitally defective eyesight.
53. F. Scott Fitzgerald–EH [Dec. 1927], Turnbull, pp. 302–3.
54. EH–F. Scott Fitzgerald, *SL*, pp. 267–9. Baker dates this letter ca. Dec. 15, 1927, but it is probably a week or two later.
55. Item 489, undated on back of 1927 envelope addressed to Pauline at Gstaad, JFK. Note goes on to say that Eliot and Pound were examples of imitators. Eliot "watered waste land and made it blossom like the rose."
56. EH–Wyndham Lewis, Oct. 24, 1927, *SL*, p. 263.
57. Wyndham Lewis–EH, Nov. 6, 1927 and [undated, ca. Nov. 17, 1927], JFK. Archibald MacLeish–Wyndham Lewis, dated [Dec. 1927?] but probably late Nov., Winnick, p. 209.

58. Wyndham Lewis, "New Novels," *The New Statesman*, Nov. 26, 1927, p. 208.
59. EH–Ezra Pound [ca. Nov. 1927], probably unmailed, JFK.
60. Archibald MacLeish–Wyndham Lewis, Dec. 8, 1927, Winnick, p. 210.
61. Item 407, JFK. This poem is not in the first edition of *88P*. There are two versions. Item 407 is a typescript with revisions to Item 406, a holograph manuscript.
62. EH–Waldo Peirce [late Dec. 1927], Baker files, PUL. The Dostoevsky books were *The Insulted and Injured* and *The Gambler and Other Stories*. Hemingway's borrower's card, Sylvia Beach Collection, PUL.
63. *transition*, 10, pp. 115, enclosed in Guy Hickok–EH, Jan. 2, 1928, JFK.
64. Grace Hemingway–EH, Dec. 16, 1927, JFK.
65. Marie Reichelt–Grace Hemingway, Nov. 27, 1927, UTex.
66. Madelaine Hemingway–EH, Jan. 6, 1928, JFK.
67. Clarence Hemingway–EH, Jan. 13, 1928, UTex.
68. EH–Ezra Pound, undated, JFK.
69. Art Moss, "With Latin Quarter Folk," Feb. 4, 1928.
70. EH–Max Perkins, Jan. 15, 1928, *SL*, p. 269; EH–James Joyce, Jan. 30, 1928, *SL*, p. 271.
71. *New York Times*, Jan. 20, 1928, p. 12.
72. Grace Hemingway–EH, Feb. 1, 1928, JFK.
73. EH–Ezra Pound [undated, ca. Feb. 12, 1928], JFK.
74. Hemingway's borrower's card, Beach Collection, PUL. Card notes he returned the Jan. *Dial* on Feb. 13.
75. EH–Max Perkins, Feb. 12, 1928, *SL*, p. 271.
76. Item 529c, JFK. This chapter is the only time the name "Breen" appears in the twenty-two original chapters and two revised chapters.
77. *New Yorker*, Dec. 24, 1927, pp. 17–18; *Bookman*, Jan. 1928, p. 560.
78. John Riddell, "A Parody Interview with Mr. Hemingway," *Vanity Fair*, 29 (Jan. 1928), p. 78.
79. T. S. Matthews, "Flatteries: Pretty Grand: By a Sincere Flatterer of Ernest Hemingway," *New Republic*, 52 (Feb. 8, 1928), pp. 323–4.
80. Constant Reader (Dorothy Parker), "Reading Writing," *The New Yorker*, Feb. 18, 1928, pp. 76–7.
81. Pauline Hemingway–Gertude Stein, Feb. 27, 1928, YUL.

82. "With Latin Quarter Folk," Feb. 18, 1928. For unknown but possibly conscious reasons the *Herald* began to misspell Hemingway's name at almost every opportunity.
83. EH–Max Perkins, Mar. 17, 1928, *SL*, p. 274.
84. "Around the Town," *Herald*, Mar. 4, 1928.
85. EH–Max Perkins, Mar. 17, 1928, *SL*, p. 273.
86. *Herald*, Mar. 6, 1928.
87. EH–Max Perkins, Mar. 17, 1928, *SL*, p. 274.

Chapter Eleven: A PIECE OF THE CONTINENT

1. US Census Reports for 1920 and 1930; various histories of Key West.
2. Christopher Cox, *A Key West Companion* (New York: St. Martin's Press, 1983), pp. 133–4.
3. Misdated ca. Mar. 28, 1928, JFK; four days out would have been 21 March.
4. Probably misdated ca. Mar. 28, 1928, *SL*, p. 275. Probably 22 March; says "five or ten days out."
5. G. A. Pfeiffer–EH, Apr. 7, 1928, JFK (sent to Piggott and redirected to Key West on April 20.)
6. G. A. Pfeiffer–EH, Jan. 22, 1928, JFK. This has sometimes been referred to as a "yellow" Ford. If it was yellow, it was a special order, for Ford had only four colors in 1928: Niagara Blue, Arabian Sand, Dawn Grey, and Gun Metal Blue.
7. EH–Max Perkins, Apr. 7, 1928, Scribner author file, PUL.
8. *AFTA*, 1957 edn, p. 3. (Further references are to this edition.) For more detailed treatment of the manuscript, read my early work, *Hemingway's First War* (Princeton: Princeton University Press, 1976; paperback Oxford: Blackwell, 1989). References to the manuscript draft are found in Item 64, JFK. Quotes have been limited to previously published material.
9. *AFTA*, p. 6.
10. Information on daily life in Key West comes from numerous sources: James McLendon, *Papa, Hemingway in Key West* (Key West: Langley Press, rev. edn 1990); the Monroe County Library; the Key West Historical Society; Christopher Cox, *A Key West Companion* (New York: St. Martin's Press, 1983); 1935 FERA *Guide Book to Key West*; Stan Windhorn and Wright Langley, *Yesterday's Key West* (Langley Press, 1973) and *Yesterday's Florida Keys* (Langley Press,

1974); US Weather Bureau local reports in the Monroe County Library; and the *Key West Citizen.*

11. This chance meeting has been much retold with varying degrees of accuracy. My version is based on letters Clarence Hemingway–EH, Apr. 11, 13, 1928, JFK. Grace Hemingway–EH, Mar. 11, 1928, redirected to Key West stamped Apr. 18, 1928, JFK; the ferry schedule from Havana published in the train schedules of the Florida East Coast Railway, 1928; photographs at the Kennedy Library; and Marcelline H. Sanford, *At the Hemingways* (Boston: Little, Brown, 1961), p. 227. The version in Leicester Hemingway, *My Brother, Ernest Hemingway* (New York: World Pub. Co., 1961), pp. 94–5, is almost all fiction.

12. Photograph, JFK.

13. McLendon, *Papa*, pp. 26–9.

14. EH–Max Perkins, Apr. 21, 1928, *SL*, pp. 276–7; John Dos Passos–EH, Apr. 18, 1927, JFK; William Smith–EH, Apr. 17, 1928, JFK.

15. *AFTA*, p. 5.

16. US Weather Bureau Report, original in Monroe County Library; "Valbanera Loss Still Is Mystery; Find No Survivors," Miami *Metropolis*, Sept. 26, 1919.

17. Max Perkins–EH, Apr. 19, 1928, JFK.

18. *AFTA* MS-128, 129A, 129B, JFK.

19. *AFTA* MS-149.

20. Robert T. Webb, *The History of Clay Country* (publisher unknown, 1933), p. 30.

21. Information on the Pfeiffer family is based on interviews with Eileen Spence in Piggott, letters, newspaper stories, and the Baker and Kert biographies. Like all family stories, it comes in several versions with contradictions. See Tom Weil's feature in St. Louis *Post Dispatch*, May 8, 1984; Noel Burton's feature in the Clinton, MO *Daily Democrat*, Jan. 7, 1983; and Ron Russell's "Chasing Hemingway's Ghost," *The Commercial Appeal* [Memphis] Sunday magazine, Aug. 27, 1978.

22. EH–Max Perkins, May 31, 1928, *SL*, p. 278.

23. Eileen Spence interview, Piggott, 1989. Years later Hemingway would have his personal priest coming to the house in Cuba.

24. EH–Clarence Hemingway, June 1, 1928, JFK.

25. EH–Max Perkins, May 31, 1928, *SL*, p. 278.

26. *AFTA* MS-201 in a section later revised extensively.

27. *AFTA* MS-208, canceled.

28. *AFTA* MS-230.
29. *AFTA* MS-232–3.
30. Grace Hemingway–EH, June 4, 1928, and Clarence Hemingway– EH, June 4, 1928, JFK.
31. *AFTA* MS-278.
32. Hoover's nomination on the first ballot came on June 15, 1928. The Hemingways drove into town the day before. A Max Perkins–EH letter (June 26, 1928, JFK) confirms Hemingway's brief visit to the convention. At one time Hemingway planned to do a convention report for Pound's *Exile*, but with his novel running smoothly, he lost interest.
33. In a letter to Guy Hickok (Sept. 28, 1928, JFK), EH refers to Ruth White Lowry as his cousin.
34. *AFTA* MS-302.
35. EH–Waldo Peirce, June 17, 1928, Baker files, PUL.
36. Guy Hickok–EH, June 19, 1928, JFK; Marcelline H. Sanford–EH, June 14, 1928, JFK; Waldo Peirce–EH, June 28, 1928, JFK. Max Perkins–EH, June 26, 1928, JFK.
37. EH–Guy Hickok, ca. July 27, 1928, *SL*, p. 280.
38. Repeated in Gus Pfeiffer–EH letter, June 29, 1928, JFK.
39. Waldo Peirce–EH, 28 June, 1928, JFK.
40. Leonore Ovitt, "Ernest Hemingway, One of Ours," *The Oak Parker*, June 29, 1928, p. 32.
41. Telegram is found on the verso of the Waldo Peirce letter cited in n–39 above and confirmed in EH–Dad and Mother, July 15, 1928, JFK.
42. Clarence Hemingway–EH, July 18, 1928, JFK; Paul Pfeiffer– Pauline Hemingway, July 1, 1928, JFK; Mary Pfeiffer–EH, July 1, 1928, JFK.
43. Turnbull, p. 220. "Hophead" was slang for a user of narcotics.
44. *AFTA* MS-355–6.
45. *AFTA* MS-359.
46. Austro-Hungrarian battle map, Italian front (October, 1917), Library of Congress.
47. EH–Grace and Clarence Hemingway, dated July 4, 1928 and added on to July 15, 1928, JFK.
48. EH–Archibald MacLeish, July 15, 1928, Library of Congress; because the top of MS-457 is clearly labeled "July 15," this letter may have preceded his day's work, but that is unlikely, given his habits.

49. *AFTA* MS-387.
50. EH–Waldo Peirce, July 23, 1928, Baker files, PUL.
51. EH–Max Perkins, July 23, 1928, *SL*, p. 280.
52. Road directions and conditions are from a variety of 1928–9 road maps in the Map Division, Library of Congress. Information on cross-country driving in 1928 comes from Albert D. Manchester, *Trails Begin Where Rails End* (Glendale, CA: Trans Anglo Books, 1987); Charles J. Finger, *Footloose in the West* (New York: William Morrow, 1932); Warren J. Belasco, *Americans on the Road* (Cambridge, MA: MIT Press, 1979).
53. EH–Waldo Peirce, Aug. 9, 1928, *SL*, p. 282. The route is speculative, based on Hemingway's statement on mileage (1,040 miles), period road maps, and routes recommended in guidebooks.
54. EH–Waldo Peirce, Aug. 9, 1928; confirmed by notations in the manuscript.
55. John Dos Passos–EH [undated], JFK; Waldo Peirce–EH, July 28, 1928, JFK; HH–EH, Aug. 4, 1928, JFK.
56. Guy Hickok–EH, Aug. 7, 1928, JFK.
57. Pauline Hemingway–EH, July 29, 31, Aug. 3, 4, 1928, JFK.
58. Pauline Hemingway–EH, Aug. 6, 1928, JFK.
59. *AFTA* MS-596.
60. Pauline Hemingway–EH, Aug. 9, 1928, JFK.
61. Pauline Hemingway–EH, Aug. 14, 1928, JFK.
62. According to the medical historian at the Duke University medical school, nitrous oxide was the gas being used during labor in 1918. Robbie Knott brought this information to my attention.
63. *AFTA* MS-615.
64. EH–Guy Hickok, Aug. 18, 1928, *SL*, p. 284.
65. By this point, Hemingway was putting dates at the beginning and end of each day's work. August 18 and 19 are conspicuously recorded with a zero after each entry.
66. *AFTA*, p. 140.
67. *AFTA* MS-629.
68. *AFTA* MS-640.

Chapter Twelve: THE DEAD

1. Owen Wister–EH, Sept. 13, 1928, JFK. It was probably on this visit that Hemingway was given the two Henry James quotes that appear on a typed page in the *AFTA* MS.

2. The book, published in July 1928, contained "The Right Honorable the Strawberries," one of Hemingway's favorite Wister stories.

3. EH–Waldo Peirce, ca. Aug. 23, 1928, *SL*, p. 284. This letter is misdated, probably written at least two weeks later. EH did not finish his first draft until 22 Aug.

4. EH–Waldo Peirce, ca. Aug. 23, 1928.

5. EH–Waldo Peirce, Aug. 9, 1928, *SL*, p. 282. In the same letter he says that Patrick "looks like a Chinese woodchuck."

6. See Verda Arnold, "The Last Frontier" (1925), reprinted Ralph Glidden, in *Exploring the Yellowstone High Country* (Cooke City, Montana: Cooke City Store, 1976), pp. 110–13.

7. See EH–Owen Wister, ca. Sept. 26, 1928, Library of Congress.

8. EH–F. Scott Fitzgerald, ca. Oct. 9, 1928, *SL*, pp. 287–8.

9. Clarence Hemingway–EH, Sept. 26, 1928, JFK.

10. EH–Owen Wister, Sept. 26, 1928, Library of Congress.

11. EH–Archibald MacLeish, Sept. 26, 1928, Library of Congress. A "Mammy song" refers to the blackface minstrel songs that Al Jolson was then making popular in his talking movies.

12. EH–Max Perkins, Sept. 28, 1928, *SL*, pp. 285–7.

13. Max Perkins–EH, Sept. 21, 1928, PUL, JFK.

14. EH–Max Perkins, Oct. 11, 1928, *SL*, p. 289–90.

15. In my *Hemingway: An Annotated Chronology* I have Pauline going with Hemingway to Chicago. In truth, she joined him there about Oct. 30. She was not with him in Oak Park.

16. In the first draft, the Fontans were called Pichots which evokes the French word *pichet*, the small wine pitcher. Fontans, in revision, calls up fountain or spring. As usual I am indebted to H. R. Stoneback's essay "Mais Je Reste Catholique," in Beegel, *Hemingway's Neglected Short Fiction*, pp. 209–24, for several insights. See also Smith's discussion of the story's development (*Reader's Guide*).

17. G. A. Pfeiffer–EH, Oct. 16, 1928, JFK. EH–Guy Hickok, Sept. 27, 1928, private collection: "I hope to vote for Al in Illnois. Will return to birth place for that alone." On election day, he was visiting MacLeish in Conway, MA.

18. "Wine of Wyoming," *CSS*, p. 347.

19. Ibid., p. 350.

20. Pauline's letter (Oct. 17, 1928; JFK) to EH indicates he left Oct. 16 and arrived in Oak Park the following day.

21. Although this trip is not mentioned in books by several Hemingway biographers, it is verified by the following letters at the JFK:

Pauline Hemingway–EH, Oct. 17, 19, 1928; Clarence Hemingway–EH, Oct. 23, 1928.

22. See Clarence Hemingway–EH, Oct. 23, 1928, JFK.
23. See Sanford, *At the Hemingways*, pp. 223–30.
24. Grace Hemingway–EH, Mar. 24, 1929, JFK.
25. Sanford, *At the Hemingways*, pp. 223–4.
26. "The Florida Madness," *New Republic*, 45 (Jan. 27, 1926), p. 258. See also Gertrude Shelby, "Florida Frenzy," *Harper's Monthly*, 152 (Jan. 1926), pp. 117–86.
27. Stella Crossley, "Florida Cashes in Her Chips," *The Nation*, 123 (July 7, 1926), p. 11.
28. *Tribune*, Sept. 21, 1926.
29. Henry S. Villard, "Florida Aftermath," *The Nation*, 126 (June 6, 1928), pp. 635–6.
30. *New York Times*, Sept. 18–23, 1928.
31. Madelaine Hemingway–EH, Sept. 26, 1928, JFK.
32. Based on two paintings in the First United Church in Oak Park and ten paintings owned by Ruth Arnold's daughter.
33. Oliver S. Ormsky–Clarence Hemingway, Oct. 3, 1928, UTex.
34. Pauline Hemingway–EH, Oct. 22, 1928, JFK.
35. Pauline Hemingway–EH, Oct. 26, 1928, JFK. In 1928, Rosenfeld published a novel, *The Boy in the Sun*, and he edited the 1927 edition of *American Caravan*.
36. Clarence Hemingway–EH, Oct. 23, 1928, JFK.
37. Booklet, dated Nov. 1, 1928 and signed in Hemingway's hand, Hemingway Miscellaneous File, JFK.
38. Gioia Diliberto, *Hadley* (New York: Houghton Mifflin, 1992), galley-188 (read in galleys).
39. HH–EH, Nov. 1, 1928, JFK.
40. EH–F. Scott Fitzgerald, Nov. 18, 1928, *SL*, p. 290.
41. Henry Strater–EH, Nov. 21, 1928, JFK. See Bruccoli (1), pp. 68–70; Mellow, pp. 323–8.
42. Evan Shipman–EH, Nov. 20, 1928, JFK. "Gans Outpointed By Glick Before 19,000 At Garden," *New York Times*, Nov. 17, 1928.
43. *New York Times*, Nov. 18, 1928.
44. Mellow, p. 325.
45. F. Scott Fitzgerald–EH, Dec. 28, 1928, Turnbull, p. 303.
46. Lorine Thompson–Pauline Hemingway [undated], enclosed in Pauline Hemingway–EH, ca. Oct. 25, 1928, JFK.
47. *Tribune*, Dec. 7, 1928.

48. Hadley Richardson–EH, Jan. 8, 1921, JFK.
49. Sanford, *At the Hemingways*, pp. 230–1.
50. Evan Shipman–EH, Dec. 13, 1928, JFK.
51. Grace Hemingway–Scribner's Publishing Company, Dec. 6, 1928, Scribner author file, first read at Scribner offices, now at PUL. Telegram read: "Try to locate Ernest Hemingway in New York. Advise him of death of his father today. Ask him to communicate with home immediately."
52. Carol Hemingway–EH, Dec. 6, 1928, JFK.
53. EH–Max Perkins, Dec. 6, 1928, timed 5.00 p.m., Scribner author file, PUL.
54. EH–F. Scott Fitzgerald, ca. Dec. 9, 1928, *SL*, p. 291.
55. Henry Strater–EH, Dec. 8, 1928, JFK.
56. EH–Max Perkins, Dec. 6, 1928, timed 8.00 p.m., Scribner author file.
57. Coroner's inquest held Dec. 7, 1928, Oak Park, IL. "The bullet pierced the brain looping under the skin, after shattering the bone of the skull in the left temple 5 cm. above and 7 cm. posterior to the external auditory meatus. There were powder burns at the point of entrance of the bullet. Blood was oozing from the bullet wound."
58. See Sanford, *At the Hemingways*, pp. 230–1; Leicester Hemingway, *My Brother, Ernest Hemingway*, p. 99.
59. EH–Madelaine Hemingway, Dec. 7, 1928, JFK.
60. Sanford, *At the Hemingways*, p. 232.
61. Leicester Hemingway *My Brother, Ernest Hemingway*, p. 99.
62. Thanks to Barbara Ballinger of Oak Park for information on the funeral home and burial of Dr. Hemingway.
63. Grace Hemingway–EH, Dec. 22, 1928, JFK.
64. Leicester Hemingway, *My Brother, Ernest Hemingway*, p. 99.
65. Note found in Baker files, PUL, undated but probably written in Kansas City in October 1931 as EH was finishing *Death in the Afternoon*.
66. EH–Max Perkins, Dec. 16, 1928, *SL*, pp. 291–2. The week in Oak Park is substantiated by this letter mailed from Corinth, Mississippi on Hemingway's return trip to Key West.
67. *AFTA* MS p. 128 says in margin: "read to here Wednesday." MS p. 202 says: "Read up to here Thursday Dec. 13 going better so far." MS p. 293 says: "Read Dec. 15 to 344 can type almost as it stands." MS p. 345 says: "went over Monday Dec. 16 [*sic*] from 345 to 400 is OK to type." Monday was the 17th.

68. For details and exact quotes see Reynolds, *Hemingway's First War*, pp. 29–30. *AFTA* MS pp. 129A and 129B.
69. Several letters between mother and son in Jan.–Mar. 1929, JFK, confirm this point.
70. Archibald MacLeish–EH, Dec. 14, 1928, JFK.
71. EH–John Dos Passos [early Jan. 1929], UVa.
72. *AFTA* MS-425 bis.
73. EH–Max Perkins, Jan. 8, 10, 1929, *SL*, pp. 292–4.
74. EH–Guy Hickok, Jan. 14, 1929, private collection.
75. EH–Max Perkins, Jan. 22, 1929, *SL*, p. 294: "Finished the book today."
76. Max Perkins–EH, Jan. 23, 1929, Scribner author file, PUL.
77. EH–Max Perkins, Jan. 23, 1929, Scribner author file, PUL.
78. EH–Grace Hemingway [undated, Jan. 1929], Lilly.
79. Grace Hemingway–EH, July 24, 1920, UTex.
80. Grace Hemingway–EH, Feb. 24, 1929, JFK.

ENVOI

1. This photograph is in the Patrick Hemingway Collection, PUL. A. C. Fabricius & Co.–EH, Mar. 15, 1929, JFK.
2. Guy Hickok–EH, Jan. 29, 1929, JFK. *New York Times*, Apr. 5, 1929, source: US Census.
3. A. G. Pfeiffer–EH, Feb. 28, 1929, JFK.
4. EH–Max Perkins, Feb. 14, 1929, Scribner author file, PUL.
5. EH–Max Perkins, Mar. 11, 1929, Scribner author file, PUL.
6. *New York Times*, Apr. 1–6, 1929.
7. Grace Hemingway–EH, Apr. 7, 1929, JFK; EH–Grace Hemingway, Mar. 30, 1929, JFK. This letter is misdated March 11, 1929 in *SL*, pp. 295–6. The biblical reference reads: "Greater love hath no man than this, that a man lay down his life for his friends."

INDEX

Adams, Henry, 26
Adams, Maud, 16
Abd el Krim, 11
Adelboden, Switzerland, 162
Aigues-Mortes, France, 124–5
Alden, John, 161
American Caravan, 99
Americans in Paris, 145
Anderson, Sherwood, 4, 16, 62–3, 81, 82, 92, 165
    response to *Torrents*, 33–4, 42–3
Antheil, George, 71, 83, 165
Antibes, France, 26, 30, 31, 43–5
Arch-Confraternity for Relief of Souls in
    Purgatory, 202
Arlberg, Austria, 97
Arlen, Michael, 88
Asch, Nathan, 2
avalanches, 97, 237 n. 30
Avignon, France, 124

Bailey, C. Thomas, 121
Baker, Josephine, 122, 144–5
Ballet Russe, 132
Barry, Philip, 45
bars, cafes, and restaurants
    Aux Deux Magots, 87, 103, 132, 164
    Café des Mariniers, 132
    Café du Dôme, 21
    Café Flore, 164
    Closerie des Lilas, 16, 21, 164
    Dingo, 7, 21
    Gypsy, 21
    Iruna, 46
    Jockey, 21
    Lavenue, 64
    Lipps, 164
    Rotonde, 21
    Select, 132
Barton, Bruce, 116

Baudelaire, Charles, 64
Beach, Sylvia, 6, 13, 75, 81
Benchley, Robert C., 10, 45, 106, 118
Berlin, Germany, 153
Berlin, Irving, 145
Bernhardt, Sarah, 144
Bird, William, 47
Black Mannikin, 73
Bocher, Main, 7
Bologna, Italy, 113
Boulogne, France, 62
boxers
    Jimmy Brown, 93
    Georges Carpentier, 93
    Gorilla Jones, 204
    Bart Molina, 93
    Al Singer, 204
Bromfield, Louis, 5, 75, 138–40, 148, 164, 165
Bromfield, Mary, 75
Brooklyn Eagle, 113
Brooks, George, 172
Brown, Curtis, 20
bullfighters
    Juan Belmonte, 49
    Lalanda, 49
    Niño de la Palma, 27, 46, 49
    Villalta, 46
    Zurito, 49
bullfights, 5, 27, 34, 46–50, 69, 133
Bullitt, Mrs. William, 137
Burkhardt (divorce lawyer), 91, 111
Butcher, Fanny, 92, 139, 246 n. 35

Chartres, France, 26, 35, 78–80, 66, 111
churches
    Cathedral of the Holy Name (Chicago), 202
    First Congregational Church (Oak Park), 211
    Nuestra Señora del Pilar (Zaragoza), 69
    St. Honoré d'Eylau (Paris), 121, 124

St. Martin-au-Val, 78
St. Mary's Star of the Sea (Key West), 170
St. Pierre-de-Montrouge (Paris), 121
St. Sulpice (Paris), 113, 164
"Cinema of a Man" (MacLeish), 70–1
Cleland, John, 85
Coates, Frances, 100
Common Reader (V. Woolf), 13, 26
Composition as Explanation (Stein), 83, 100
Connelly, Marc, 45
Cooke City, Montana, 194
Coolidge, Calvin, 145
Crosby, Harry, 103–4
Crowley, Aleister, 41
cummings, e. e., 104

"Daisy Miller" (James), 52
Defoe, Daniel, 26
Dempsey, Jack, 57
Descriptions of Literature (Stein), 57
Dijon, France, 115
Donaldson, Scott, 230 n. 2
Dos Passos, John, 9–12, 14, 45, 47, 71–2, 100–1,
   129, 136, 172–3, 188, 215
Dreiser, Theodore, 22
Dry Tortugas, 172, 174
Dubliners (Joyce), 235 n. 59
Duncan, Isadora, 87, 144
Dunn, Clara, 143

Early Autumn (Bromfield), 138–9
election of 1928, 179, 197, 204
Eliot, T. S., 6, 21, 23, 82, 83, 127, 163, 180
Ellerslie Mansion (Fitzgerald), 203–4
"Elucidation, An" (Stein), 112
Enormous Room, The (cummings), 104
"Ernest Hemingway" (Walsh), 15
"Ernest Hemingway, One of Ours," 182–3

"Family Group" (MacLeish), 94
Fanny Hill (Cleland), 85
"Farm, The" (Miró), 53
fascism, 108–9, 110, 113
Fez (Morocco), 11
Finch, Edith, 57
Firenze, Italy, 113
Fitzgerald, F. Scott, 4, 12, 16–17, 22, 31–5, 38–9,
   45, 57, 68, 81, 88, 117–18, 141, 157–8, 183,
   195, 196, 203–4, 209
   critique of The Sun Also Rises, 40–2
Fitzgerald, Zelda, 37, 38–9, 42, 45–6, 203–4
"Fixer, The," 161
Flechtheim, Alfred, 153
Fleming, Robert E., 231 n. 15
Florida land boom, 73
"For Approximately the Same Reason That a Man
   Can't Marry His Widow's Sister," (Guthrie),
   153
Ford, Ford Madox, 18, 41, 43, 74, 75, 82, 106, 165
Forest Home Cemetery, 211
Fournier, Nina, 235 n. 8

Friend, Krebs, 102
Fuller, Loie, 144

Galantière, Lewis, 75, 165, 196
Gaschurn, Austria, 9–12
Genova, Italy, 113
Gentlemen Prefer Blondes (Loos), 8
Grant, Robert, 24
Grau-du-Roi, Le, France, 124–5
Gris, Juan, 125
Gstaad, Switzerland, 97–104, 157–62
Guffey, Carlos, M.D., 180–1, 194
Guthrie, Ramon, 153
Gypsies, 125

Haines, Lett, 18
Hamlet of A. MacLeish, The, 158
Hammet, Dashiell, 136
Harcourt, Alfred, 5
Hemingway, Anson, 211
   death of, 72–3
Hemingway, Carol, 207, 211
Hemingway, Clarence Edmonds, 34, 71–3, 91, 92,
   141, 179, 195, 202, 219–20
   appearance, 171, 199–201
   behavior, 199–201, 210
   coroner's inquest, 209
   Ernest's divorce, response to, 91, 116, 137
   financial condition, 210–12, 233 n. 24
   Florida, retirement investments, 72–3, 171,
   199–201, 210
   funeral, 211, 219
   Key West, visit to, 171, 252 n. 11
   medical condition, 146, 171, 199, 209, 212
   suicide, 206–7, 257 n. 57
Hemingway, Ernest
   Biographical
   accidents, 142, 157, 166–7
   affair with Pauline Pfeiffer, 6, 26–7, 29–30,
   31–4, 38–40, 49–50, 59, 61–2
   androgony, 65, 133
   apartments and houses, 113–14, 121, 133, 143,
   205
   appearance, 1–3, 45, 47, 97–8, 171
   art, 27, 53, 62, 153, 164
   automobiles, 113–15, 218
   behavior, 7, 53–4, 70, 75–6, 92–3, 120, 143
   Berlin trip, 153
   biography, dislike of, 106–7
   Catholicism, 34–5, 70, 114, 123–5, 133–4, 156,
   170, 177, 189, 197–8, 202
   changes in life style, 74–5, 83, 86, 98–9, 109,
   115–16, 121–2, 131–2, 143, 205, 219–20
   character traits, 1–2, 102–3, 194, 196; alienation
   of friends, 83, 86, 92–3, 165, 236 n. 23;
   competitiveness, 10–11; female
   companionship, need for, 30, 62, 65, 143, 196,
   206; humor, 22, 85–6, 158, 195; loneliness,
   26–7, 36, 65; male companionship, need for,
   108–9, 172–6, 215; money, worries about,
   32, 35, 121–2, 196, 205; papers, accumulation

of, 114−16, 189; wives blamed for problems, 30, 81, 196
Christmas: 1926, 90−7; 1927, 157−62
divorce: begins, 79−80; effect of, 75, 100, 105−6, 110−11, 122, 143−4; terms of 80−1, 91
father's suicide and funeral, 207−14
Hadley, separation from, 51−60
Hundred Days, 60−80
income, 57, 58, 88, 128, 130, 174, 194, 215, 218, 226 n. 21
Italian trip, 112−15
Kansas City, trip to, 179−80
Key West, arrival in, 168−76
media, appearance in, 13, 16, 60, 74, 102, 106−7, 111−12, 120, 131, 148, 151−2, 161, 162, 163−6, 239 n. 62
meets Hadley and Bumby in New York, 204−6
mental state, 3, 76
need to return to the U.S., 165−6
New York, trip to, 203−4
nicknames, 30, 69, 78, 79, 80, 195
Oak Park, visit to, 198−201
parents, relationship with, 91, 104−6, 137, 141, 171, 202, 215−16, 220
Paris, attitude toward, 20−1, 51−2, 131−2, 144
reading, (authors): Adam, Edward, 196; Aiken, Conrad, 196; cummings, e. e., 104; Dostoevsky, 160; Henry, O., 161; James, Henry, 17, 52, 160, 163, 197, 230 n. 10, 254 n. 1; Joyce, James, 70, 104; Mann, Thomas, 202; Rosenfeld, Paul, 202; Thomason, John, 68; Wister, Owen, 193, 197
reading, (texts): American Caravan, 202; The Awkward Age, 160; Before the Bombardment, 157; Costumes By Eros, 196; Descriptions of Literature, 57; The Enormous Room, 104; Fix Bayonets, 68; The Gambler and Other Stories, 250 n. 62; Grandmothers, 152; The Great Gatsby, 16−17; The Insulted and Injured, 250 n. 62; "Kenneth MacLeish's Path to Glory," 93; Lawrence and the Arabs, 163; The Life, Work and Evil Fate of Guy de Maupassant, 68; Nigger to Nigger, 196; Parnell, 130; "The Real Frenchman," 138−40; Recollections of the Irish War, 163; Riddle of the Irish, 163; "The Right Honorable the Strawberries," 197; The Spanish Journey, 112; "Twa Corbie," 147, 247 n. 14; Ulysses, 70, 104; War and Peace, 22; When West Was West, 193
return to Europe, 218−20
sickness, 22, 157, 163; fear of, 31, 228 n. 14
sporting events and outdoor activities: bike races, 19−20, 61, 115, 120, 153; boxing matches, 66, 204; bullfights, 5, 34, 48−9, 69, 133; fishing, 135, 170, 172−4; football, 204; skiing, 9−12, 162
suicide, contemplation of, 1, 6, 76, 96, 103, 212
summer of: 1925, 47; 1926, 26−50
wedding plans, 114, 121
wedding and honeymoon with Pauline, 123−8, 242 n. 43, 244 n. 57

World War One experiences, 34−5, 70, 156−7
Wyoming, trip to 186−94
Zaragoza, trip to, 68−71
Literary
Bromfield satire, 138−40
censorship, 24−5, 193
Hearst offer, rejects 135−6
iceberg theory, 82, 234 n. 49
Liveright contract, 4−5
new novel stalls, 152−7, 166
parodies of Hemingway, 161, 163
prototypes, use of, 83, 88−90, 101−2, 150, 173
references and allusions, 25
relationships, literary: Sherwood Anderson, 33−4, 42−3, 62−3, 81, 92; Louis Bromfield, 138−40, 148; T. S. Eliot, 82, 163; F. Scott Fitzgerald, 22, 40−2, 57, 81, 88, 117−18, 157−8; James Joyce, 21, 29, 70, 99; Wyndham Lewis, 159−60; Archibald MacLeish, 70, 104, 107−8; Ezra Pound, 82−3, 95−6, 99−100, 112; Gertrude Stein, 57, 81, 83−6; Owen Wister, 136, 193; Glenway Wescott, 55, 151−2, 154
reviews, response to, 9, 153, 155, 183
satire, use of, 81, 83−6, 102, 118−19, 138−40
Scribner contract, 4−5
short story award, 163
unable to write, 135−8
Books
A Farewell to Arms: writing of, 66−8, 167, 170, 173, 175−6, 177−9, 180−1, 183−6, 187−91; revisions, 212−17; serialization, 194, 218−19
Fiesta, 112
in our time (1924), 117
In Our Time (1925), 4, 13, 20, 75, 166
Men Without Women, 143, 156, 166; writing of, 107, 117, 121, 122−3, 128; galley proofs, 133−4; publication, 152; reviews of, 152−3, 155, 159; sales, 155−6, 174
The Sun Also Rises, 4, 12, 20, 23−5, 40−2, 81, 100−1, 135, 136, 166, 193; revisions, 5, 10, 16−19, 42; dedication of, 22, 31, 56; editorial changes, 55−6; galley proofs, 54−6; publication, 73; reviews of, 71−2, 73−4, 81, 88, 92, 97, 105, 116−17; sales, 99−100, 130
The Torrents of Spring, 4, 23, 33−4, 57, 118, 138; revisions, 16; galley proofs, 19−20; reviews of, 43, 62−3
Short Stories and Essays
"An Alpine Idyll," 57, 95−6, 99
"A Banal Story," 122
"A Canary For One," 51−3, 230 n. 2
"A Divine Gesture," 85
"The End of Something," 147
"Fifty Grand," 10, 42, 57, 74, 112, 119
"Hills Like White Elephants," 126−8, 135, 244 n. 67
"How I Broke With John Wilkes Booth," 85−6, 99
"In Another Country," 77−8, 88, 94
"Italy, 1927," 119−20, 122, 130

INDEX

"The Killers," 28, 56–7, 136, 163, 219, 231 n. 15
"The Matadors," 28
"Mr. and Mrs. Elliot," 101–3
"Now I Lay Me," 88–90
"A Pursuit Race," 107–8, 123
"The Real Spaniard," 139–40, 147
"A Simple Enquiry," 108
"Ten Indians," 28–9, 122, 126, 227 n. 10
"Today is Friday," 27, 57
"Up In Michigan," 107, 123, 126
"The Wine of Wyoming," 197–8
Poetry, 66, 160
"Neothomist," 65–6, 83
"The Rail Ends Do Not Meet," 132–3
"They All Made Peace," 234 n. 50
"Tragic Poetess," 81–2
"Valentine," 155
Unpublished Writing, 3, 118–19, 126, 158–9, 160, 212, 223 n. 1
"After the War," 93–5
"Crossroads," 52, 230 n. 4
"A Lack of Passion," 123, 126
"A New Slain Knight" 141, 145–52, 152–7, 163, 247 n. 10
Subject Matter
abortion, 126–8
boxing, 93
homosexuality, 18–19, 102, 108, 126, 154
marriage, 51–3, 77–8, 88–90, 93, 95, 101–3
military, 67–8, 77–8, 88, 93–5, 108
revolutions, 145–52
Themes
betrayal, 29, 130
father and son, 28–9, 88–90, 145–52, 249 n. 41
loss, 77–80, 93
male–female relationships, 28–9, 51–3, 77–8, 88–90, 95, 126
Hemingway, George, 200, 209, 219
Hemingway, Grace Hall, 171, 210–12
character, 104–5, 201
Ernest's divorce, response to, 91, 116
financial problems managed by Ernest, 215–16
painting, 104–5, 161, 199, 201
reaction to *The Sun Also Rises*, 92
Hemingway, Hadley Richardson, 7, 30–5, 54–5, 58–9, 90–1, 101, 141, 188, 203, 204–6, 213
Chartres, trips to, 78–80, 111
divorce, 80–1, 100, 110–11, 122
Hundred Days, calls off, 79–80
Paul Mowrer, relationship with, 31, 60, 90, 98, 100, 204–5
new apartment, 53–4, 247 n. 17
nicknames, 30, 78, 80, 98
Pauline, attitude toward, 30–1, 38–40, 49–50, 61, 114
separation from Ernest, 59–60, 61–2, 71–2
trip to U.S. 122, 130–1, 148
Hemingway, John Hadley (Bumby), 31–5, 40, 122, 148, 204–6, 208
Hemingway, Leicester, 163, 199

Hemingway, Madelaine (Sunny), 122, 130, 161–2, 199, 201
Hemingway, Marcelline *see* Sanford, Marcelline
Hemingway, Patrick, 181–2, 189
Hemingway, Pauline Pfeiffer, 6–9, 12, 71, 96–7, 113–14, 171–2, 188–9
affair with Ernest, 13–14, 29–30, 33–4, 46–50, 82
appearance, 6–7
Catholicism, 8
caesarean delivery, 181–2
character, 98
education, 8
money, 7–8, 224 n. 14
pregnancy, 152, 164, 174, 177
separation from Ernest, 62–80
reading, 6, 8–9, 160
wedding, 114, 121
Hemingway, Ursula, 199
Hemingway, Willoughby, 171, 207
Hendaye, France, 138
Herald (Paris edition), Hemingway information, 60, 73–4, 102, 120, 111, 131, 162, 164–5, 165–6
Hickok, Guy, 101, 108–9, 112–15, 118, 119, 120, 130, 136, 156, 157, 161, 181, 188, 190, 195, 215
homosexuality, 18–19, 38, 70, 102, 154, 160
Hoover, Herbert, 179, 204
Horne, William, 156–7, 185, 187
hotels
Alpine (Gstaad), 97
Beauvoir (Paris), 59
Brevoort (New York), 204
Earle Hotel (New York), 206
Folly Ranch (Wyoming), 187
Grand Hôtel de France (Chartres), 78
Metropole (London), 203
Meurice (Boulogne), 62
Hotel de la Pineda (Juan les Pins), 40
Over Sea Hotel (Key West), 173
Pension Aguilar (Madrid), 31
Quintana (Pamplona), 46
Rossli (Gstaad), 97
Shaw's Camp (Cooke City), 194
Taube Inn (Schruns), 5
Vénétia (Paris), 16
Waldorf Astoria (New York), 71
Zum Rössle-Post (Gaschurn), 10–12
Huddleston, Sisley, 233 n. 28

Imola, Italy, 115
Imperia, Italy, 115
"irony and pity," 23

James, Henry, 17–18, 25, 52, 55–6
Johnson, Dossie, 71
Jolas, Eugene, 99
Joyce, James, 21, 34, 70, 75, 99, 104, 112
Juan les Pins, France, 36–46
Junkins, Donald, 230 n. 7

Kessler, Arnold, 10
Key West, Florida, 168–76
Kiley, Jed, 233 n. 26
Knott, Robbie, 254 n. 62
Komrof, Manuel, 71
Kreymbourg, Alfred, 99
Krutch, Joseph Wood, 152

La Coruña, Spain, 133
La Spezia, Italy, 113
Leger, Fernand, 44–5
Lenk, Switzerland, 162
lesbianism, 86, 98
Levine, Charles, 132–3
Lewis, Sinclair, 101, 153
Lewis, Wyndham, 159–60
Lindbergh, Charles, 125, 130
Liveright, Horace, 4
Loeb, Sophie Irene, 22
Long, Ray, 196
Loos, Anita, 8
Lowry, Malcolm and Ruth, 179–80

McAlmon, Robert, 131
MacDonald, Olive, 101–3
MacKenzie, Vernon, 39
MacLeish, Ada, 38, 46, 81, 113, 124
MacLeish, Archibald, 38, 43–5, 68–71, 75, 81, 90,
   93–5, 104, 107–8, 112, 129, 135, 136–7, 158,
   161, 185, 195–6, 203, 214, 215
   analysis of Ernest, 159–60
MacLeish, Kenneth, 69, 93–5, 233 n. 14
Madrid, Spain, 133
Magador, Morocco, 11
Magdalene, Mary, 125
Marrakesh, Morocco, 11
Marx, Harpo, 132
Maupassant, Guy de, 64
Meaux, France, 66
Mencken, H. L., 19–20, 117
Mencken, S. Stanwood, 19–20
Menton, France, 115
Milan, Italy, 77
Miller, Linda P., 230 n. 7
Mitchell, Charles, 145
Modena, Italy,
Moll Flanders (Defoe), 26
Moon Is A Gong, The (Dos Passos), 11
Moorhead, Ethel, 165
Morris, Cedric, 18
Moss, Art, 144, 147, 165
Mowrer, Paul, 30, 60, 79, 98, 100, 103, 203
Mowrer, Winifred, 60, 78–80, 98, 111, 203
Mr. Pamame: A Paris Fantasy (Huddleston), 233 n.
   28
Mrs. Dalloway (V. Woolf), 6, 8–9, 13
Murphy, Gerald, 2, 9–12, 14, 32–5, 38–9, 43–5,
   46–50, 58–9, 62, 71, 130, 132
   appearance, 45, 47
   character, 44–5
   studio, 53–4, 114, 121
   Villa America, 44

Murphy, Sara, 32–5, 38–9, 43–5, 46–50, 71
   feelings for Ernest, 58–9
   view of Hadley, 58–9
Mussolini, Benito, 110, 115, 145

National Security League, 20
Nicaragua, 151
neo-Thomism, 83

Oedipus Rex (ballet), 132
O. Henry Award, 163
"On Those Synthetic States" (Hickok), 120

Pamplona, Spain, 5, 46–50, 133
Paris, France, 20–1, 51–2, 131–2, 144–5
Paris That's Not In The Guide Books, 21
Parker, Dorothy, 45, 81–2, 106, 118, 119, 152,
   163–4
Parma, Italy, 115
Paul, Elliot, 138, 165
Peirce, Waldo, 120, 157, 160, 172–3, 180–2, 186,
   188, 194, 195, 215
periodicals
   American Mercury, 19
   Atlantic Monthly, 116
   Auto, 115
   Black Mask, 136
   Bookman, 163
   Boulevardier, 138–40, 147
   Colliers, 10
   Commerce, 107
   Cosmopolitan, 39
   Dial, 162–3
   Exile, 82–3, 95, 99, 112, 115
   Field and Stream, 115
   Harper's, 112
   Lazrus, 116
   Liberty, 10
   Nation, 4
   New Masses, 39, 57, 95
   New Republic, 62, 163
   New Yorker, 99, 118, 163–4
   Ring, 115
   Saturday Evening Post, 10
   Saturday Review of Literature, 68, 97, 115, 152
   Scribner's Magazine, 4, 57, 88, 95, 99, 115, 122,
      181, 194
   This Quarter, 4, 15, 74
   Time, 107, 152
   Toreros, 115
   transatlantic review, 74, 118, 161
   transition, 99, 112, 115, 138
   Vanity Fair, 36, 99, 118, 163
   Vogue, 7, 96–7
Perkins, Max, 10, 16, 22, 39, 40, 57, 68, 107,
   122–3, 128, 135, 136, 153, 156, 163, 166, 170,
   172, 181, 195–6, 203, 208
   response to The Sun Also Rises, 23–5, 55–6
Pfeiffer, Augustus (Gus), 7–8, 113, 121, 169, 242
   n. 29
   character, 117, 154

INDEX

Pfeiffer, Mary, 76, 134, 143–4, 145, 177
Pfeiffer, Paul, 8, 76, 134, 174, 196–7
Pfeiffer, Pauline,
    see Hemingway, Pauline
Pfeiffer, Virginia (Jinny), 8, 75, 80, 90, 98, 124,
    134, 143, 237 n. 31
Picasso, Pablo, 45, 119
Piggott, Arkansas, 34, 75–6, 176–9, 195–8
Pisa, Italy, 113
Porter, Cole, 44, 145
Possession (Bromfield), 138
Pound, Ezra, 17, 74, 82–3, 99, 109, 110, 113, 136,
    157, 161, 162–3, 188
Prado Museum, 27
publishers
    Boni & Liveright, 4–5, 75, 122
    Charles Scribner's Sons, 4–5, 24–5, 75
    Hearst Publications, 135–6
    Jonathan Cape, 20, 57, 112

Raeburn, John, 239 n. 63
Rapallo, Italy, 109, 113
Rascoe, Burton, 153
Rebecca Shoals, 174
Republican convention of 1928, 179
Research Hospital, 181
revolution, 11, 46, 150–1
Rimini, Italy, 113
Rivera, Primo de, 11
Rodker, John, 112
Rogers, Cameron, 156
Rohrback, Marie, 32–3, 40, 114
Roosevelt, Theodore, 193
Ruby Tuesday, 131
Rudge, Olga, 110, 196
Russell, Joe, 173
Ryan, Red, 145

Sacco and Vanzetti case, 72, 129
Sacred Wood (Eliot), 6
Saintes-Maries-de-la-Mer, France, 125–6
Salome (Wilde), 85
Sandinistas, 151
San Fermin, festival of, 12, 46–50, 133
Sanford, Marcelline Hemingway, 106, 181, 199,
    210
Sanford, Sterling, 212
San Remo, Italy, 115
San Sebastian, Spain, 133, 142
Santiago de Compostela, Spain, 133–7
Saunders, Eddie (Bra), 174
Schruns, Austria, 3–5
Scribner, Charles, 24–5
"Seine Also Rises, The," 165–6
Shakespeare and Co., 6, 13, 21, 26, 62–3, 68, 85,
    112, 151
Shell, Wyoming, 193
Sheridan, Wyoming, 187–8, 190
Shipman, Evan, 112, 195, 204
ships
    Berengaria, 213

Cleveland, 97
Ile de France, 205, 206
Orita, 169
Pennland, 61
Maurentania, 56
Yorck, 218
Smith, Al, 145, 181, 197
Smith, Chard Powers, 87, 239 n. 54
Smith, Katherine, 30, 215
Smith, Paul, 235 n. 4, 238 n. 47
Smith, William, 172–3
Spence, Eileen, 252 n. 21
Standish, Miles, 161
Stearns, Harold, 41
Stein, Gertrude, 17, 57, 74, 83–6, 112, 119, 144,
    164, 165, 196, 206
Stewart, Donald Ogden, 60, 72, 82, 156
Stoneback, H. R., 241 n. 16, 255 n. 16
Strater, Henry ("Mike"), 2, 172, 203–4, 208, 215
Stravinsky, Igor, 132
suicide, 3, 6, 52, 76, 96, 206–7
Sweeney, Charles, 150

Tate, Allen, 4
This Side of Paradise (Fitzgerald), 24, 204
Thompson, Charles, 172
Thompson, Lorin, 172, 205
Thompson, Virgil, 116
Thurber, James, 163
Thus Spake Zarathustra (Nietzche), 30
Titus, Edward, 73
Toklas, Alice B., 86, 164, 165
Tribune (Paris edition), references to Hemingway,
    13, 16, 74, 111–12, 148, 151–2
Twysden, Duff, 12, 47

Valbanera, sinking of, 174
Valencia, Spain, 50, 133
Valentino, Rudolph, 45
Valéry, Paul, 21
Velodrome d'Hiver, 19–20
veterans, American, 144
Villa Paquita, 36–7, 38
"Visit From Saint Nicholas (In the Manner of
    Ernest Hemingway), A" (Thurber), 163
Von Kurowsky, Agnes, 173, 175

Walloon Lake, 146, 212
Walsh, Ernest, 15
Ward, Michael, 123–4
Waste Land, The (Eliot), 23, 127, 180
Watson, "Sliding Billy," 19
What Price Glory (Stallings), 144, 157
Wheelock, John, 24
Whitman exhibit, 21
Wilde, Oscar, 85
Winter, Ella, 100
Within the Quota (Murphy and Porter), 44
Woolf, Virginia, 6, 13, 26, 152–3

Zaragoza (Spain), 68–71